Grammar and vocabulary of language spoken by Motu tribe (New Guinea)

W. G. Lawes

Alpha Editions

This edition published in 2019

ISBN : 9789353898922

Design and Setting By
Alpha Editions
email - alphaedis@gmail.com

GRAMMAR AND VOCABULARY

OF

LANGUAGE SPOKEN BY MOTU TRIBE
(NEW GUINEA),

BY

REV. W. G. LAWES, F.R.G.S.,

WITH INTRODUCTION BY THE REV. GEORGE PRATT.

SECOND AND REVISED EDITION.

SYDNEY : CHARLES POTTER, GOVERNMENT PRINTER, PHILLIP-STREET.
1888.

a 15—88

PREFACE TO FIRST EDITION.

THE following pages represent the first attempt to classify and reduce to a written form the grammar and vocabulary of the language spoken by the Motu tribe of New Guinea. As a first attempt it is necessarily imperfect, but I need make no apology for its publication. The first step towards accuracy and correctness is only taken when the result of observation and study is put into print.

The vocabulary in both parts would have been more full if I had been able, while in New Guinea, fully to prepare it for the Press. When I came to Sydney three months ago, I brought with me in MS. the material for the following pages, but had no intention of printing it. The ready promise of the Hon. A. Stuart, on behalf of the New South Wales Government Press, and the kindly offer of the Rev. G. Pratt to arrange the work and prepare it for the printer, induced me to give to the public that which would have been better for another year's research and preparation.

But for Mr. Pratt's experienced pen and unwearied patience, the work would not have been half so good or complete as it is.

My knowledge of the language has been acquired during seven years residence among the people who speak it.

My colleague, Mr. Chalmers, has contributed largely both to grammar and vocabulary, but must not be held responsible for anything I have published, as there has been no opportunity of submitting the work to him for revision before going to press.

In carrying out the provisions of the Protectorate, which has been proclaimed over part of New Guinea, it will be of the first importance that all who have to do with the natives in an official capacity should be able to speak to the people in their own language. This little work will, I hope, be of some use to those who may be located in the Port Moresby district. From the knowledge we have of the dialects spoken in the Hood Bay and South Cape districts, there is every reason to believe that the grammar of the language of the S.E. Coast, from Maiva to the East Cape, is practically the same, the only difference being in the vocabulary. The consonantal changes in the different dialects are remarkable. Consonants of different classes taking the place of each other, as for instance *t* being exchanged for *l* or *r*.

In the Motu dialect the sibilant never occurs before an *a*, *o*, or *u*, but at South Cape we meet with the *s* before all vowels, and find the Samoan words—*isu*, nose, and *susu*, breast.

On my return I hope to be able to prepare something like a comparative grammar and specimen vocabulary of the different dialects spoken in the districts where we have mission stations established. I have to ask all using the following pages kindly to supply me with any additions or corrections they may discover, so that the next edition may be a much nearer approach to accuracy and completeness.

W. G. LAWES.

Sydney, March 24th, 1885.

PREFACE TO THE SECOND EDITON.

THE present edition has been revised, corrected, and enlarged. A good many new words have been added, and a few pages of phrases likely to be of use to beginners or visitors.

The comparative vocabulary will be of interest to philologists. It comprises 400 words in seven dialects of the south-east coast, and illustrates the difference which exists, as well as the changes which a word passes through by dropping or changing its consonants.

The New South Wales Government, through the Hon. J. Burns, have kindly consented to print the following pages, and so enabled me to share with others the results of my study and research.

W. G. LAWES.

Sydney, 15th February, 1888.

INTRODUCTION.

BY Rev. G. PRATT.

In the grammar of the Motu dialect of New Guinea one peculiarity is in the use of letters so much alike as to be scarcely distinguishable, *e.g.*, the letters b and p, *keboka* or *kepoka* ; d and t, *bāda* or *bāta* ; g and q, *qanua* or *guanua* ; r and l, *ara* and *ala*.

The pronunciation of t before e and i as ts, is also a recent introduction to Niue or Savage Island. When we first went there we found the young people generally using it, whilst the old men, especially on public occasions, pronounced the t. In the same way, the Tahitians have changed b into p ; the Sandwich Islanders have changed t into k, and the Samoans are endeavouring to do the same. As these islands had little or no communication with one another, how is it that these changes, as if by common consent, have been made ?

The Motuan language seems to be a strange mixture of Papuan and Eastern Polynesian. The grammar is Papuan, the dictionary is Eastern Polynesian. The suffixed pronoun and the method of counting by two threes for six, and two fours for eight, is Papuan. Very peculiar is the declension of the noun by means of pronouns ; also, the use of both the separate and the suffix pronoun with the noun, *Lau aegu*, my leg, mine.

Suffix pronoun.	Duke of York Island.
gu, I	g
mu, your	m
na, his	n

These are evidently Papuan roots, made to conform to Eastern Polynesian by adding a vowel to the termination.

Many of the words seem to have Papuan roots, but all take the form of Eastern Polynesian.

The formation of the noun by adding *na* to the verb is like the Samoan ga, used in the same way. The use of a, in relation to food, *adia* for edia, corresponds with the Samoan lau for lou.

Some of the numerals are Eastern Polynesian—*tu*, one; *rua*, two; *hitu*, seven. *Hui*, a hair used for ten, resembles the fulu hair or feather in Samoan, and seems to indicate the same use of a tally in counting. The singular pronouns, *lau*, *oi*, *ia*, are Eastern Polynesian (au, oe, ia). The plural are Papuan.

Having different words for counting different articles, is, as far as I know, in use only in the East.

A Tahitian idiom is seen in the word *hanamoa* (lit., to make good) to praise. In Tahitian, haamaitai.

The dearth of particles, and the arrangement of words in a sentence, seem to make the sense obscure. " He Jerusalem journey made, he towns and villages passed through, he them taught went." That is a literal translation of Luke 13, 22.

In arranging and copying out the Dictionary, I was struck with the numerous divergencies from the Eastern Polynesian dialects, and with the very large number of words which have no counterpart there.

Though th is much used, it is often changed to d, as *daudu* for tautu. It is also prefixed to some words beginning with a vowel or h, as *diho* for ifo or hifo, *dae* for ae or hake. In the same way l is prefixed, as lahi for afi, and is often omitted in the beginning or middle of a word, as *tui* for tuli, *ima* for lima.

G being nasal in Eastern Polynesian, is omitted, as *tai* (to cry) for tagi, *taia* (an ear) for taliga, *lao* for lago (a fly). On the contrary g hard is inserted, as *tage* for tae.

M is substituted for g, as *matama* for amataga. Again it is prefixed, as in *miri* (gravel) for ili. N is omitted, as *maino* for manino. Having no f, p or h is substituted for it, as *pata* for fata.

Yet more strange is the alteration of vowels. A long is put for short a, as *māta* (the eye) for măta, *mānu* (a bird) for mănu. O is put for u, as *namo* (a mosquito) for namu, *ramu* (to chew) for lamu.

Some words change their meaning, as *lele* (to swim) means to fly in Eastern Polynesian. *Hanua* (a village) for fanua (land). *Tunua* (to burn Pottery) for tunu (to roast). *Sinarai* (a river) for a water-fall.

The following are from pure Eastern Polynesian roots :—

New Guinea.	Eastern Polynesian.	English.
adorahi	ahiahi	evening
gauaia	gau	to chew cane
gahu	asuasu	mist, fog
hetuturu	tutulu	to drip
hekalo	tālo	to beckon
huahua	fua	fruit
hururu	sulu	torch
kanudi	anu	to spit
kaubebe	pepe	butterfly
kalo	alo	to paddle
sisina	sina	small piece
papapapa	papapapa	flat rock
tamana	tama	father
tupuna	tupuga	ancestors
laoevaeva	evaeva	to go about
laka	laka	step
mavamava	mavava	to yawn
motu	motu	to break
motumotu	motu	an island
mu	gu	dumb
noho	nofo	to sit
nohu	nofu	stinging fish
noinoi	faanoi	to beg
qalahu	ahu	smoke
raroa	vailaloa	flood
rua	rua	two
sinana	tinā	mother
taoatao	taotao	to press down
tari	foe talitali	steer oar
togo	togo	mangrove

The number of compound words and of doubled words is very observable. In the latter case they were not satisfied, as their Eastern brethren are, with doubling part of the word, but repeated the whole, as *hekisehekise.*

From the meanings of the words of the Dictionary many of the customs of the people may be learnt. We find there, that though naked savages, they are fond of adorning themselves with feather head dresses and chaplets with strings of teeth, shell armlets, and a bone passed through the nose as a "nose-jewel." In addition to these, they paint their bodies, and also tattoo ; this is done by making a black paint with burnt resin and water. With this they mark the design on the body of the young man who is to be operated on. Then the skin is punctured by an instrument dipped in the black paint and driven in by a tap with the mallet.

b

Besides the usual articles of food, consisting of taro, yams, bananas, sugarcane, and cocoanuts, they have sago, which they make into puddings with bananas. They cook their food by boiling in an earthenware pot ; or if an animal, they roast it on a spit. Banana leaves serve for plates. In times of scarcity they eat the stem of the banana.

Fish is grilled on a gridiron of sticks. They also cook with heated stones after the manner of the Eastern Polynesians. The Elema people cook sago in hard cakes, which they sell.

When going to fight they paint their faces red. Their weapons are a spear, bow and arrows, a stone headed club, and the man-catcher. This last article consists of a loop at the end of a pole, which being put over the head of the retreating foe, on to his neck, held him back. It is armed with a sharp point so as to pierce the back of the neck. A newly married man is exempt from war.

They make earthenware pots and other vessels for domestic use. In order to shape them, in one hand they hold a stone, and insert it inside of the vessel, while with the other hand they fashion the outside with a small piece of flat wood. Their pottery has an ornamental marking on the edge of the bowl, which is equivalent to the trade mark of civilized nations. Dry banana leaves are used for packing when exported.

Besides pottery, they use the cocoanut shell for a drinking cup. To keep oil or fat, they carve a cocoanut shell, and make a cover to it.

A kind of ship is made by lashing several canoes together. Caulking is effected with banana leaves and the gum of a tree. On the top of these canoes is erected a platform with a house at either end. In these houses they stow away the crockery which is taken to be exchanged for sago. The captain has a separate place in which to stow away his crockery. In these ships they make long voyages. Before starting a farewell dance of an indecent character is held.

To assist the steering of these unwieldly structures, large long paddles are let down by the side, and they act as centre-boards.

Like Eastern Polynesians, they beat out the inner bark of the paper-mulberry, with which they make cloth. They also plait mats. Large netted bags are used by the women in which to carry their children, and smaller bags of the same kind are used for carrying other articles. They have nets for fishing, and also for catching kangaroos, wild pigs, and dugong. Fish are also speared.

Charms are used, such as a smooth stone to make the yams grow. Also one particular leaf of the banana, that nearest the bunch of fruit (*gōgō*) is thought to make yams fruitful. Coming events are foreshown by sneezing or by quivering of the body. By cracking the fingers they predict the coming home of a ship. During the absence of the men on a voyage, a sacred woman performs certain rites to ensure the safe return of the voyagers. Incantations are used to bring misfortune and death on an obnoxious partly. A man in a fit is supposed to be possessed of a demon. The spirits of those killed are believed to appear to survivors in some dreadful form. They believe in spirits who are malevolent; and that certain persons have influence over them, so as to secure their services in executing vengeance on enemies. In sickness the soul leaves the body, and it is the province of the sorcerer to find and bring it back. Passes are made by the sorcerer over the body of the sick man. He receives a payment for his services.

Some of the prevalent diseases are, abscess, ulcers, yaws, rash, rheumatism, whitlow, erysipelas, thrush, vomiting, constipation, fits, palsy, dropsy, and elephantiasis. Sickness is sometimes caused by sleeping on the place where visitors have slept a night or two previously. Villages were sometimes deserted on account of sickness often occurring in it. In drawing blood they use a flint pointed instrument like a small arrow; with this they lanced the forehead by repeatedly discharging it from a small bow. This was the cure for headache. Friends pay visits to their sick friends.

Suicide is committed either by drowning or hanging, or by leaping from a tree or a cliff. Hired assassins are made use of. When grieving for the dead they scratch their faces, so as to draw blood, or else they cut themselves with a flint or shell. A coarse cloth is worn as a mourning garment, or a cane is plaited round the body. The beat of a drum answers to the funeral knell. On the death of a husband, an enclosure of mats is made round the grave; inside of this the widow sits and mourns. They bury their dead.

By way of sports, they have a spinning top. They have a low swing, and also a very high one depending from the top of a high leaning cocoanut palm. They practice throwing the spear, and they run races. A musical instrument is made of reeds; and a drum by stretching a green skin over a hollow wooden frame. Native poets compose songs, for which they are paid. The betel nut is chewed.

They marry and are polygamists. Divorce is common. The woman is betrothed to a husband; but breaches of promise are iu vogue. Gifts are made in expectation of a return gift. Like civilized people, credit is sometimes given. The stomach is considered to be the seat of the affections ; hence, to feel pity is to have the stomach-ache. Cocoanuts are made taboo as in Eastern Polynesia by plaiting a cocoanut leaf round a tree. Fences for their gardens are made by sticks, or split bamboos, placed lengthways, like a hurdle fence. The waterpot is carried either on the head or shoulder. To pass along in front of a chief is regarded as a mark of disrespect.

Hospitality is shown to strangers ; but treachery is practised to an enemy. He is invited to partake of food, and then killed, as Amnon was by Absalom.

They have distinguishing terms for the hospitable, kind-hearted, good-tempered, courteous man ; and also for the abusive, churlish man. The industrious man, the one who stores up for future use, is praised ; while the lazy man and the thief are abused. Thus " they show the law written in their hearts, their conscience bearing witness therewith, and their thoughts one with another accusing or else excusing them."

GEO. PRATT.

GRAMMAR OF MOTU LANGUAGE.

THE Motu language is spoken by the Motu tribe living at Port Moresby, Pari, Borebada, Lealea, and Manumann; also by natives of Delena, Boera, Tatana, Vabukori, Tupuselei, Kaile, and Kapakapa. There are considerable local differences in pronunciation,

LETTERS.

The Motu alphabet consists of nineteen letters, viz.,—*a, e, i, o, u, b, d, g, h, k, l, m, n, p, q, r, s, t, v.*

A is pronounced,—

    1st. Long, as in "father"; *vāra*, to grow.

    2nd. Short, as in "mat"; *harihari*, to-day; *varavara* relations.

E, i, o, u, are pronounced as in Italian.

There are slight differences in quantity for which no rules can be given.

    Usually *e* is sounded as *a* in take.

i	,,	*ea* ,,	eager.
o	,,	*o* ,,	no.
u	,,	*oe* ,,	shoe.

The consonants are for the most part pronounced as in English.

B, native name *bi*. This is generally sounded as *b* in bad; but in some cases it approaches nearly to the *p* sound, and when pronounced quickly is scarcely distinguishable from *p*.

D, native name *di*, as *d* in dip. Like *b* this has the rougher and softer sound; sometimes it is almost *t*.

G, native name *ga*, as *g* in good. In some words it has a sound between the ordinary *g* and *k*; as *āu ginigini*, a nettle; but *āu ginigini* (almost *k*), a thorny tree.

H, native name *eti* (pronounced *etsi*). (The reason for the name of this letter being at variance with rule is that a large number of natives who speak the Motu language drop the *h*, the name to them would be the same as the vowel *e*.) This is the nearest a native can pronounce to the English name of the letter. It is a characteristic of the Pari and some other natives to drop the *h* entirely; they pronounce *hanua, anua; haine, aine,* &c.

A

K, native name *ke*, as *k* in key.

L, native name *la*, as *l* in lady.

M, native name *mo*, as *m* in man.

N, native name *nu*, as *n* in now.

P, native name *pi*, as *p* in pig.

Q, native name *kiu*, as *q* in queen. The *q* in Motuan does not take an *u* after it.

R, native name *ro*, as *r* in robber.

S, native name *sa*, as *s* in sing. *S* never occurs in Motuan before before an *a* or *u*, and rarely before *o*.

T, native name *ti*. Before *a*, *o*, or *u* it is sounded as *t* in take. Before *e* or *i* it becomes *ts*, like the Tsade in Hebrew, *raruoti* pronounced *raruotsi*.

V, native name *vi*, as *v* in victor.

Of diphthongs there are two:—

>   *ai*, pronounced like English *ai* in aisle.
>   *au*   ,,   ,,   *ow* in cow.

No two consonants can ever stand together without a vowel between.

SYLLABLES.

Every syllable must end in a vowel, hence every syllable is an open one, and in introducing foreign names or words this should be remembered. The natives will always so divide a word that each syllable will end in a vowel.

ACCENT.

As a rule the accent is on the penultima; but there are exceptions.

When suffixes are added the accent is shifted forward, as *haìne*, hainèna, mèro, meròna.

Reduplicated words have the two accents of the simple form, as *kadàra, kadàra-kadàra.*

The natives of Tupuselei, Kapakapa, and Kaile, are known by the peculiarity of raising the voice on the last syllable of the sentence.

WORDS.

1. THE ARTICLE.

There does not seem to be any distinctive definite article.

Harī, an adverb of time, now, is often used as a definite article. *Hari kekeni*, the girl.

In the same way, *varani*, yesterday, *vanegai*, the other day, and *idaunegai*, a long time ago, are used, where in other languages an article would be employed. *Varani lakatoi*, the ship, the particular ship which came yesterday, or about which we talked yesterday. *Vanegai ira edeseni ?*—Day before yesterday, hatchet, where ?

Ta (an abbreviation of *tamona*) one, is used as indefinite article, as, *Lakatoi ta vata emaimu*, a ship is coming.

2. THE NOUN.

Nouns are primitive, as *au*, a tree; *nadi*, a stone; or derivative, as *igui*, a bundle ; from *guia*, to tie.

Nouns are formed from verbs by prefixing *i* to the verb root, as *kokoa*, to nail ; *ikoko*, a nail ; *lapaia*, to smite ; *ilapa*, a sword. When the noun is the agent performing the action of the verb, *tauna* is added, as *kaha*, to help ; *ikahana tauna*, a helper. Also by *he* prefixed, as *dibagani*, to tempt ; *hedibagani*, a temptation ; *nanadai*, to question ; *henanadai*, a questioning.

Some nouns are formed from verbs by suffixing *na*, as *doko*, to end ; *dokona*, the end.

GENDER.

Gender is sometimes expressed by different words :—

Tau, man.	*Haine*, woman.
Mero, boy.	*Kekeni*, girl.
Dabari, male wallaby.	*Miara*, female wallaby.

When there is no distinct word the gender of animals is distinguished by adding *maruane*, male, and *haine*, female, respectively, as, *boroma maruane*, boar, *boroma haine*, sow.

NUMBER.

The plural is sometimes indicated by reduplicating one syllable, as

Mero, boy.	*Memero*, boys.

Or by dropping one or even two syllables, as

Tauhau, a young man.	*Uhau*, young men.
Haniulato, maiden.	*Ulato*, maidens.

There seems to be no certain means of indicating the plural, *nadi*, is stone or stones ; *ruma*, house or houses. As soon, however, as they can be put in the possessive, then the termination *dia* distinguishes the plural, as *uma nadidia*, the stones of the garden ; *hanua rumadia*, village houses, *i.e.*, the houses of the village.

Dia is sometimes added to the simple noun as, *tau*, man; *taudia*, men; *haine*, woman; *hainedia*, women. In most cases perhaps another noun is understood, as in *taudia* in the above example, *hanua* village, or *iduhu* family may be understood. *Dia* is the pronominal suffix of third person plural (see below). It may in some cases be the first syllable of *diagau* many. Words signifying multitude are also used with the singular to denote plural, as

> *Au momo*, many trees.
> *Mānu diagau*, many birds.
> *Hanua logora*, many towns.

CASE.

Case is indicated by prepositions and suffixes. The *nominative* is the simple form, and may be known by its position in the sentence, always standing first, *Qarume umui o abia vata namo*, the fish you have taken are good.

The *Genitive* is expressed by adding the suffix *na* singular and *dia* plural for parts of the body, and family relations, as

> *Lohiabada aena*, chief leg his, *i.e.*, the chief's leg.
> *Mero sinana*, boy mother his, *i.e.*, the boy's mother.

In other cases, such as property, land, weapons, &c., *ena* is placed after the principal noun, and before that of which it is possessed.

Lohiabada ena ruma, chief his house, *i.e.*, the house of the chief.

Kekeni ena dabua, girl her dress, *i.e.*, the dress of the girl.

Plural nouns take the plural suffix *dia* instead of *na* in the singular, and *edia* for *ena*, as :—

Memero aedia, boys leg theirs, *i.e.*, the legs of the boys.

Hanua taudia edia rumadia, village men their houses, *i.e.*, the houses of the villagers.

Food takes *ana* and *adia* instead of *ena* and *edia*, as :—

Haine ana maho, woman her yam, *i.e.*, the yam of the woman.

Memero adia tohu, boys their sugar cane, *i.e.*, the sugar cane of the boys.

The *Dative* is expressed by *ena* following the noun or *ana* if food, as :—

Dabua sinada ena, dress our mother hers, *i.e.*, the dress is for the mother.

Bigu tamada ana, banana our father his, *i.e.*, the banana is for the father.

For plural see genitive above.

The *Accusative* is known by its position in the sentence, and also by *dekena* an adverb of proximity.

Lohiabada dekena lao, chief by side of go ; go to the chief.

Dekena is often shortened into *ena*.

The *Vocative* is indicated by *e* sometimes *o* following the noun.

Tamagu e! O my father.

Sinagu e! O my mother.

The *Ablative* is governed by *amo* from, as :—

Guba amo mai, heaven from come, *i.e.*, from the heaven.

By addition of *lalona* inside, as :—

Ruma lalona ai, house inside it, *i.e.*, in the house.

By *laia* suffixed to the verb of which it is the agent or instrument, as :—

Ia mero heaulaia, he, child ran away with, *i.e.*, he ran away with the child.

Dabua hurilaia ranu, clothes wash with water, *i.e.*, water to wash clothes with.

The noun with its cases is as follows :—

Singular.

Nom.	*Haine*, woman.
Gen.	*Haine ena*, of a woman.
Dative.	*Haine ena*, for a woman.
Accus.	*Haine dekena*, to a woman.
Voca.	*Haine e*, O woman !
Abla.	*Haine amo*, from a woman.
	Haine lalonai, in a woman.

Plural.

Nom.	*Hainedia*, women.
Gen.	*Hainedia edia*, of women.
Dative.	,, ,, for women.
Accus.	,, *dekedia*, to women.
Voca.	*Hainemui e*, O women !
Abla.	*Hainedia amo*, from women.
	,, *lalodiai*, in women.

3. THE ADJECTIVE.

The adjective is known rather by its position in the sentence than by anything distinctive in its form. It follows its noun, as, *ira namo*, a good hatchet. Personal qualities are most frequently expressed by two nouns in apposition, the person following the quality, as :—

Goada tauna, a strong man, literally, strength of man. *Tau goada* is less frequently used.

A kind of compound adjective is used by union of a noun with an adjective, as, *Haine udu mauri*, a live-mouthed woman ; *Lalo auka tauna*, a hard-stomached man.

Diminutives are frequently expressed by reduplication, as, *kekeni*, girl ; *kekenikekeni*, little girl.

Adjectives expressive of colours are all reduplicated, as, *kuro-kuro*, white ; *koremakorema*, black. By the addition of *ka* the quality is modified ; *kurokakuroka*, whitish ; *gano*, sharp edge ; *ganokaganoka*, sharpish ; *paripari*, wet ; *parikaparika*, damp.

Comparison is effected by using two adjectives in the positive state, as, *inai namo*, this is good ; *unai dika*, that is bad.

Also by using the word *herea*, to exceed, as, *namo herea*, very good, the best.

Also by using *sibona*, only, as, *ia sibona namo*, he only is good.

NUMERALS.

The cardinals are :—

Tamona,	One.
Rua,	Two.
Toi,	Three.
Hani,	Four.
Ima,	Five.
Tauratoi,	Six.
Hitu,	Seven.
Taurahani,	Eight.
Taurahani ta,	Nine.
Qauta,	Ten.
Qauta ta,	Eleven.
Qauta rua,	Twelve.
Rua ahui,	Twenty.
Toi ahui,	Thirty.
Hari ahui,	Forty.
Ima ahui,	Fifty.
Tauratoi ahui,	Sixty.
Hitu ahui,	Seventy.
Taurahani ahui	Eighty.
Taurahani ta ahui,	Ninety.
Sinahu	One hundred.
Sinahuta rua,	One hundred and two, &c.
Sinahu rua,	Two hundred.
Daha,	One thousand.
Gerebu,	Ten thousand.
Domaga,	One hundred thousand.

ORDINALS.

Same as cardinals after the first, which is generally *guna.*

Numeral adverbs, twice, thrice, &c., are expressed by *ha* prefixed to cardinals, as, *harua,* twice; *hatoi,* thrice, &c.

Things of length, such as spears, poles, &c., are counted differently. The numerals have *au* prefixed, as, *auta, aurua,* and so on up to nine, which is *autaurahaniauta,* and ten, *atalata.*

Rabu rua,	20	*Rabu hitu,*	70
Rabu toi,	30	*Rabu taurahani,*	80
Rabu hani,	40	*Rabu taurahani ta,*	90
Rabu ima,	50	*Sinahu,*	100
Rabu tauratoi,	60		

Fish and some other things are counted differently to ordinary things.

Of fish, pigs, and wallaby, the ordinary numerals are used up to ten, which is *bala ta*; 20, *bala rua*; and so on up to 100, which is the same as ordinary, *sinahu.*

Cocoanuts are counted by *raro* (strings), as, *raro ta,* 10; *raro rua,* 20, &c.

4. PRONOUNS.

The cases of Pronouns are expressed by suffixes. The dual is formed by adding *raruoti* to the corresponding plural, as, *umui raruoti,* you two.

There are two pronouns for the first person plural, one inclusive (*ita*) which is used when the person addressed is included, the other exclusive (*ai*) which excludes the person addressed.

PERSONAL PRONOUNS.

Lau,	I.
Oi,	Thou.
Ia,	He or she.
Ai,	We (exclusive).
Ita,	We (inclusive).
Umui,	You.
Idia,	They.
Ai raruoti,	We two (exclusive).
Ita raruoti,	We two (inclusive).
Umui raruoti,	You two.
Idia raruoti,	They two.

POSSESSIVE PRONOUNS.

Lauegu,	My.
Oiemu,	Thy.
Iena,	His.
Ai emai,	Ours (exclusive).
Ita eda,	Ours (inclusive).
Umui emui,	Yours.
Idia edia,	Theirs.

All kinds of food take *a*, as:—

Lauagu ligu,	My banara.
Oiamu bigu,	Thy ,,
Iana ligu,	His ,,
Ai amai bigu,	Our ,, (exclusive).
Ita ada bigu,	Our ,, (inclusive).
Umui amui bigu,	Your ,,
Idia adia bigu,	Their ,,

For parts of the body and relations the personal pronoun precedes the noun, and the following terminations are suffixed to it:—

Gu,	1st person singular.
Mu,	2nd ,,
Na,	3rd ,,
Mai,	1st person plural (exclusive).
Da,	,, ,, (inclusive).
Mui,	2nd ,,
Dia,	3rd ,,
As *Lau aegu,*	My leg.
Oi aemu,	Thy leg.
Ia aena,	His leg.
Ai aemai,	Our (exclusive) legs.
Ita aeda,	Our (inclusive) legs.
Umui aemui,	Your legs.
Idia aedia,	Their legs.

DISTRIBUTIVE PRONOUNS.

Ta ta,	Each, as *Idia ta ta koau,* they each spoke.
Umui ta,	One of you, &c.

DEMONSTRATIVE PRONOUNS.

Inai,	This	⎞ Singular
Enai,	That—close to.	⎬ and
Unai,	That—distant or opposite to.	⎠ Plural.

INDEFINITE PRONOUNS.

Haida,	Some—others.
Ta,	Any one.
Idau,	Another.

INTERROGATIVES.

Daika,	Who? *Daidia,* who? plural.
Dahako,	What? Singular and plural.
Edana,	Which?
Edananegai,	When?

5. VERBS.

Verbs are for the most part primitive or underived words, as *gini*, to stand; *noho*, to dwell. Some are derived from adjectives by prefixing the causative and adding *a*, as *namo*, good; *hanamoa*, to make good.

PERSON.

There is no change in the verb itself for person. It is expressed by the pronoun and a vowel or particle placed between it and the verb, as :—

1st person	*Lau na diba,*	I knew.
2nd ,,	*Oi o diba,*	You knew.
3rd ,,	*Ia e diba,*	He knew.

Plural.

1st person	{ *Ai a diba,*	We (exclusive) knew.
	{ *Ita ta diba,*	We (inclusive) knew.
2nd ,,	*Umui o diba,*	You knew. ;
3rd ,,	*Idia e diba,*	They knew.

TENSE.

Tense is indicated by particles placed immediately before the verb.

PRESENT : *vata rada*; used also of past when the action is finished and complete, as *Lau vata diba*, &c., &c., I know.

PAST by the following particles :—

1st person *na*	1st plural (exclusive) *a*
	,, ,, (inclusive) *ta*
2nd ,, *o*	2nd ,, *o*
3rd ,, *e*	3rd ,, *e*
As *Lau na diba,*	I knew.
Oi o diba,	You knew, &c., &c.

A particle *me* is often added in both past and future tenses, but without adding anything to the meaning, as *Lau name diba*, *Oi ome diba*, &c.

CONDITIONAL PAST.

Lau bama diba,	If I had known.
Oi boma diba,	If you had known.
Ia bema diba,	If he had known.

Plural.

Ai baiama diba,	If we (exclusive) had known.
Ita baitama diba,	If we (inclusive) had known.
Umui boma diba,	If you had known.
Idia baema diba,	If they had known.

FUTURE is known by the following words preceding the verb, viz :—

1st person	*baina*	1st plural (exclusive)	*baia*
		,, ,, (inclusive)	*baita*
2nd ,,	*la*	2nd ,,	*ba*
3rd ,,	*baine*	2rd ,,	*bae*

As : —

Lau baina diba,	I shall know.
Ia baine diba,	He shall know, &c., &c.

It is often used as a conditional, possible, future. When certainty is expressed *do* is placed before it :—

Lau do baina diba.	I shall (certainly) know.

The *b* of the above is dropped to express an immediate future, as :—

Ita aita mate,	We shall (soon) die.

The *do* above is often used with the negative to signify "not yet," but implying that it will take place :—

Ia do mai lasi,	He hasn't yet come.

There is a present participle ending in *mu*, which always takes the vowels of the past tense before it, as :—

Lau na dibamu,	I am knowing.
Oi o dibamu,	You are knowing.
Ia e dibamu,	He is knowing, &c., &c.

There is also a past participle ending in *va* which also takes the same vowels before it as the present participle :—

Lau na nohova,	I was dwelling, &c , &c.

IMPERATIVE MOOD.

Expressed by *a* and *ba* both in singular and plural. In entreaty *ame* and *bame* are often used.

Oi a kamonai,	Hear thou.
Oi ba itaia,	Look thou.
Oi ame bokamai hisi,	Have mercy on us.

INFINITIVE MOOD.

This has no distinctive form, but takes *baina*, &c., as in the future, as :—

Baina diba,	} To know, &c., &c.
Ba diba,	

The word *totona* is also often used to express object, where in English we should use the infinitive, as :—

Ia vata mai kamonai totona,	He came to hear.

The Passive

Is sometimes expressed by the suffix of the person who is the subject of the verb being added to it, as :—

Henao, to steal.	*Henaoa,* to be stolen.
Lakatani, to leave.	*Lakatanigu,* I am left.

Sometimes by the auxiliary verb to give, as :—

Dagedage lau henigu, I am persecuted.

Literally, persecution me given to me.

The Causative.

This is formed by prefixing *ha* to the root, as :—

Diba, to know.   *Hadiba,* to cause to know.

The Reciprocal.

This is expressed by prefixing *he* and suffixing *heheni* to the verb, which is also generally reduplicated, as :—

Hebadubaduheheni, To be angry with one another.

There is no verb *to be.* It is expressed by the pronoun and noun or adjective with a verbal particle as copula, as :—

Lau vata dika, I am bad.   *Lau baina gorere,* I shall be sick.

Mai, and, is sometimes used, as :—

Bosea mai anina hani ? Is there anything in the basket ?

Ma used before the verb signifies continued action, as :—

Ma tahua, To continue seeking.
Ma koau, To continue speaking.

Reduplication also signifies continued action, as :—

Kadarakadara, To continue playing.

Lai or *rai* with the suffix of the person added to the verb denotes the instrumental " with" or objective " at," as :—

Dabua hurilaia ranu, The water the clothes are washed with.
Ia niu ta lau koilaigu, He deceived me with a coacoanut.
Umui lau kirikirilaigu, You laugh at me.

Sometimes it means " of," as :—

Koaulaia, To speak of or about.

PARADIGM OF VERB.

Itai, to look.

INDICATIVE MOOD.

PRESENT TENSE.

Singular.

Lau vata itaia,	I look.
Oi vata itaia,	Thou lookest.
Ia vata itaia,	He looks.

Plural.

Ai vata itaia,	We (exclusive) look.
Ita vata itaia,	We (inclusive) look.
Umui vata itaia,	You look.
Idia vata itaia,	They look.

PAST TENSE.

Singular.

Lau na itaia,	I saw.
Oi o itaia,	Thou sawest.
Ia e itaia,	He saw.

Plural.

Ai a itaia,	We (exclusive) saw.
Ita ta itaia,	We (inclusive) saw.
Umui o itaia,	You saw.
Idia e itaia,	They saw.

me is often added to the vowel, as *Lau name itaia, Oi ome itaia,* &c.

FUTURE TENSE.

Lau baina itaia,	I shall see, or If I see.
Oi ba itaia,	Thou shalt see, or If thou dost see.
Ia baine itaia,	He shall see, or If he sees.
Ai baia itaia,	We (exclusive) shall see, or If we see.
Ita baita itaia,	We (inclusive) shall see, or If we see.
Umui ba itaia,	You shall see, or If you see.
Idia bae itaia,	They shall see, or If they see.

Another form is sometimes used for a more immediate future in which the *b* is dropped—

Lau aina itaia.
Oi a itaia.
Ia aine itaia, &c.

PAST CONDITIONAL TENSE.

Lau bama itaia,	If I had seen.
Oi boma itaia,	If thou hadst seen.
Ia bema itaia,	If he had seen.
Ai baiama itaia,	If we (exclusive) had seen.
Ita baitama itaia,	If we (inclusive) had seen.
Umui boma itaia,	If you had seen.
Idia bema itaia,	If they had seen.

PARTICIPLES.

Itaiamu,	Looking.
Itaiava,	Was looking.
Itaia koaulaia,	Was about to look.

These are declined like the other parts of the verb.

Lau na itaiamu,	I am looking.
Oi o itaiamu,	Thou art looking.
Ia e itaiamu,	He is looking.

Plural.

Ai a itaiamu,	We (exclusive) are looking.
Ita ta itaiamu,	We (inclusive) are looking.
Umui o itaiamu,	You are looking.
Idia e itaiamu,	They are looking.

PAST PARTICIPLE.

Lau na itaiava,
Oi o itaiava, &c., &c.

IMPERATIVE MOOD.

The same as the Future Indicative, as :—

Oi ba itaia, Look thou.

More commonly—

Oi a itaia.

In entreaty and invocation another form is used, as :—

Oi ame itaia, Do thou look.

and

Oi bame itaia, &c.

INFINITIVE MOOD.

The same as the future—*Baine itaia,* To look.

The objective suffix is used with the verb, as follows :—

Lau oi itamu,	I look at you.
Oi lau itagu,	You look at me.
Ia ai itamai,	He looks at us (exclusive).
Ai ia itaia,	We look at him.
Ia ita itada,	He looks at us (inclusive).
Ita umui itamui,	We look at you.
Oi idia itadia,	Look (thou) at them.

PASSIVES.

are expressed as above by the objective suffix, as

Oi lau itagu,   I am looked at by you.

Also by the auxiliary verb to give, *henia* with suffix,

Badu lau henigu,   Literally anger is given to me, *i.e.,* I am hated.

There is no distinctive form or termination for the passive.

The verbs, *mai* to come, and *lao* to go, are irregular in past and future as :—

Lau nama,	I came.
Oi oma,	Thou camest.
Ia ema,	He came.
Ita tama,	We (inclusive) came.
Ai ama,	We (exclusive) came.
Umui oma,	You came.
Idia ema,	They came.
Lau bainama,	I will come.
Oi baoma,	Thou wilt come.
Ia bainema,	He will come.
Ita baitama,	We (inclusive) come.
Ai baiama,	We (exclusive) come.
Umui baoma,	You come.
Idia baema,	They come.

Lao to go is the same substituting *l* for *m*, thus :—

Lau nala,
Oi ola,
Ia ela, &c., &c.

6. ADVERBS.

There is nothing in the form of adverbs to distinguished them from adjectives. Almost every adjective can be used as an adverb.

iniseni,	here.	*edeseni,*	where ?
unuseni,	there.	*dohore,*	presently.
hari,	now.	*haragaharaga,*	quickly.
io, oibe,	yes.	*edeheto,*	how ?
lasi,	no.	*initomaia,*	thus.
edana negai,	when.	*iniheto,*	thus.

&c., &c , &c.

7. PREPOSITIONS.

amo,	from.	*unukā,*	beyond.
lalo,	within.	*inikā,*	on this side.
muri,	without.	*vaira,*	in front.
atai,	above.	*madi be,*	on account of,
henu,	below.		&c., &c., &c.

8. CONJUNCTIONS.

mai,	and.	*garina,*	lest.
ā,	but.	*ida,*	together with,
danu,	also.		&c., &c., &c.

9. INTERJECTIONS.

ināi,	Oh! exclamation of wonder.
inā,	Oh! exclamation of dissent or reproof.
lau dahakai nado,	exclamation of indignation.
hī,	pish! get out!
	&c., &c., &c.

SYNTAX.

Much that belongs properly to the syntax has been already stated under the different parts of speech. The following notes on the order of words in a sentence, &c., will complete it.

The noun or pronoun in the nominative case usually precedes the verb, as, *Mero vata heau,* The boy runs. *Ia bainema,* He will come. With verbs active, the agent is always put first, and the subject acted upon next, followed by the verb, as *Lau ia dadabaia,* I he beat him, that is, I beat him. *Ia natuna lau hadikagu,* He his child I abused me.

Observe the suffix agreeing with the object is always added to the verb. In the above examples, *Lau ia dadabaia,* I he beat him. *Ia natuna,* his child, *lau,* I, *hadika-gu,* abused me. The suffix to a noun requires its corresponding pronoun to precede it, as, *Lau imagu,* I hand my, my hand. *Idia matadia vata hapapadia,* their eyes them were opened them. Also in such sentences as these, *Hanua taudia idia edia rumadia,* Village men their houses them. *Mero idia tohu baine henidia,* Boy they sugarcane will give them.

Compound verbs take the suffix after the first word, as, *Hatoreguisi,* I am raised up. *Oi butumutao,* Thou art caught.

The genitive of material is made by putting the two nouns together, and suffixing *na* to the qualified noun, as *biri rumana,* palm leaf house his, a palm leaf house. The plural takes *dia,* as *nara vanagidia,* cedar canoes theirs. Also nouns signifying the use to which a thing is applied, as, *Kohu rumana,* goods house his, a store-house. *Ira segea gauna,* hatchet sharpen thing, a hatchet sharpener.

Hani the sign of a question is always put last in the sentence. *Mero vata gorere hani?* The boy ill is? It is like the English, Eh? A pause is made before *hani.* A question is often indicated by tone of the voice solely.

Interrogative adverbs come last in sentence, as *Ia be daika?* Who is he? *Idia edeseni ai?* Where are they? &c.

A peculiar idiom is used to express, "on account of." *Ia bigu baduna badu,* he bananas anger [is] angry, *i.e.,* he is angry on account of the bananas. *Idia boroma garidia gari,* They pigs their fear [are] afraid. They are afraid because of the pigs. *Oi lau garigu gari,* Thou I my fear [art] afraid. You are afraid of me. *Mero hitolo taina tāi,* Boy hunger his crying cries, *i.e.,* the boy cries from hunger.

Another peculiar idiom is the breaking up of a sentence, and putting the negative before each member, as in Luke xi, 7. I will not rise to you, I will not give.

The negative is put between the two nouns, as *Umui idia garidia basi o gari,* You they fear their do not fear, *i.e.,* do not be afraid of them. See also Luke xxiii, 28.

The personal pronoun and its noun must agree in person. A pronoun of the singular number cannot take a noun with a plural suffix. When in English we should say "my eyes," in Motuan it is "my eye" only, two must be added to make its dual, as *Lau matagu rua.* "My children" will be *Lau natu-gu.* If plural has to be expressed particularly, a noun of multitude will be added, as *verina* the company, or *logora* all.

A long speech quoted requires to be followed by, "he said so." See Luke xvi, 24. *Ia ini e koautoma.*

ENGLISH MOTU VOCABULARY.

A

A or An, Ta.
Abandon, Negea. Lakatania.
Abandoned, Vata negea.
Abase, Hamanaua.
Abash, Ahemaraia.
Abate, Hamaragia.
Abbreviate, Haqadogia.
Abdomen, Boka.
Abet, Durua.
Abhor, Lalo dika henia.
Abhorrence, Lalo dika.
Abide, Noho.
Ability, Diba. Aonega.
Abject, Dika rohoroho.
Able (*to do, &c.*), Karaia diba.
Ablution, Digu. Hadigua.
Abode, Noho gabuna. Ruma.
Abolish, Haorea.
Abominable, Dika rohoroho.
Abominate, Lalo dika henia.
Abortion, Mara dika.
Above, Atai.
Abound, Diagau. Hoho. Momo.
About, *adv.* Hegege (*round about*).
  Lao evaeva (*to go about*).
Abreast (*to walk*), Laka bou.
Abridge, Haqadogia.
Abrogate, Ruhaia. Koauatao.
Abscess, Veto.
Abscond, Heau.
Absent, Noho lasi. Lasihia.
Absolve, Koauatao.
Absorb, Dodo.
Abstract, Abia-lasi. Veria-lasi.
Absurd, Kavakava.
Abundance, Momo. Diagau.
Abuse, Hadikaia.
Accede, Ura henia. Gadudae.
Accept, Abia.
Access, Mai dalana.
Accompany, Bamoa. Ida lao (*preceded by person accompanied.*)
Accomplice, Bamona.
Accomplish, Karaia vaitani.

According, Hahegeregere. Bamona
  (*following thing or speech with
  which it accords.*)
Account, Hereva. Sivarai.
Accumulate, Haboua.
Accurate, Maoromaoro.
Accurse, Uduguilai.
Accuse, Habade. Loduhenia.
Accustom, Hamanadaia.
Ache, Hisihisi.
Acid, Iseuri.
Acknowledge, Koau. Hegore lasi.
Acquiesce, Kamonai. Ere tamona.
Acquire, Abia.
Acrid, Hegara.
Across (*to go*), Hanai.
Act, Kara.
Active, Goada. Mauri.
Adage, Idaunegai hereva.
Adapt, Halaoa. Hahegeregere.
Add, Haboua.
Adhere, Kamoa.
Adjacent, Badibadina.
Adjoin, (*of houses, &c.*) Gini hetabila.
Adjourn, Ununega koaulaia.
Adjudge, Ahemaoro henia.
Adjure, Ominuo *adopted from the
  Greek.*) Koauhenia.
Adjust, Hagoevaia. Gabunai atoa.
Admirable, Namo herea.
Admire, Hanamoa.
Admit, Iduara kehoa.
Admonish, Sisiba henia.
Adopt, Butuaoho.
Adore, Hanamoa.
Adorn, Hera karaia. Hagoevaia.
Adrift, Hure.
Adult, Sinana. Tamana.
Adultery, Henaohenao.
Adversary, Inai.
Adverse, Nega didadika.
Adversity, Nega dika.
Advise, Sisiba henia.
Advocate, Ahemarumaru tauna.
Adze, Ira. Omu (*introduced.*)
Afar, Daudau.

B

Affable, Gado namo tauna.
Affection, Lalokau henia. Ura henia.
Affirm, Koau.
Afflict, Hahisia.
Affright, Hagaria.
Affront, Hadikaia.
Afloat, Heilu.
Afoot, Tanoa mo lao.
Afraid, Gari.
After, Gabea. Murina.
Afterbirth, Momo.
Afternoon, Dina gelona.
Afterpains, Mariva.
Again, Lou (*following verb*); Ma, (*preceding.*)
Against (*opposite*), Hegagaheheni.
Age, Lagani, (*followed by number of years.*)
Aged, Tau or Haine bada.
Agent, Boloa tauna *and* Ibodohi tauna.
Aggravate, Habadaia.
Aggressor, Ima guna tauna.
Agitate (*as water in a bottle*), Qadaqadaia.
Ago (*long ago*), Idaunegai.
Agony, Hisihisi bada.
Agree, Koau bou. Lalo tamona.
Agreement, Taravatu.
Aground, Qihohoa.
Aha! Hi! Hinā!
Ahead, Vairanai. (*to go*), Laka guna.
Aid, Durua.
Aim, Havevea.
Air, Lāi (lit. wind).
Alarm, Hagaria.
Alas! Ināi. Inaio!
Albino, Gahukagahuka tauna. Hurokahuroka tauna.
Alien, Idau tauna.
Alike, Hegeregere. (*of persons*) Heidaida.
Alive, Mauri.
All, Idoinai. Ibounai. Logora.
Alleviate, Hisihisi hamaragia.
Allot, Haria. Karoa.
Allotment, Ahuna.
Allow, Mia Koauatao lasi.
Allure (*by deceit*), Koia.
Ally, Durua tauna. Hekaha tauna.
Almost, Moko (*before the verb.*)
Aloft, Ataiai.
Alone, Sibona.
Also, Danu.
Alter, Haidaulaia.
Alternate, Hadava.
Although, Enabe,

Altogether (*to do*), Karaia hebou. (*to stay*) Nohobou.
Always, Nega idoinai.
Amass, Haboua.
Amazed, Hōa. Laumadaure.
Amazing, Hahoaia gauna.
Ambassador, Isiaina tauna.
Ambiguous. Hereva maoro lasi.
Ambition, Heagi tahua.
Ambush, Banitao.
Amend, Kara hamaoromaoro.
Amends, Davana.
Amidst, Bokaragina.
Amiss, Kererekerere.
Amongst, Bokaragina.
Ample, Bada.
Amuse, Hamoalea.
Anchor, Doko.
Anchorage, Hedoko gabuna.
Ancient, Gunana. Idaunegai gauna or tauna.
Aucle, Ae komukomu.
And, Mai.
Anger, Badu.
Animal, Boroma (*literally pig*).
Annoy, Gādegāde. Dāuahuahu.
Annul, Negea. Haorea.
Anoint (*head*), Ehoro. (*body*) Hetahu.
Another, Ma ta. Idau.
Answer, Haere.
Ant, Bilailo. Demaile (*very small*); Mutuma (*white*).
Anxious, Lalo he siku.
Any, Haida. Taina.
Apart, Idauhai.
Apartment, Daeutu. Daehudu.
Apologize, Maino noinoi. Hamarumarua.
Apparel, Dabua.
Apparition, Lauma. Vatavata.
Appeal, Noinoi henia.
Appear (*as a spirit*), Hanihia. Hahedina.
Appease, Hamarumarua.
Applaud, Hanamoa.
Apply (*ask*), Henanadai.
Appoint, Koaulaia.
Approach, Laka kahila.
Approve, Namo koaulaia.
Arbitrate, Ahemaoro karaia.
Architect, Ruma iseuna tauna.
Arduous, Metau. Malakamalaka.
Areca (*tree and also nut*), Buatau.
Argue, Hepapahuahu.
Arise, Toreisi.
Arm, Ima.
Arm *v.*, Ima gaudia abia.

Armpit, Kadidia.
Arms, Ima gaudia.
Army, Tuari.
Around, Hegege.
Arouse, Haoa.
Arrange (things), Kokosi. Atoa namonamo.
Arrest, Rosia. Dabaiatao.
Arrive, Lasi.
Arrogance, Hekokorogu.
Arrow, Diba.
Arrowroot, Rabia.
Artery, Varovaro.
Artifice, Hedibagani.
As, Bamona.
Ascend, Daradae, (mountain). Daekau.
Ashamed, Hemarai.
Ashes, Rahurahu. Gahu.
Ashore, Tano ai.
Ask, Henanadai.
Aslant, Marere.
Asleep, Mahuta.
Assault, Hadikaia.
Assemble, Habona.
Assent, Namo koaulaia. Gadudae.
Assiduous, Goada.
Assist, Durua.
Associate s., Bamona. v. Bamoa.
Asthma, Roē.
Astonish, Habōa. Lauma hadaurea.
Astray, Laka kerere ; (of pig, &c.) Dobi.
Astride, Helai dagadaga.
Asunder, Idau hai atoa. Parara.
Asylum, Magu.
At (place), Unuseni ai.
Atone, Davana benia.
Atonement, Davaraia.
Attack, Alala henia.
Attain, Abia. Davaria.
Attempt, Karaia toho.
Attend (to listen), Kamonai ; (to attend to a person) Isiai laoheni.
Attest, Hamomokanilaia.
Attracted, Veria.
Audience, Kamonai taudia.
Austere, Koautoratauna.
Authority, Siahu.
Avarice, Kohu hekisehekise bada.
Avenge, Davana karaia.
Avert, Helaoahu.
Avoid (spear, &c.), Dekea.
Await, Naria, Helaro.
Awake, Noga.
Away, Idauhai.
Axe, Ira.

B.

Babe, Natuna karukaru.
Back, Dolu.
Backbite, Murina hadikaia.
Backbone, Turia mava.
Backside, Kunu.
Backslide, Dedi dobi.
Backwards, Laka muri.
Bad, Dika.
Bag (small netted), Vaina ; (large) Kiapa ; (canvas) Nulu ; Moda.
Bait, Guma.
Bake, Hamudoa.
Bald, Boha ; " qara boha," Lama boha.
Bale, v. (if thrown without dipping) Petaia ; (dipped and then poured over the side) Ranu seia.
Bale, s. Ikumi.
Ballad, Ane.
Bamboo, Ban.
Banana (fruit), Bigu ; (tree) Dui.
Bananas, different kinds of. See Appendix.
Band, Guia gauna.
Bandage, Hilia dabuana.
Bang, Regena bada. Poudagu.
Banish, Lulua.
Banishment, Idauhai lulua.
Bank (of river), Popoto.
Banner, Pepe.
Banter, Hevasea.
Bar (of wood), Au.
Barb, Igara.
Bard, Ane sisibaia tauna.
Bargain, Taravatu.
Bark, s. Au kopina.
Bark, v. Qaru.
Barren, Gabani (of animals).
Barricade, Dara kouahu gauna.
Barter, Hoihoi.
Base the, Badina.
Bashful, Hemarai. Igodiho.
Basket, Bosea.
Bason, Oburo. Biobio.
Bastard, Ariara natuna.
Bat, Mariboi.
Bathe, Digu.
Battle, Alala karaia.
Bay, Dogudogu. Tabero.
Beach, Kone.
Beads, Akeva.
Beak, Udu.
Beam, Mukulo.

Bear, v. (as fruit) Dobi ; (give birth) Mara ; (to endure) Aheauka ; (to carry) Huaia ; (down, as in labour) Lado.

Beard, s. Hadehuina.

Bearer, Huaia tauna.

Beast, Boroma.

Beat, Dadaba.

Beat out (as native cloth), Tadaia.

Beautiful, Namoherea. Raho namo.

Becalmed, Vea (if by day) ; Gaima (if by night).

Because, Madi be.

Beckon, Hekalo.

Become, Halaoa.

Becoming, Namo herea.

Bed, Mahuta gauna.

Bedridden, Ruma noho.

Beetle, Manumanu.

Before, Vairanai.

Beg, Noi hegame.

Beget, Havaraia.

Beggar, Hegame tauna.

Begin, Matama.

Beginning, Matamana.

Begone, Baola. Lao.

Beguile, Koia.

Behaviour, Kara.

Behead, Qara utua.

Behind, Murina.

Behold, Ba itaia. Interj. Inäi.

Belch, Gado lohilohi.

Believe, Kamonai.

Bell, Gaba.

Bellow, Lolo. Tai lolololo.

Belly, Boga or Boka.

Bellyful, Boka kunu.

Belong (to him) Iena.

Beloved, Lalokau tauna.

Below, Henuai.

Belt, Gaba gauna.

Bench, Pata.

Bend, Hagagevaia.

Beneath, Henuai.

Beneficial, Namo.

Benevolence, Harihari bada.

Benight, Hanna eme boi.

Beseech, Noinoi.

Beside, Badibadinai.

Besiege, Tuari hegegedae.

Besmear, Hedahu.

Bespeak, Koauamata.

Best, Namo herea.

Bestow, Henia.

Betray, Taotore.

Betroth, Maoheni.

Better, Inai namo (thing compared with), Unai dika.

Between, Ihuanai.

Bewail, Tāi.

Beware, Itaia namonamo.

Beyond, Unuka.

Bible, Buka helaga.

Bid (command), Hahedua. Hagania.

Bier, Mate tauna patana.

Big, Bada.

Bigamy, Hodara.

Billow, Sinaia.

Bind, Guia.

Bird, Mānu. For names of different kinds, see Appendix.

Birth, Vara.

Bit (a piece), Sisina. (horse's) Hosi udu koria gauna.

Bite, Koria.

Bitter, Idita.

Black, Koremakorema.

Bladder, Posi.

Bladebone, Larolaro turiana.

Blame, Koau henia. Hadikaia.

Blaspheme, Dirava badikaia.

Blaze, Hururu. Paitapaita.

Blaze, v. (trees) Daroa. (fire) Lahi-huruhuru.

Bleed, Rara diho. (from the nose), Udu makohi.

Blemish, Dika.

Bless, Hauamoa.

Blessed, Namo.

Blind, Matakepulu.

Blink, Varirivariri.

Blister, Goua.

Blood, Rara.

Bloody, Rara karaia.

Blossom, Au huahua.

Blossom, v. Burea.

Blow, v. (as wind) Tōa. (with the mouth) Hihiria. (nose) Iluhai.

Blue, Gadogadoga, and also green.

Blunder, Kererekerere.

Blunderbuss, Ipidi.

Blunt, Gāno lasi. Buru.

Boar, Boroma maruane.

Board, Leilei.

Boast, v. Heagi.

Boat, Bosi.

Body, Tāu. Anitarana.

Bog, Kopukopu.

Boil, Daidai.

Boil, s. Iholuln. (blind) Atuahu.

Bold, Goada.

Bold-faced, Kopi hemarai lasi.

Bone, Turia.

Bonnet, Qara gauna.
Bony, Hevăgo.
Book, Buka. (*Introduced*.)
Booty, Dadidadi gaudia *or* Kohudia.
Border, Isena.
Bore, *v.* (*a hole*) Budua.
Borrow, Koautorehai.
Bosom, Geme.
Both, Rua davana.
Bother, Haraivaia.
Bottle (*native*), Ahu. (*Foreign*) Kavapu.
Bottom (*of sea*), Qari.
Bough, Rigi.
Boundary, Hetoa.
Bow, *s.* Peva.
Bow (*to string*), Rohea.
Bow and Arrow (*for bleeding*) Ibasi.
Bow down, *v.* Tomadiho.
Bowels, Bokalau.
Bowl (*wooden*), Dihu. (*Earthenware*) Nău.
Bows (*of canoe*) Itama.
Bowstring, Maora.
Box, Măua.
Boy, Mero,
Boyish, Merobamona.
Brackish, Măga.
Brag, Heagi herevana.
Brain, Hara. " Qara harana."
Branch, Rigi.
Brandish, Hare.
Brave, Goada.
Brawl, Lolo.
Breadfruit, Ūnu.
Breadth, Lababana.
Break (*string*), Motu. (*Spear, &c.*) Qaidu. (*Pottery, &c.*) Huaria.
Breaker (*in sea*), Sinaia.
Breast, Geme.
Breastbone (*of bird*), Abagoro. *Of mammal*) Gemegeme.
Breath, Laga.
Breath (*short*), Lagatuna.
Breath (*deep*), Hahodi.
Breathe, Laga.
Breathless, Lagatuna.
Breeches, Biribou. (*Introduced*.)
Breed, Mara (*act of bringing forth*).
Breeze, Lăi.
Bridge, Nese hanai pătana.
Bright, Hururuhururu. Kiamakiama.
Brimful, Honuhonudae.
Bring, Mailaia.
Bring forth, Mara.
Brink, Isena.
Brisk, Lega haraga tauna.

Bristle, Boroma huina.
Brittle, Makohi haraga.
Broad, Lababana bada. Gamoga bada.
Broil, Nonoa. Gabua.
Brood, *s.* Serina.
Brood, *v.* Hadetari. Laloa.
Brother, Tadikăka. (*younger*), Tadina. (*elder*), Kakana.
Brother-in-law, Ihana.
Brown, Korema.
Browse, Rei ania.
Bruise, Rara arukubou.
Brush, *n.* Iareva. Hedaro gauna.
Brushwood. Au maragimaragi.
Bubble, Lohilohia.
Bud, Komukau.
Buffet, Tutua.
Build (*a house*), Ruma karaia. (*a wall*), Nadi larebaia.
Builder, Ruma karaia tauna.
Bullet, Ipidi nadina.
Bully, Dagedage tauna.
Bunch, Igui. (*of fruit*), Takona.
Bundle, Ikumi.
Buoy, Uto.
Burden, Maduna (*if carried on a stick*.)
Burn, *v.* (*food*) Halaka. (*grass*), Doua. (*house*), Alaia.
Burn, *n.* Lahi alaia.
Burnish, Hahururuhururua.
Burrow, Tahia.
Burst, Păpa. Pou.
Bury, Guria.
Bush, Uda. (*fallow ground*), Vahu.
Business, Gau karaia. Totona.
Busy, Heqarahi.
But, Ā.
Butterfly, Kaubebe.
Buttock, Kunu.
Button, Pitopito (*introduced word.*)
Buy, Hoihoi.
By (*instrument*),—laia (*suffixed to verb.*)
By (*near*), Badibadina. Dekena.
By-and-bye, Dohore.

C

Cable, Mataboi. Gadea.
Cackle, Tăi.
Cadaverous, Raborarabora.
Cage, Ruma.
Cajole, Hanamoa koikoi.
Cake, Mone.

Calamity, Dika.
Calculate, Duahia.
Caldron, Uro bada.
Calf (of leg), Doku.
Calk, Demaia.
Call, v. Boiboi.
Call, n. Boiboi.
Calm (in the day), Vea. (at night), Gaima.
Calm, v. Hamarumarua.
Calumniate, Hadikaia.
Camp, Taruha hebou.
Camp, v. Taruha.
Can, Karaia diba.
Cancel, Rohoa.
Cane, Oro. Vagoda.
Cannibal, Taunimanima aniatauna.
Cannon, Ipidi bada.
Cannot, Karaia diba lasi.
Canoe (small), Vanagi. (large), Asi.
Canoe maker, Ikede tauna.
Cap, Qara gauna.
Capable, Karaia diba. Aonega.
Capacious, Gabana bada. (of house) Lababana bada.
Cape, Iduka.
Capsicum, Urehegini, Oboro (introduced name.)
Captain (of ship), Lakatoi tauna.
Captive, Abi mauri tauna.
Care, Lalo he siku (to take care of), Dōsi. Naria.
Careful, Namonamo, Dōsi.
Careless, Kererekerere. Matalahui.
Carpenter, Au idibaka tauna.
Carry (on the shoulder), Huaia. (Pick-a-back), Geia. (On a pole between two), Huaia horoma. (As water pot), Ehea. (On the head), Oraia. (Astride on neck), Udua.
Carve, Ivaia.
Cast, Tohoa.
Cast away, Tahoa daure.
Cast down, Tahoa dobi.
Castigate, Dadabaia.
Castle, Magu.
Castrate, Abona abia.
Cat, Posi (introduced.)
Catch, Butuatao.
Catch (by contagion), Kara (with suffix) karagu, &c.
Catch hold, Abia. Kahua.
Catechize, Henanadai.
Caterpillar, Bulelamo.
Cause, s. Koauna. Badina.
Cause, v. Havaraia.
Causeway, Dala.

Caustic, Hegara.
Cautious, Metailametaila.
Cave, Kohua.
Cavil, Koauatubu.
Cease, Doko. Vadaeni.
Cedar, Besele.
Cede, Henia.
Celebrate, Hanamoa.
Cemetery, Mate guria gabuna.
Censure, Koau henia. Sisiba henia.
Census, Taunimanima duahia.
Centipede, Aiha.
Centre, Bokaragi.
Certain, Momokani etomamu.
Certify, Koaulaia.
Chain, Gadoa.
Chair, Helai gauna.
Challenge, Boi gagadae. Haré henia.
Chamber, Daehudu.
Change, Boloa.
Channel, Mātu.
Chant, Ane.
Character, Kara.
Charcoal, Gida.
Charge, v. Hetamanu.
Charge (a gun), Ipidi anina.
Charity, Heboka hisi.
Charm, (cocoa nut), Biobio.
Chaste, Igodiho haniulato. Se mata dikana.
Chat, Hereva.
Chatterer, Udn mauri.
Chase, v. Hāvaia.
Chasm, Koupa.
Chastise, Dadaha.
Cheap, Hoihoi davana maragi.
Cheat, Koia.
Check, Dokoatao. Laoahu.
Cheek, Vaha.
Cheer, Tauhalō.
Cheerful, Lalo namo tauna.
Cherish, Ubua. Naria.
Cherisher, Iubuna tauna.
Chest, Geme. (a box), Māua.
Chestnut, Omada.
Chew, Ganaia. (the pandanus), Oria.
Chicken, Kokorogu natuna.
Chide, Koaukoau. Sisiba henia.
Chief (thing), Herea gauna.
Chief, s. Lohiabada.
Child, Natuna.
Childbirth, Mara, natuna abia.
Childish, Meromero bamona.
Chill, v. Hakerumaia.
Chin, Ade.
Chip, Memeuse.
Chip, v. Siria.

Chirp (*as lizard*), Tanatana.
Chisel, Vadu.
Chisel (*small*) Pāko.
Choice, *adj.* Namo herea.
Choke, Gādo ai hetara. (*by another*), Gado gigia.
Choose, Abia hidi. (*by inspection*), Ita hidi.
Chop, Talai.
Churlish, Koautora tauna.
Circular, Kubolukubolu.
Clammy, Parikaparika.
Clamour, Helogohelogo.
Clang, Hataia.
Clap (*hands*), Ima patapata.
Clash, Huaria.
Clasp (*in arms*), Rosia.
Class, Verina.
Clatter, Regeregena.
Claw, Ima.
Clay, Raro.
Clean, Goevagoeva.
Cleanse, Hagoevaia.
Clear, Nega.
Clear (*away*), Abiaoho. Laohaia.
Cleave to, Badinaia.
Cleave (*to split*), Hapararaia.
Clever, Aonega.
Cliff, Hagahaga.
Ciimb, Urua.
Cling, Hekamokau.
Clip, Haqadogia.
Close (*near*), Kahilakahila.
Close, *v.* Ahu. Kouahu.
Cloth, Dabua.
Clothe, Dabua hadokilaia.
Clothing, Dabua.
Cloud, Dagadaga. Ori.
Cloudy, Dagahu.
Cloven, Parara.
Clownish, Guni tauna bamona.
Cloy, Laloalu.
Club (*stone*), Gahi ; (*wood*) Kaleva.
Cluck, Tāi.
Clump (*of trees*), Uda motu.
Clumsy, Ima mamano.
Cluster (*of fruit*), Takona.
Clutch, Hekamotao.
Coagulate, Hetari. Hemani.
Coarse (*cloth*), Nulu.
Coarse (*rough*), Butubutu.
Coast, Tano isena.
Coat, Pereue (*adopted from the Tahitian*).
Coax, Noinoi.
Cobweb, Valavala.
Cock, Kokorogu maruane.

Cockcrowing, Kokorogu tāi.
Cockfight, Kokorogu heatu.
Cocoanut, Niu. (*young fruit*) Gāru.
Coequal Hegeregere.
Cogitate, Lalo. Lalo haguhi.
Coil (*in hand*), Tāia ; (*on deck*) Kekea.
Cold, Keru.
Colic, Boka hisihisi.
Collar-bone, Dōa.
Collect, Haboua.
Collection (*of things*), Senusenu. Hegigibon.
Collision, Tatakau.
Comb, Iduari.
Combat, Heatu.
Combine, Haheboua.
Combustible, Lahi haragaharaga.
Come, Mai. Aoma.
Come (*in sight*), Vata dina.
Comet, Hisiu bada.
Comfort *v.* Tauhalō.
Command, Hagania. Haduaia.
Commandment, Ahegani herevana,
Commemorate, Ahelaloa.
Commence, Matamaia.
Commend, Hanamoa.
Commerce, Hoihoi karaia.
Commit, Henia.
Common (*to make*), Petapetalaia.
Commotion, Herouherou.
Compact, Taravatu.
Companion, Bamona.
Company, Hutuma. (*visitors*) Vadi-vadi.
Compare, Hahetoho. Hahegeregere.
Compassion, Hehokahisi.
Compel, Hahedua.
Compensate, Davana henia.
Compete, Goada karaia daika herea.
Competent, Karaia diba.
Complain, Maumau.
Complete, Idoinai.
Compliment, *v.* Hanamoa henia.
Comply, Gadu dae. Oi he koaulaia.
Compose (*a song*), Ane sisibaia.
Comprehend, Diba.
Compute, Duahia.
Comrade, Bamona.
Conceal, Ehuni.
Conceited, Heagi tauna. Hekoko-rogu tauna.
Conceive, Rogorogo.
Conch, Kibi
Conciliate, Hamarumarua.
Concise, Qadogi.
Conclude, Hadokoa.

Conclusion, Dokona.
Concourse, Hegogo bada.
Concur, Koaubou.
Condemn, Revaia. Rataia.
Condescend, Hamanaua.
Conduct, s. Kara.
Conduct, v. Hakaua.
Confer, Herevahereva.
Confess, Koaulaia. Ahedinarai.
Confide, Hamaoroa.
Confirm, Hamomokania.
Conflict, Heatu. Alala.
Confounded, Laumadaure.
Congregate, Haheboua.
Conjecture, Lalo koau.
Conquer, Qalimu.
Conscience, Lalona.
Consecrate, Ahelagaia.
Consent, Gadudae. Namo koaulaia.
Consider, Laloa.
Consign, Henia.
Console. Tauhalō.
Consort, s. Adavana.
Conspicuous, Vata dina.
Conspire, Hereva ehuni.
Constantly, Nega idoinai.
Consternation, Kudou hetaha.
Constipation, Tupuahu.
Constrain, Hahealo.
Construct, Karaia.
Consult, Ida hereva (preceded by the person consulted).
Consume (by fire), Lahi alaia ore. (To eat), Ania ore.
Contagious, Dāi hanai hisina.
Contemn, Hadikaia.
Contemplate, Laloa.
Contend, Heatu. Hepapahuahu.
Content, Boka kunu.
Contents, s. Anina.
Contention, Hepapahuahu.
Contest, Heatu. Alala.
Contiguous, Badibadina.
Continual, Nega idoinai.
Continue, Mia hanaihanai.
Contract, s. Taravatu, Koauhamata.
Contract, v. (from cold), Hegogo.
Contradictory, Hegeregere lasi.
Contribute, Henia.
Contribution, Gau vata henia.
Control, Hakaua. Dokoatao.
Controversy, Hepapahuahu.
Contumacy, Ura dika.
Convalescent, Mauri maragimaragi.
Convene, Haheboua.
Conversant, Vata diba.
Conversation, Herevahereva.

Convert, Haloua.
Convey, Laohaia.
Coo, Mu.
Cook, s. Nanadu tauna.
Cook v. Nanadu.
Cookhouse, Nanadu ruma.
Cool, Kerumakeruma.
Coop (for fowls), Kokorogu ruma.
Copious, Gaubadabada.
Copper, Veo (introduced).
Copulation, Gagaia.
Copy, s. Oromana.
Coquette, Hegera.
Coral, Irigi. Nadi kuro. Lade.
Cord, Qanau.
Core (of boil), Komutu.
Cork, Iqadobe.
Corner, Daeguni.
Corner-stone, Nadi daegunina.
Corpse, Tau mate.
Corpulent, Nuana bada.
Correct, Maoromaoro.
Corrupt, v. Hadikaia.
Corrupt, adj. Dika.
Cost, Davalaia.
Costive, Boka tubuahu.
Costly, Hoihoi bada.
Cottage, Ruma maragi.
Cotton (introduced word), Vavae.
Couch, Hekure gauna.
Cough, Hūa.
Council, Taubadadia hegogo.
Counsel, v. Sisiba henia.
Count, Duahia.
Countenance, Vaira.
Counteract, Koauatubu. Laoahu.
Counterfeit, v. Koia.
Countermand, Koauatao.
Countless, Duahia lasi.
Country, Tano.
Countryman, Tano tauna.
Couple, Ruaoti.
Courage, Goada.
Courteous, Gado namo.
Courtezan, Ariara haine.
Cousin (younger), Tadina. (Elder), Kakana.
Cove, Dogudogu.
Covenant, Taravatu.
Cover, Kaluhia. Bubuni.
Covet, Hekisehekise henia.
Covetous, Mata ganigani.
Coward, Manokamanoka tauna. Gari tauna.
Cower, Rāki karaia.
Coy, Hemarai.
Crab, Kokoba. Bava.

Crack, Māka.
Crackle, Hepoupouahu.
Craft, Dagi.
Crafty, Hedibagani tauna.
Crag, Haga.
Cramp, Hegagiudae.
Crash, Makohi.
Crave, Noinoi.
Crawfish, Ura. Depuru.
Crawl, Rāu.
Creak, Koke.
Crease, Magugu.
Create, Karaia.
Creep, Laka helada.
Creeper, Au hilia.
Creepy, Hemaihemai.
Crevice, Maka.
Crew (of ship), Lakatoi memero.
  Neseriki memero.
Crime, Kara dika. Taravatu
  tataiautu.
Crimson, Kakakaka.
Cringe, Raki karaia.
Crinkle, Magugu.
Cripple (lame), Ae sike.
Crockery, Uro. Hodu, &c.
Crocodile, Uala.
Crook, v. Hagagevaia.
Crookback, Doruqagugu. Doru laoho.
Cross, Au hiri baribara. Satauro.
  (Introduced).
Crossway, Dala katakata.
Crouch, Rāki karaia.
Crow, v. Kokorogu tai.
Crowbar, Isiva.
Crowd, Hutuma.
Crown, Qara gegea gauna.
Crown (of head), Qara tupua.
Cruel, Dagedage.
Crumb, Momoruna.
Crumple, Magugu kainekaine.
Crush (under foot), Aemoia.
Cry, Tai.
Cubit, Kubita (introduced).
Cuff, Huaria.
Cultivate, Uma hadoa.
Cunning, Aonega.
Cup, Kehere. (Shell), Bio.
Cure, Hamauria.
Curly, Hui tuma.
Current (of river, &c.), Aru.
Curse, Hadikaia. Uduguilai.
Curve, n. Gagevagageva.
Custom, Kara.
Cut (up), Ivaia. (Off), Utua.
Cutlass, Ilapa.
Cuttlefish, Urita.

D

Daily, Daba daba idoinai.
Damage, Hadikaia.
Damp, Parikaparika.
Dance, Mavaru.
Dandle, Harohoa.
Dare, Goada.
Dare (to defy), Hare.
Dark, Dibura.
Darling, Lalokau tauna (man), or
  natuna (child).
Dart, v. Qanua.
Dash (on ground), Tahoa dobi.
Daub, Hetahu. Tabaiahu.
Daughter, Kekeni. Natuna haine.
Daunt, Hagaria.
Dawn, Daba e kinia.
Day, Dina.
Dazzle, Mata paia.
Dead, Mate.
Deaf, Taia kudima.
Deaf (to make), Akudimaia.
Deal, Hoihoi karaia.
Deal out, Hagana.
Dear (in price), Hoihoi davana bada.
Dear (beloved), Lalokau.
Dearth (of food), Doe.
Death, Mate.
Debate, Herevahereva. Hepapa-
  huahu.
Debauch, Hadikaia.
Debilitate, Hamanokaia.
Debility, Manokamanoka.
Debt, Abitorehai davana. Dodi.
Debtor, Abitorehai tauna.
Decapitate, Qara utua.
Decay, (fruit), Pouka. (wood),
  Houkahouka.
Decease, Mate.
Deceit, Koikoi.
Deceive, Koia.
December, Biriabada.
Decent, Namo.
Decide, Koaulaia.
Deck, v. Ilaha karaia. (With orna-
  ments) Hera karaia.
Deck, s. Ilaha.
Declare, Koaulaia. Hedinarai.
Decline, Dadaraia.
Decorate, Hera karaia. Hairaina
  karaia.
Decorous, Kara namo.
Decoy, Koia.
Decrease, Hamaragia.
Decree, Lohiabada hereva. Ahe-
  gani hereva.

Dedicate, Ahelagaia.
Deep, Dobu.
Deface, Hadikaia.
Defame, Eredika koaulaia.
Defeat, Darere.
Defect, Dika.
Defend, Naria. Gimaia.
Defer, Dohore koaulaia
Deference, Hemataurai
Defiance, Hare.
Deficient, Idoinai lasi.
Defile, Hamiroa. Hadikaia.
Define, Koaulaia maoromaoro.
Deformed, Tāu dika.
Defraud, Koia.
Defy, Heqada karaia.
Degrade, Hadikaia.
Delay, Halahe. Haraga lasi.
Deliberate, Herevahereva.
Deliberately, Metailametaila.
Delicious, Namo herea.
Delight, Moale.
Delirium, Lalona e boio, Koau kava.
Deliver, Hamauria.
Delude, Koia. Hagagevaia.
Deluge, Ututu bada.
Delusion, Koikoi.
Demand, Noinoi.
Demolish, Haorea. Buatari (as town, &c.)
Demon, Demoni. (Introduced.)
Demonstrate, Ahedinarai.
Denial, Hegore.
Denounce, Loduheheni.
Depart, Idauhai lao.
Depend, Abidadama henia.
Depopulate, Taunimanima haorea.
Depose, Doria dobi. Abiaoho.
Deprave, Hadikaia.
Deprive (take away), Idauhai laohaia.
Depth, Dobu.
Deputy, Boloa tauna.
Deride, Gonagonalaia.
Descend, Diho. (Mountain) Hekei.
Descendant, Tubuna.
Descent, Hekei darana.
Describe, Hamaoroa.
Desecrate, Hadikaia.
Desert, v. Lakatania.
Desert, s. Tano gagaena or deke-dekenarahu.
Design, Lalokoau.
Desire, Hekisehekise. Urana ura.
Desist, Doko.
Desolate, Dekedekenarahu.
Despatch, s. Siaia.
Despicable, Dika rohoroho.

Despise, Hadikaia.
Despond, Lalo dika.
Destination, Totona gabuna.
Destitute, Asi gauna. Ogogami.
Destroy, Haorea. Buatari.
Detach, Kahuanege.
Detail, Koaulaia hegege.
Detain, Rūa.
Detect, Abia. Davaria.
Determine, Lalona ura hamaoroa.
Detest, Inai henia.
Devastate, Hadikaia rohoroho.
Deviate, Idauhai lao.
Devoid (of sense), Asi aonega.
Devote, Ahelagaia.
Devour, Ania.
Dew, Hunu.
Diadem, Qara gegea gauna.
Dialect, Gādo.
Dialogue, Herevahereva heheni.
Diarrhœa, Boka hekukuri
Dictate, Ahegani hereva.
Did, Karaia.
Die, Mate.
Die (red color), Hakakakakaia ; (black), Hakoremakoremaia.
Differ, Idau.
Difficult (to do, open, &c.), Āuka.
Diffident, Hemarai.
Diffuse, Buloa.
Dig, Geia.
Dilapidate, Hamakohia.
Dilatory, Haraga lasi.
Diligent, Goadagoada.
Dilute, Ranu buloa.
Dim, Valahuvalahu.
Diminish, Hamaragia.
Dip, Uruadiho.
Dip up, Kadoa.
Dire, Dika bada.
Direct, v. Hadibaia. Hamaoroa.
Direction (towards), Hagerea.
Directly, Haragaharaga. Harihari.
Dirt, Miro.
Dirty, Miro.
Disagree, Hereva tamona lasi.
Disappear, Boio. Lasihia.
Disapprove, Hanamoa lasi.
Disaster, Dika butuatao.
Disband, Karoho.
Disbelieve, Hedalo kepokipoa.
Discern, Diba.
Discharge, v. Lulua. Siaia lao.
Disciple, Hadibaia mero.
Disclose, Hamaoroa. Koaulaia.
Discompose, Haraivaia. Turiariki.
Discord, Helogohelogo.

Discourage, Lalona hamanokaia.
Discourse, Haroro.
Discourteous, Eredika.
Discover, Ahedinarai.
Discreet, Aonega.
Discriminate, Hasinadoa.
Disdain, Badu henia.
Disease, Gorere.
Disembowel, Bokaia.
Disfigure, Hadikaia.
Disgrace, Ahemaraia.
Disgraceful, Hemarai kara.
Disgust, Lalo dika.
Dish, Nāu.
Dishearten, Hagaria. Hamanokaia.
Dishevelled, Hui karaia lasi.
Disinter, Guria tauna abiaisi.
Disjoin, Ruhaia nege.
Dislike, Lalo dika henia.
Dislocated, Heladaoho. Helide.
Dismiss, Siaia lao.
Dismount, v. a. Abiadobi.
Dismount, v. n. Diho.
Disobedient, Kamonai lasi.
Disown, Dadaraia.
Disperse, Karoho.
Dispirit, Hamanokaia.
Display, Hedinarai.
Displease, Habadua.
Dispossess, Dadidadi abiaoho.
Dispute, Koauatubu.
Disregard, Itaia lasi.
Disreputable, Harina dika.
Disrespect, Lagāua.
Dissatisfy, Lalo namo lasi.
Dissemble, Hedibagani karaia.
Dissent, Heiriheiri.
Dissever, Utua nege.
Dissimilar, Hegeregere lasi.
Dissolve, Veve.
Distant, Daudau.
Distemper, Gorere.
Distend, Kuroro.
Distinguish, Toana diba.
Distress, Nega dikadika.
Distribute. Henia hagauhagau.
District, Kahana.
Disturb, Hahoaia.
Disturbance, Heai karaia.
Ditch, Koupa.
Dive, Hedai.
Diverse, Idau.
Divide, Karoa. Haria.
Division, Karoa ahuna.
Divorce, v. Hadihoa.
Divulge, Koaulaia.
Dizzy, Gagala. Mata madaimadai.

Do, Karaia.
Docile, Manada.
Doctor, Muramura tauna.
Doctor, v. Muramura henia. (by native sorcerer), Daroa.
Dodge, v. Dekea.
Dog, Sisia.
Dolt, Kavakava.
Dominion, Basileia. (Introduced.)
Doom (to death), Rataia.
Door, Mu.
Doorway, Iduara.
Dot, Toutou.
Dotage, Garugaru bamona.
Double, Ere rua.
Double-minded, Lalo rua.
Double-up, Lokua.
Doubt, Daradara.
Dove, Pune.
Down, Diho. Dobi.
Downward, Henuai.
Doze, Mahuta.
Drag, Veria. Dabuia. (as anchor), Dadaroha.
Drake, Mokora maruane.
Draught (fluid drank), Gurita.
Draw, Veria.
Draw near, Laka kahila.
Draw-rope (of well), Itudobina varona.
Dread, Gari.
Dream, Nihi.
Dregs, Nurina.
Dress, Dabua.
Drift, v. Hure.
Drill, s. Ibudu gauna.
Drink, Inua.
Drip, Hetuturu.
Drive, Ahavaia.
Drivel, Tāba.
Drizzle, Sisimo.
Droop, Marai.
Drollery, Hevaseha kara.
Drop, Hetuturu.
Dropsy, Rara dika e dae.
Drown, Maloa.
Drowsy, Mata e gara.
Drum, Gaba. (bamboo) Sede.
Drunk, Muramura heala. Kekero.
Dry, Kaukau.
Dry, (to, in the sun), Raraia.
Duck (tame), Mokorā.
Duck (wild), Ohuka. Bala.
Dull (of tools), Ganolasi. Buru.
Dumb, Mu.
Dunce, Kavakava.
Dung, Tage.
Durable, Auka bada.

Dusk, Mairumairu.
Dust, Gahu.
Dwell, Noho.
Dwelling, Noho gahuna. Ruma.
Dwindle, Hamaragia. Hagadoia.
Dyspnœa, Laga tuna.

E

Each, Ta ta, Hagauhagau.
Eager, Ura bada.
Ear, Taia. (of corn), Boga.
Early (in the morning), Daba matana.
Earn, Gau kara davana.
Earnest, Momokani.
Earth, Tano.
Earthquake, Laga karaia.
Earthworm, Biruka.
Ease, v. (to be at) Noho namonamo.
East, Maireveina.
Eastward, Mairieveina kahana.
East-wind, Lai mairiveina.
Easy, Haragaharaga.
Eat, Ania.
Eat together, Anibon.
Eat up, Aniore.
Eatable, Aniani gauna.
Eaves, Seasea.
Ebb, Gui.
Ebulition, Lohilohia.
Echo, Hetohotoho.
Eclipse (sun) Dina gobaiahu.
        (moon) Hua gobaiahu.
Eddy, Aru. Kavabulobulo.
Edge, Isena.
Edible, Aniani gauna.
Edict, Ahegani herevana.
Edge, Matana.
Educate, Hadibaia.
Eel, Daqala.
Efface, Hamatea. Rohoa.
Effigy, Laulau.
Effort, Karaia toho.
Effulgent, Hururuhururu.
Egg, Katoi.
Eight, Taurahani.
Eighteen, Quata taurahani.
Eighty, Taurahani ahui.
Either, Iava, as, namo e iara dika.
Eject (from the mouth), Pururua.
        (from the house) Doria lāsi.
Elate, Hamoalea.
Elbow, Diu.
Elders, Taubadadia.
Eldest, Vara guna.

Elect, Koaulaia hidi.
Elegy, Sesera.
Elephantiasis, Badau (preceded by the member), as, ae badau.
Elevate (as a pole from the ground.) Piuaisi.
Eleven, Qauta ta.
Elongate, Halataia.
Elude, Heau.
Emaciate, Tau gadili.
Emasculate, Abona e abia.
Embalm, Muramura hetahu.
Embark, Lakatoi gui.
Embassy, Hesiai taudia.
Embellish, Hanamoa.
Embers, Gida.
Embrace, Rosia.
Embrocation, Hetahu muramura.
Emerge (from diring), Sesedaeroha.
Emetic, Hamumutaia.
Eminence, Ataina.
Emissary, Isiaina tauna.
Emmet, Dimaili.
Employ, v. a. Siaia.
Employment, Gau karaia.
Empty, Asi anina.
Encamp, Taruha karaia.
Enclose, Gegea. Hegege madai.
Enclosure, Ara. Ikou.
Encompass, Hegege.
Encounter, s. Alala.
        v. Toia hedavari.
Encourage, Hahealo.
Encumber, Hametaua.
End, Dokona.
Endeavour, Karaia toho.
Endless, Asi dokona.
Endure, Aheauka.
Eoemy, Inai.
Enfeeble, Hamanokaia.
Enforce (to instigate), Havaraia.
Engage (to work) Taravatu karaia.
Engagement, Taravatu.
Engrave, (wood), Koloa.
Enjoin, Hetamanu.
Enjoy, Moale. Lalo namc.
Enkindle, Haraia.
Enlarge, Habadaia.
Enlighten Hadiaria. (With torch), Hakedea.
Enmity, Inai henia.
Enough, Davana.
Enough ! Vadaeni.
Enquire, Nanadai.
Enrage, Hahadua.
Ensign, Pepe.
Ensnare, Idoa.

Entangle, Hiria.
Enter, Vareai.
Entertain, Hagerea. Heabidae.
Entice, Hedibagani.
Entire, Idoinai.
Entrails, Bokarau.
Entrance, Iduara.
Entrap, Doa.
Entreat, Noinoi.
Entwine, Hiria.
Euumerate, Duahia. Koaulaia.
hegege.
Envelope, Kumia.
Envious, Hebore karaia.
Envoy, Hesiai.
Envy, Vagege. Hebore.
Epidemic, Hisi karaia.
Epilepsy, Tororotororo.
Equal, Hegeregere.
Equivalent, Davana.
Erect, Gini.
Err, Kererekerere.
Errand, Koaukau.
Eruption (on skin), Lari.
Escape, Heau.
Escort, Hakaua taudia.
Essay, v. Karaia toho.
Establish, Badinaia.
Eternal, Hanaihanai.
Evasive, Hedibagani hereva.
Even, Manada. Hegeregere.
Evening, Adorahi.
Ever, Hanaihanai.
Every, Idoidiai.
Evident, Dina.
Evil, Dika.
Evil speaking, Koau dika.
Eulogy, Hanamoa herevana.
Exact (to be), maoromaoro.
Exalt, Abiaisi.
Examine, Nanadaia. Tahua.
Example, Oromana kara.
Exasperate, Hadagedagea.
Exceed, Herea.
Excel, Sibona namo.
Excellent, Namo herea.
Exchange, Davana.
Excite, Haloa.
Exclaim, Koau. Lolo dagu.
Excoriated, Hekopa.
Excrement, Tage.
Excuse, v. Ahekora.
Execrate, Hadikaia.
Execute, Karaia.
Exempt, Tabu.
Exert, Hagoadalaia.
Exhibit, Ahedinarai.

Exhort, Hahealo.
Exile, Lulua oho tauna.
Exorbitant (in price), Davana bada.
Expand, Habadaia.
Expect, Naria. Laroa.
Expectorate, Kanudi.
Expedient, Namo baine karaia.
Expedite, Haragaia.
Expel, Luluaoho. Halasia.
Expert, Lega haraga.
Expiate, Davana henia.
Expire, Mate.
Explain, Hamaoroa.
Explode, Hapoua. Poudagu.
Expose Ahedinaraia.
Expound, Hadibaia. Hamaoroa.
Extend, Habadaia.
Extend (the neck), Hauogo.
Exterior, Murina.
Exterminate, Haorea. Alaia ore.
Extinct (as fire), Bodo.
Extinguish, Habodoa.
Extirpate, Alaia ore.
Extol, Heatolaia. Hanamoa.
Extraordinary, Hoa gauna.
Extremity, Dokona.
Extricate, Ruhaia. Hamauria.
Exuberant, Vara roho roho.
Exult, Heagi.
Eye, Mata.
Eyeball, Mata anina.
Eyebrow, Ibuni mata.
Eyelid, Mata kopina.

F

Fable, Hereva hegeregere.
Face, Vaira.
Face, v. Vaira henia.
Fade, Marai.
Faint, Matelea. Manori.
Fair (wind), Lai namo.
Faith, Kamonai. Abidadama henia.
Faithful, Kamonai bada. Momokani.
Faithless, Kamonai lasi.
Fall, Keto. (from height), Moru.
(of tree, &c.), Gari.
Fallow, Vabu.
False, Koikoi.
Falsehood, Hereva koikoi.
Falter, Manokamanoka.
Famed, Harina bada.
Family, Iduhu.
Famine, Doe.
Famish, Hitolo mate.

Fan, Itapo gauna.
Fan, v. Tapoa.
Far, Daudau.
Farewell, Ba mahuta !
Farewell (to bid), Ahetoni.
Farthest, Dokona gauna (thing), tauna (man).
Fashion, Oromana.
Fast, v. Anivāga.
Fast (to make) Ahunua. Qadua.
Fast, Kona kunukakunuka.
Fasten, Koua. (As string), Qadua.
Fastening, Koua gauna.
Fasthanded, Lega haraga.
Fastness, Magu.
Fat, adj. Digara.
Fat, s. Digara.
Father, Tamana.
Fathom, Roha.
Fatigue, Manori. Tau e boera.
Fatigue, v. Aheboera. Aheqarahia.
Fault, Kererekerere.
Favour, Harihari.
Favourite, Lalokau natuna (child).
Fear, Gari.
Feast, Aria. (Of cooked food), Anibou.
Feather, Hui.
Feeble, Manokamanoka.
Feed, Ubua. (to feed him), Ana henia.
Feel (to grope), Darahu. To feel a thing whether hard or soft), Dauatoho.
Feign, Hedibagani.
Felicity, Moalena. Lalo namo.
Fell, Hagaria.
Fellow, Bamona.
Female, Haine.
Fence (of upright sticks), Ara. (lengthwise), Kahi.
Ferment, Tubu.
Ferocious, Dagedage.
Fertile, Tano namo.
Fetch, Mailaia. (A person) Maihenia, Laohenia.
Fetid, Bodaga.
Feud, Heai.
Fever, Gorere siahu. (Intermittent) Tau harihari.
Few, Gadoi.
Fibre (coconut) Buru.
Fickle, Hereva momo.
Fierce, Dagedage.
Fifteen, Quatu ima.
Fifth, Ima.
Fiftieth, Ima ahui.

Fifty, Ima ahui.
Fig, Suke (introduced).
Eight, Heatu. Alala karaia.
File, Iliili.
Fill, Ahonua.
Fillip, Pidia.
Filth, Miro.
Fin, Taiana.
Final, Dokona.
Find, Davaria.
Fine (weather) Dina namo.
Finger, Ima qagiqagi.
Fingernail, Ima qagiqagi kahauna.
Finish, Hadokoa. Vadaeni.
Fire, s. Lahi.
Fire, v. Dona.
Fire (a gun), Ipidi karaia.
Firefly, Kobo. Kobokobo.
Fireplace, Rahurahu.
Fireshovel, Rahurahu kadoa gauna.
Firewood, Āu.
Firm (not loose), Āuka. Tutuka-tutuka.
First, Gunaguna.
Firstborn, Natuna roboa.
Firstfruits, Uma anina roboa.
Fish, s. Qarume. Different kinds of, see Appendix.
Fish, v. Haoda. Alatone.
Fisherman, Haoda tauna.
Fishhook, Kimai.
Fissure, Maka.
Fist, Ima kahua kubolukubolu.
Fit, adj., Namo.
Five, Ima.
Fix, Atoa goevagoeva.
Flabby, Aukalasi,
Flame, Lahi hurnruhururu.
Flame, v. (to cause), Ahnrurua.
Flannel, Dabua mamoe. (Introduced.)
Flash (as lightning), Kevaruaisi.
Flat, Palakapalaka.
Flatter, Hanamoa hedibagani.
Flavour, Mamina.
Flay, Ivaia.
Flea, Sei.
Flee, Heau.
Fleet, adj. Ae haraga.
Fleet (of fishing canoes), Haoda bada. (Of large trawling canoes), Hiri badabada.
Flesh, Anina.
Flexible, Perukaperuka.
Fling, Tahoa.
Flint, Vasika.
Flirt, Hekela or Hegera.

Float, *s.* Uto
Float, *v.* Hure.
Flock, *v.* Arua mai.
Flock, *s.* Serina.
Flog, Dadaba.
Flood, Ututu.
Flow, *v.* Veve.
Flow (*tide*), Hagaru.
Flower, Au huahua.
Fluent, Hereva namo.
Fluid, Ranu.
Flute, Ivirikou.
Fly, Roho.
Fly, *s.* Lao.
Foam, Qaraqara.
Foe, Inai.
Fog, Ninoa, Gahu.
Foil, Laoahu.
Fold, *v.* Lokua.
Follow, Murina laka.
Follower, Imurina tauna.
Folly, Kavakava.
Fond, Lalokau henia.
Food, Malamala. Aniani gauna.
Food (*cold*), Malamala bahuna.
Food (*for voyage or journey*), Laqa.
Fool, Kava. Bobo.
Foot, Ae palapala.
Footpath, Dara.
Footprint, Ae gabu.
For, Egu and Agu. Emu and Amu, &c.
Forage, *v.* Anianitahua.
Forbear, Aheauka.
Forbid, Koauahu. Koauatao.
Ford, *v.* Turu hanai.
Forefinger, Qagiqagi dodori.
Forego, Koauatao.
Forehead, Bagu.
Foreign, Idau.
Foreland, Iduka.
Foremost, Gunalaia.
Forenoon, Daha.
Forest, Uda.
Foretell, Koaulaia dose vara negana.
Forget, Reaia. Lalo boio.
Forgive, Koauatao.
Fork, Dinika.
Forked, Gada.
Forlorn, Iharcha.
Form, Oromana.
Former, Gunana.
Formerly, Gunaguna.
Fornication, Rahea.
Forsake, Lakatania.

Fort, Magu.
Fortitude, Lalo auka.
Fortunate, Nega namonamo.
Forty, Hari ahui.
Forward, *adv.* Vairanai.
Foul, Dika.
Found, Davaria.
Foundation, Badina.
Founder, Maloa.
Four, Hani.
Fourfold, Ere hani.
Fourfooted, Ae hani.
Fourteen, Qauta hani.
Fowl, Kokorogu.
Fowlingpiece, Ipidi. (*Introduced.*)
Fragile, Makohi haraga,
Fragrant, Bonana namo.
Frail, Manokamanoka.
Frantic, Kava bamona.
Fraud, Koikoi. Hineri.
Free, Dokoatao lasi.
Freight, Lakatoi-anina.
Frequent, Loulou.
Fresh, Matamata.
Freshwater, Ranu.
Fretful, Tai momo.
Friend, Turana.
Fright, Gari.
Frighten, Hagaria.
Fringe, Rimuna.
Frisk, Mavaro.
Frivolous, Kiri tauna.
Frizzy, Hui tuma.
Frog, Paroparo.
From, Amo.
Front, Vaira.
Front, *v.* Vaira henia.
Froth, Qaraqara.
Frown, Vaira hua.
Frugal (*to be*), Abia namonamo.
Fruit, Au huahua.
Fruitlessly, Abia lasi.
Frustrate, Koauatubu.
Fry, *v.* Hadedea.
Fuel, Lahi auna.
Fulfil, Hamomokanilaia.
Fulgent, Hururuhururu
Full, Honu.
Fumble, Lega metau.
Fun, Kadara. Hevasea.
Furious, Dagedage bada.
Furniture, Ruma gaudia.
Further, Unuka.
Futile, Abia lasi.
Future, Ununega.
Fy! Ina!

G

Gad, Loa.
Gale, Guba. Ore.
Gall, s., Aotuna.
Gambol, Kadara.
Gaol, Ruma koua.
Gape, Udu hagaia.
Gardening, Biru.
Gargle, Hegomogomo.
Garment, Dabua.
Garrulous, Udu mauri.
Gash, Bero.
Gasp, Lagadae lagadae.
Gate, Koko.
Gateway, Ikokou.
Gather (as fruit), Bitua. Bulukia.
Gaze, Raraia.
Geld, Apo ivaia.
Generation, Uru.
Gentle, Manada.
Gentleman, Lohiabada.
Genuine, Korikori.
Germinate, Havaraia.
Get, Abia.
Ghost, Vatavata.
Giddy, Mata madaimadai. Lagaga.
Gift, Harihari gauna. Herahia gauna.
Gill, Lada.
Gimlet, Ibudu gauna.
Ginger, Agi. Sioha.
Gird, Rioa. Gegea.
Girl, Kekeni. Haniulato.
Give, Henia.
Glad, Moale.
Glare (of sun), Dina tara.
Glass, Varivari.
Glisten, Hururuhururu.
Globular, Kubolukubolu.
Gloom, Dagahu.
Glorify, Heatolaia.
Glow, Kiamakiama.
Glutton, Aniani bada tauna.
Gnash, Ise hahedai.
Gnaw, Koria.
Go, Lao.
Go about, Loa.
God, Dirava.
Godliness, Dirava urana ura kara.
Good, Namo.
Goodbye, Bamahuta.
Goodnight, Bamahuta.
Goods, Kohu.
Gore, v. Pina.
Gorge, Koupa.
Gossip, Herevahereva.

Gourd, Ahu.
Govern, Siahu karaia.
Government, Siahu karaia taudia.
Grace, Harihari.
Gradually, Metailametaila.
Grain (of wood), Idiho.
Grant, Henia.
Grapple, Rosia.
Grasp, Kahua.
Grass, Rei.
Grass (different kinds of)—
  Honehone, Short.
  Dibagadi, Long.
  Kudekude, Long.
  Kurokuro, Long (used for thatch).
Grasshopper, Qadi.
Grate, v., Lilia. (Cocoanut), Oria.
Grave, Guri.
Gravel, Miri baroku.
Graze, Helaqahia.
Greasy, Dedidedi.
Great, Bada.
Greedy, Anianidika
Green, Gadogagadoga.
Green (unripe), Karukaru.
Greet, Hanamoa.
Greyhair, Hui buruka.
Grieve, Tai. Boka hisihisi.
Grind (axe, &c.), Segea.
Grindstone, Uro.
Gripe, v.n., Pudipudi.
Groan, Ganagana.
Groin, Dagadaga.
Grope, Darahu.
Ground, Tano.
Groundless, Badina lasi. Koauna lasi.
Grove (of cultivated trees), Imea.
Grow, Vara. (Of children), Badahobadaho.
Growl, Koaukoau.
Grumble, Maumau.
Grunt, Ruku.
Guard, Gima. Naria. Kito.
Guess, Koau kava, koau kava.
Guest, Vadivadi.
Guide, Hakaua.
Guide, s., Hakaua tauna.
Guilt, Dika.
Guilty, Dika tauna.
Gullet, Gado baubau.
Gulp, Hatono.
Gum, Tode, "au todena."
Gums, Mao.
Gun, Ipidi. (Introduced).
Gunpowder, Pauda. (Introduced).

Gunwale, Iscise.
Gush, Larelarea.
Gush out (*as blood*), Budia lasi.
Gut, *s.*, Bokarau.
Gut, *v.*, Bokaia.

H

Habit, Kara.
Habitation, Ruma.
Habitual, Dina idoinai.
Habituate, Hamanadaia.
Hack, Tarai hepatapata.
Haft, Halala.
Hair, Hui.
Hairy (*man*), Dera tauna.
Hale, Tāu namo.
Half, Karoa rua.
Half-full, Hekābi.
Half-moon, Hua lokaloka.
Half-way, Bokaragina. Ihuana.
Hallow, Ahelagaia.
Halt, Lagaani.
Halve, Karoa rua. To cut in half,
    Bokaraginai ivaia.
Hammer, *v.*, Hodoa.
Hammer, *s.*, Hamara (*Introduced*).
Hammock, Ivitoto.
Hamper, *v.*, Dokoatao.
Hand, Ima palapala.
Handful, Ima honu.
Handkerchief, Muko.
Handle, *v.*, Halalana karaia.
Handle, *s.*, Auauna. (*Of hatchet*),
    Halala.
Handsaw, Iri.
Handsome, Raho namo (*of men*), Hane
    namo (*of women*).
Handwriting, Revareva.
Hang, Tauadae.
Hanker, Hekischekise.
Happy, Lalo namo. Moale.
Harangue, Haroro. Koau henia.
Harbour, Ao.
Hard, Auka.
Harden, Aheauka.
Hardly (*enter*), Heloge.
Hark, Kamonai.
Harlot, Ariara haine.
Harm, Dika.
Harpoon, Karaudi.
Harsh, Koautora. Koaudika.
Haste, Haragaharaga.
Hasty, Badu kava.
Hat, Qara gauna.
Hatch (*eggs*), Pāpa.

Hatchet, Ira. (*American axe*), Qara
    qaitu.
Hatchet-head, Ira.
Hate, Badu henia.
Haughty, Kokorogu.
Haul, Veria. Haroro.
Have, Abia.
Haven, Medai gabuna.
Havoc, Haorea.
Hawk, Bogibada. Bivai.
Haze, Gahu. Ninoa.
He, Ia.
Head, Qara.
Head, *adj.*, Qarana.
Headland, Iduka.
Headlong, Moru hedaqa.
Headstrong, Ura dika.
Heal, Hamauria.
Health, Gorere lasi.
Heap, Senusenu.
Hear, Kamonai.
Heart, Kudou (*physical*).
Hearth, Rahurahu.
Heat, Siahu.
Heated, Hasiahua.
Heathen, Etene. (*Introduced*).
Heave, *v.a.*, Tahoa.
Heave, *v.n.*, Heudeheude.
Heaven, Guba.
Heavy, Metau.
Heel, Ae gedu.
Height, Gau lata. Dorivadorivanai.
Helm, Tari gauna.
Help, Kahaia. Durua.
Helve, Auauna.
Hem, Isena.
Hen, Kokorogu haine.
Henceforth, Harihari ela.
Her, Ia.
Herd, Serina.
Here, Iniseni. Inai.
Hereafter, Gabea.
Hero, Goada tauna.
Heron, Nogo.
Hesitate, Daradara.
Hew, Tarai. Utua.
Hide, Kopina.
Hide, *v.*, Hunia.
High, Gaulatalata.
Highminded, Hekokorogu.
High-water, Davara bada. Hagaru
    (*rising*).
Highway, Dala korikori.
Hill, Orooro komuta.
Hillock, Orooro berutaberuta.
Him, Ia.
Hinder, Laoahu.

C

Hindermost, Murina tauna. Gabea tauna.
Hinge, Hinere, (*Introduced*). Garugaru.
Hip, Koekoe.
His, Iena. (*Of food*), Ana.
History, Idaunegai herevana.
Hit, Huaria. Tutua. Pataia.
Hither and Thither, Ini mai unu lao.
Hoard, Haboua.
Hoarse, Gado dika.
Hobble, Ae guia.
Hog, Boroma.
Hoist, Daralaia. (*sail of canoe*) Diua ; (*ship*), Hekida.
Hold, Abia. Kahua.
Hold ! Vadaeni.
Hole, Matu.
Hollow, Asi anina.
Home, Noho gabuna korikori.
Homesick, Hanua tāi.
Honest, Henao lasi.
Honour, *v.*, Hematauraia.
Hoof, Ae kahauna.
Hook, Kimai.
Hooked, Igāu.
Hoop, Ava keikei.
Hoop, *v.*, Lolo.
Hope, Laroa.
Hopeless, Baia.
Horizon, Guba dokona.
Horn, Doa.
Hornbill, Bobolo.
Hornet, Ubama.
Horrible, Dikabada.
Horse, Hosi. (*Introduced*.)
Hospitable, Gaiho namo. Heabidae tauna.
Hot, Siahu.
Hotheaded, Kara kererekerere.
House, Ruma.
Household, Ruma taudia.
Householder, Ruma biaguna.
How ? Ede heto.
Howl, Tāi.
How many ? Hida.
Hubbub, Helogohelogo.
Hug, Gugubaia.
Huge, Gaubadabada.
Hum, Hu.
Humane, Hebokahisi.
Humble, *adj.*, Manau.
Humorous, Hevasea tauna.
Humpback, Doru qagugu.
Hundred, Sinahu.
Hunger, Hitolo. (*for meat*), Gādo.
Hunt, Rabana.

Hurl, Tahoa.
Hurricane, Orebada.
Hurry, *v.*, Haragaia.
Hurt, Hahisia.
Husband, Adavana.
Hush ! Asi regeregena.
Hush, *a child, v.*, Hadoloa.
Husk, Kopina.
Husk, *v.* (*cocoanuts*), Isia ; (*with teeth*), Daria.
Hut, Ruma.
Hymn, Ane.
Hypocrisy, Kara koikoi. Hedibagani.
Hypocrite, Koikoi tauna.

I

I, Lau.
Idiot, Kava tauna.
Idle, Lahedo. Bokamate.
If (*past*), Bema ; (*fut.*), Baine.
Ignite, Haraia,
Ignorant, Kavakava.
Iguana, Ariha.
Ill, Gorere.
Ill-treat, Hadikaia.
Ill-nature, Dagedage.
Illumine, Hadiaria.
Image, Laulau.
Imagine, Lalo koau.
Immature, Garugaru.
Immediately, Harihari.
Immerse, Bulubulu.
Immorality, Kara dika.
Immortal, Mate diba lasi.
Immovable, Auka bada. Tutukatutuka.
Immutable. Lalo lou lasi.
Impatient, Aheauka lasi.
Impede, Laoahu.
Impenitent. Helalo karaia lasi.
Imperfect, Idoinai lasi.
Imperious, Hekokorogu.
Impertinent, Koau dika.
Impetuous, Ura dika.
Implicate, Habadelaia.
Implore, Noinoi.
Impolite, Lagaua.
Importune, Noinoi.
Impose. (*cheat*) Koia.
Impossible, Karaia diba lasi.
Improper, Namo lasi.
Improve, Hanamoa.
Impudent, Ere dagedage.
Impure, Miro.

In, Lalonai.
Inaccessible, Dala lasi.
Inactive, Lahedo.
Inarticulate, Logologo.
Incapable, Karaia diba lasi.
Incessant, Nega idoinai.
Incision, Ivaia.
Incite, Hāloa.
Incivility, Ere dika.
Inclined, Lalona ura.
Incomparable, Ta ia bamona lasi.
Incomplete, Idoinai lasi.
Incomprehensible, Diba lasi.
Inconsolable, Tauna halōa lasi.
Incorrect, Maoromaoro lasi.
Incorrigible, Matagani lasi.
Increase, Habadaia.
Incumber Hametaua.
Indecent, Hemaraikara.
Indecision, Daradara mo.
Indeed, Etomamu.
Indefatigable, Goada bada.
Indelible, Rohoa lasi.
Indemnify, Qara henia.
Indicate, Hamaoroa.
Indifferent, Ura lasi.
Indigent, Ogogami.
Indignant, Badu.
Indignity, Hadikaia.
Indiscreet, Aonega lasi.
Indiscriminate, Kererekerere.
Indistinct, (speech) Logologo.
Indolent, Lahedo.
Industrious, Hulo tauna.
Inexhaustible, Ia basine ore.
Inexpedient, Namo lasi.
Inexperienced, Manada lasi.
Infamous, Harina dika.
Infant, Karukaru.
Infect, Hisi dāihanai.
Infirm, Manokamanoka.
Influenza, Kulu karaia.
Inform, Hadibaia. Koau henia.
Ingratitude, Hanamoa lasi.
Inhabit, Noho.
Inhale, Hohoa.
Inhospitable, Gaiho dika.
Inhuman, Hebokahisi lasi.
Iniquity, Kara dika.
Injunction, Ahegani herevana.
Injure, Hadikaia.
Injustice, Maoromaoro lasi.
Ink, Inika. (Introduced.)
Inland, Gunika.
Inlander, Guni tauna.
Innocent, Dia dika.
Innumerable, Duahia lasi.

Inquire, Nanadai.
Inquiry, Henanadai.
Insane, Kāva.
Insatiable, Boka kunu lasi.
Insecure, Auka lasi.
Inseparable, Kahuanege lasi.
Inside, Lalonai.
Insignificant, Maragimaragi.
Insincere, Momokani lasi.
Insipid, Mamina lasi.
Insist, Koaulaia loulou.
Insnare, Idoa.
Insolent, Ere dagedage.
Inspect, Itaia tarikatarika.
Instantly, Harihari.
Instead, Boloa.
Instep, Ae ganagana.
Instigate, Havaraia.
Instruct, Hadibaia.
Instrument, Iaia or raia *post-fixed to the verb.*
Insufficient, Davana lasi. Seme davana.
Insult, Hadikaia.
Inter, Guria.
Intercede, Herohemaino. Noinoi.
Intercept, Laoahu, Vairalao.
Interdict, Koauahu.
Interior, Lalonai.
Intermediate, Bokaraginai.
Interminable, Asi Dokona.
Internal, Lalona.
Interpret, Gādo hanaia, or hahe-geregerea.
Interrogate, Henanadai.
Interrupt, Hereva tataiautu.
Interval, Ihuanai.
Interview, Ia ida hereva.
Intestine, Bokarau.
Intimate, to, Hamaoroa.
Intimidate, Hagaria.
Into, Vareai.
Intoxication, Muramura heala. Kekero.
Intrepid, Goada.
Intrust, Henia baine legua.
Inundation, Ututu.
Inure, Hamanadaia.
Invalid, *n.*, Gorere tauna.
Invert, Hurea.
Investigate, Tahua. Henanadai.
Invisible, Itaia lasi.
Invite, Koaulaia.
Invoke, Hahane. Noinoi.
Inward, Lalona.
Ire, Badu.
Iron, Auri. (Introduced.)

Iron, *v.*, Dabua hamanadaia.
Irreconcilable, Maino lasi.
Irresistable, Goada bada.
Irresolute, Daradara.
Irreverent, Boka toto tauna.
Irritable, Badukava badukava.
Irritate, Hadagedagea.
Island, Motumotu.
Itch, *v.*, Hemaihemai.

J

Jabber, Hereva momo.
Jaded, Tau e boera. Manori.
Jail, Ruma koua.
Jaw (*the lower*), Auki.
Jealous, Vagege.
Jeer, Kirikirilaia.
Jerk, Veria dagu.
Jest, Hevasea.
Jester, Havasea tauna.
Jog, Doria.
Join (*as two pieces of wood*), Hiriakau.
Joint, Garugaru.
Joint (*of meat*) Regena.
Joist, Lava.
Joke, Hevasea.
Jostle, Hesede matemate.
Journey, Laolao.
Joy, Moale.
Judge, Heuanadai, *v.*, Ahemaoro karaia.
Judgment, Henanadai karaia, ahemaoro karaia.
Judicious, Aonega.
Jug, Siagi. (*Introduced.*)
Juice, Ranuna.
Jump (*up*), Rohoisi. (*Down*) Rohodobi.
Junction (*of roads*), Dala katakata.
Jurisdiction, Siahu.
Just, Kara maoromaoro.
Justice, Kara maoromaoro.
Justify, Hamaoromaoroa.

K

Kagaroo, Magani. (*Male*) Tapari. (*Female*) Miara.
Keen (*edge*), Gano.
Keep, Abia.
Keeper, Gima tauna. Ileguna tauna.
Kernel, Anina.
Kick, Helaha.

Kid, Goti natuna. (*Introduced.*)
Kidney, Nadinadi.
Kill, Alaia.
Kin, Varavara.
Kingdom, Basileia. (*Introduced.*)
Kind, Harihari bada. Hebokahisi.
Kindle, Haraia. Bania.
King, Gaubada.
Kinsman, Varavara.
Kiss, Aherahu.
Kitten, Pose natuna. (*Introduced.*)
Knee, Tui.
Knead, Kuia.
Kneel, Tuihadaia.
Knife, Kaia. (*Introduced.*)
Knock, Pidipidi.
Knot, Qadua.
Knotted, Qaduaqadua.
Know, Diba.
Knuckle, Ima garugaru.

L

Labour, Heqarahi.
Labourer, Karakara tauna. Gau karaia tauna.
Lack, Dabu.
Lad, Mero.
Ladder, Vatavata.
Lade, Atoakau.
Lady, Lohiabada haine.
Lagoon, Gohu.
Lame, Ae sike.
Lament, Tai.
Land, Tano.
Land, *v.*, Hedoa. Tano ai diho.
Landing-place, Doa gahuna.
Landslip, Hevarure.
Language, Gado.
Languish, Manokamanoka.
Languor, Tau manokamanoka.
Lap, Kopa.
Larboard, Dalima kahana.
Lard, Digara.
Large, Bada. (*Of thread, &c.*) Baroko.
Larynx, Gado baubau.
Lascivious, Mata dika.
Lash, *v.*, Dadaba.
Lash (*to fasten*), Mataia. Qadua.
Lass, Kekeni.
Last, Dokona. Gabena.
Last, *v.*, Mia hanaihanai.
Lasting, Mia hanaihanai.
Last night, Varani hanuaboi.
Late in the day, Dina diho.
Laud, Heatolaia. Heagilaia.

Laugh, Kiri.
Launch, Davea dae.
Laundress, Dabua ihurina haine.
Law, Taravatu. Doha. (*Introduced meaning.*)
Lawful, Koauahu lasi.
Lawless, Bokatoto.
Lazy, Lahedo.
Lead, *v.*, Hakaua.
Leader, Hakaua tauna. Igunalaina tauna.
Leaf, Rau.
League, Taravatu.
Leak (*in a canoe*), Dudi.
Lean, *v.* (*on a stick*), Hetotao. (*On a table, &c.*), Gorukau. (*Against*), Dabikau.
Lean, *adj.*, Hidiho. (*Person*), Tau varotavarota.
Leap, Roho.
Learn, Hadibaia.
Least, Maragina.
Leather, Boroma kopina.
Leave, *v.*, Lakatania.
Leave off, Vadaeni ! Mia !
Leaven, Hatubua ganna.
Leavings, Aniani orena.
Lecherous, Mata dika.
Left (*side*), Lauri.
Left behind, Hetavauhe. (*Persons*), Lakatania.
Left-handed, Ima lauri tauna.
Leg, Ae (*entire leg and foot.*)
Legend, Gori.
Leisure, Noho kava negana.
Leisusely, Metailametaila.
Lend, Henitorehai.
Length, Lata.
Lengthen, Halataia.
Lenity, Hebokahisi.
Less, Unai bada (*that is big*) ; inai maragi (*this is small.*)
Lessen, Hamaragia.
Lest, Garina.
Let (*allow*), Gadudae.
Let (*hinder*), Laoahu.
Letter, Leta. (*Introduced*), Revareva.
Level, Manadamanada.
Level, *v.*, Hataoraia.
Levity, Kiri momo.
Lewd, Mata dika.
Liar, Koikoi tauna.
Liberal, Harihari bada.
Liberty, Haduaia lasi, ia sibona.
Lick, Demari.
Lid, Kaluhia gauna. Itoreahu.
Lie, *s.*, Koikoi.

Lie, *v.* (*down*), Hekure. (*On the side*), Enodele. (*On the back*), Hekuregaga.
Lie (*in wait*) Banitao.
Life, Mauri.
Lift, Abiaisi.
Light, *s.*, Diari.
Light, *v.*, Rohokau. (*A fire*), Haraia.
Light, *adj.*, Haraga.
Lightheaded, Koaukava.
Lightning, Kevaru.
Like, Bamona.
Like, *v.*, Ura henia. Hekisehekise.
Likeness (*portrait*), Laulau.
Lily (*large white*), Repati.
Lime, Ahu.
Limit, Toana.
Limp, Ae sike.
Limpid, Neka.
Line fishing, Varo.
Linger, Halahe.
Liniment, Hedahu muramura.
Lip, Udu bibina.
Liquefy, Haveve.
Liquid, Ranu.
Liquor amnii. Aru.
Listen, Kamonai.
Litter, *s.*, Momo.
Little, Maragi.
Live, Mauri.
Liver, Ase or ate.
Lizard, Vaboha.
Lo ! Inai !
Load, *s.*, Maduna.
Load, *v.* (*on shoulder*), Paga ai atoakau.
Loaf, Mone.
Loathe, Lalo dika henia.
Lock, Ki karaia. (*Introduced.*)
Lofty, Latalata.
Log, Au.
Loins, Koekoe.
Loiter, Halahe.
Lonely, Sibona noho. Dara doko.
Long, Lata.
Long, *v.*, Ura henia. Hekisehekise.
Look, Itaia. (*Up*), Gagaisi. Rohadae. (*Down*), Igodiho. (*About*), Roharohalou.
Look ! A itaia !
Looking glass, Varivari.
Loop, Budia.
Loose, Heladohelado.
Loosen, Ruhaia.
Looseness (*diarrhœa*), Hekukuri.
Lop, Utua.

Loquacious, Hereva momo. Udu mauri.
Lord, Biaguna. Lohiabada.
Lose, Reaia.
Lost, Boio.
Loud, Regena bada. Gado bada.
Lounge, Hekure.
Louse, Utu.
Love, Hebokahisi. Lalokau henia.
Low, Qadogi.
Lower, v., Abia dobi.
Lower (the sky), Goeahu.
Lowly, Manau tauna.
Low-water, Komata gui. Davara maragi.
Lucky, Dirava namo.
Lug, Veria.
Lukewarm, Siahusiahu.
Lull (in wind), Lai gavena.
Luminous, Diaridiari.
Lunatic, Kāva tauna.
Lungs, Baraki.
Lure, Hedibagani.
Lurk, Banitao.
Lust, Mata dika.
Luxuriant, Vara bada. Mauri bada.

M

Mad, Kāva. Dagedage.
Maggot, Uloulo.
Magistrate, Gima tauna. Ahemaoro tauna.
Magnify, Habadaia.
Magnitude, Badana.
Maid, Kekeni. Haniulato.
Maidservant, Hesiai haine.
Maimed, Doko (preceded by the member, as "ima doko").
Maintain, Abia tarikatarika.
Majority, Hutuma.
Make, Karaia.
Malady, Gorere.
Male, Maruane.
Malediction, Uduguilai.
Malice, Lalo dika.
Mallet, Lavu. (for beating out native cloth), Itadara.
Man, Taunimanima. Tauna.
Mangle (to tear), Hetare.
Mangrove (edible), Kavera.
Manifest, Dina.
Manifold, Eremomo.
Mankind, Taunimanima.
Manner, Kara.
Mansion, Ruma bada.

Manslaughter, Taunimanima alaia.
Many, Hutuma. Diagau. Momo.
Mar, Hadikaia.
Mare, Hosi haine.
Margin, Isena.
Mark, Toana.
Marriage, Headava.
Married, to be, Adavaia.
Marry, Headava.
Marsh, Kopukopu.
Marvel, Hoa.
Massacre, Alala.
Mast, Autubua.
Master, Biaguna.
Masticate, Gauaia.
Mat, Geda.
Match, v. Hahegeregerea.
Match, s., Masisi. (Introduced.)
Matchless, Sibona herea.
Mate, Bamona.
Materials, Karalaia gaudia.
Matron, Sinana. Haine bada.
Matter (pus), Hula.
Mature (of animals), Tamana, Sinana. (Of fruit, &c.), Lō. Lokaloka.
Mean, Gaihodika.
Meaning, Anina.
Meanness, Gaiho dika kara.
Measure, Hahetoho gauna.
Measure, v., Hahetoho karaia.
Mediate, Herohemaino.
Mediator, Herohemaino tauna.
Medicine, Muramura.
Meditate, Lalo haguhi.
Meek, Manada tauna.
Meet, v. Hedavari. (To go to meet), Vaira lao. (On the road), Toia hedavari.
Meeting (an assembly), Hegogo.
Melancholy, Vaira huaia.
Melt, Haveve.
Menace, Heqata karaia.
Mend (nets), Laumea. (Mats, &c.), Bania.
Mention, Koaulaia.
Merchant, Hoihoi tauna.
Merciful, Hebokahisi tauna.
Merciless, Hebokahisi lasi.
Merry, Lebulebu.
Mesh, Māta.
Message, Koaukau.
Metal, Nadi.
Metaphor, Hereva hegeregere.
Methought, Lau lalogu koau.
Metropolis, Hanua bada.
Midday, Dina tupua.

Middle, Ihuana baine raka.
Middle-aged, Eregabe.
Middling, Namo bada lasi.
Midnight, Malokihi.
Midriff, Valavala.
Midst, Bokaragina.
Midway, Bokaragina.
Might, Goada.
Mild, Manada.
Mildew, Valavala.
Milk, Rata.
Mimic, Hetohotoho.
Mind, *s.* Lalona. Aonega.
Mind, *v.* Kamonai. (*Take care of*), Naria.
Mine, Lauegu.
Mingle, Buloa.
Minister, *v.* Isiai laoheni. Legua.
Minute, Minuta. (*Introduced.*)
Mire, Kopukopu.
Mirror, Varivari.
Mirth, Lebulebu.
Misapprehend. Kamonai kerere.
Misbehave, Kara kererekerere.
Miscarry (*in birth*), Mara dika.
Mischievous, Ima mauri.
Miscount, Duahia kerere.
Misdemeanour, Kara dika.
Miserable, Lalo dika. Meale lasi.
Misfortune, Nega dika.
Misgive, Daradara.
Misguide, Hakaua kerere.
Misinform, Hadibaia kerere.
Mislead, Koia.
Miss, *v.*, Daradoka.
Missionary, Haroro tauna.
Mist, Ninoa. (*At sea.*), Gahu.
Mistake, Reaia. Kererekerere.
Mistrust, Daradara.
Misunderstanding, Diba lasi.
Mitigate, Hamaragia.
Mix, Buloa.
Moan, Ganagana.
Mock, Gonagonalaia.
Moderate, Bada lasi. (*Of sun or wind*), Gavena.
Modest (*woman*), Igodiho haine.
Moist, Parikaparika.
Moisten, Hapariparia.
Mole, Toutou.
Mollify, Hamarumaru.
Monarch, Gaubada.
Monday, Monedei. (*Introduced.*)
Money, Moni. (*Introduced.*)
Month, Hūa.
More, Haida.
Morning, Daba.

Morning star, Hisiu bada.
Morrow, Kerukeru.
Morsel, Taina. Sisina.
Mosquito, Namo.
Moss.
Moth, Gaubebe.
Mother, Sinana.
Mother of Pearl, Maire.
Motherly, Sinana bamona.
Mouldy, Valavala.
Moult, Helata.
Mound, Orooro beruta.
Mountain, Orooro.
Mountainous, Orooro mo.
Mourn, Tāi.
Mouth, Udu.
Mouthful, Udu honu.
Move, Raivaraiva.
Much, Bada.
Mud, Kopukopu.
Muddy, Kopukopu.
Mulberry (*paper*), Sihi.
Multiply, Habadaia.
Multitude, Hutuma. Aru.
Mumble, Maumau.
Munificent, Harihari bada.
Murder, Roromaia.
Murderous, Alala tauna.
Murmur, Maumau.
Musket, Ipidi. (*Introduced.*)
Musty, Valavala.
Mute, Asi regeregena.
Mutilate, Ivaia.
Mutter, Maumau.
Mutual, He prefixed, and heheni suffixed.
My, Lauegu.
Myself, Lau.

N

Nail, Ikoko (*finger or toe*), Kahau.
Naked, Sihi lasi.
Name, Ladana.
Name, *v.* Ladana hatoa.
Nape, Lokolu.
Narrate, Koaulaia.
Narrative, Sivarai.
Narrow, Hekahihekahi.
Nasty, Dika.
Native, Hanua taudia korikori.
Native custom, Hanua kara.
Naughty, Kara dika.
Nausea, Gado lohilohi.
Nauseate, Gado lohilohi mo karaia.

Navel, Udo.
Nay, Lasi.
Near, Kahilakahila.
Nearly, Moko na.
Neck (*of animals or man*), Aio.
Necklace (*shell*), Taotao. Aio
    gauna.
Needle, Kobi.
Needy, Ogogami.
Neglect, Itaia lasi.
Neighbour, Dekena tauna.
Nest, Manu rumana.
Net (*fine*, *fishing*), Reke. (*Larger*)
    Ole. (*Very large for dugong, &c.*)
    Varo. (*Kangaroo*) Huo. (*Pig*)
    Koda. (*Bag*) Daqai.
New, Matamata.
Next, Murinai. Gabenai.
Niggard, Harihari lasi.
Nigh, Kahilakahila.
Night, Hanuaboi idoinai.
Nimble (*in work*) Lega haraga.
Nine, Taurahani ta.
Ninefold, Ere taurahani ta.
Nineteen, Qauta taurahani ta.
Ninety, Taurahani ta ahui.
Nip, Hegigi.
Nipple, Rata matana.
No, lasi.
Noble, Namo herea.
Nobody, Asi tauna.
Nod, Aio mareremarere. (*With*
    sleep) Ladorāi.
Noise, Regena.
Nominate, Ladana hatoa.
None, Lasi vaitani.
Noon, Dina tupua.
Noose, Idoa.
North, Mirigini.
North-east wind, Totōdae.
Nose, Udu.
Nostril, Udu maduna.
Not, Asi (*before the verb*). Lasi
    (*after v.*).
Notch, Koloa (*in edge of knife, &c.*),
    Hamakaia.
Noted, Harina bada.
Nothing, Asi anina.
Notify, Koaulaia.
Notorious, Harina bada.
Notwithstanding, Enabe.
Nought, Lasi vaitani.
Nourish, Ubua.
Nourishment, Aniani gauna.
Novel, Matamata.
November, Biriakei.
Novice, Matamata tauna.

Now, Harihari.
Nowadays, Inai negana.
Noxious, Dika.
Nudity, Sihi lasi.
Nuisance, Taia goegoe gauna. Dika.
Numb, Tamoru.
Number to, Hagaua, Duahia.
Numberless, Momo hamona.
Numerous, Hutuma bada.
Nurse, Rosia.
Nut, Huahua mai koukouna.
Nutriment, Aniani gauna.
Nutshell, Ikoukouna.

O

Oar, Bara.
Oath, Ominuo. (*Introduced.*)
Obdurate, Ura dika.
Obese, Boka hada.
Obey, Kamonai.
Object to, Koauedeede.
Obscure, Valabuvalahu.
Observe, Itaia.
Obstacle, Helaoahu gauna.
Obstinate, Ura dika.
Obstruct, Helaoahu.
Obtain, Abia. Davaria.
Occasion, Badina.
Occupation, Dagi. Kara.
Occupy, Noho.
Ocean, Gādo bada.
Odious, Dika bada.
Odour, Bonana.
Offence, Hadikaia.
Offer, Henia koaulaia.
Offering, Herahia.
Office, Dagina.
Offspring, Natuna.
Often, Nega hoho. Loulou.
Oh! Inā!
Oil, Diaranu.
Old, Gunana.
Omen, Toana.
On, *prep.* Dorinai. Latanai.
On, *adv.* Latanai. Dorinai.
Once, Tamona.
One, Tamona.
Onerous, Metau.
Only, Sibona. Mo.
Open, Kehoa, (*the mouth*). Aha-
    gaia.
Openhanded, Harihari bada.
Opening, Mādu.
Openly, Hedinarai.
Ophthalmia, Mata hisihisi.

Opinion, Koau.
Opponent, Inai.
Opportune, Nega namo.
Oppose, Koauatubu.
Opposite, Hegagaheheni.
Oppress, Dagedage henia.
Opulence, Kohu diagau.
Or, E. Iava.
Orange (wild), Vauto.
Oration, Haroro.
Orator, Haroro tauna.
Ordain, Siaia. Haduaia.
Order, v. Ahegani. Haduaia.
Order (class). Verina.
Ordure, Tage.
Orifice, Matuna.
Origin, Badina.
Ornament, Hera gauna.
Orphan, Ihareha.
Other, Idau.
Our, Ita eda (inclusive). Ai emai (exclusive.)
Ourselves, Ita.
Oust, Lulua.
Out, in composition, Lasi, as, Laka lasi.
Out of, Halasia.
Outcast, Ihareha tauna.
Outcry, Lolo dagu.
Outer, Murina.
Outlet, Dala.
Outrun, (to be) Heautania.
Outside, Murimuri.
Outward, Murimuri kahana.
Oven, Amu.
Over, adv. Atai ai.
Overcast, Dagahu.
Overcome, Qalimu.
Overdone (in cooking), Halaka. (Of yams) Herata.
Overflow, Hepulai dobi.
Overhang, Hereaherea.
Overhead, Atai ai.
Overlay, Enoatao.
Overpower, Qalimu.
Overrun, Heautania.
Overshade, Goruahu.
Oversleep, Mahuta bada.
Overspread, Latanai lahaia.
Overtake, Gavaia.
Overthrow, Uheahebubu.
Overturn, Uheahebubu.
Owe, Dodi. Abitorehai davana.
Owl, Baimumu.
Own, Korikori (following noun).
Owner, Biaguna.
Oyster, Silo.

P

Pacify, Hamarumarua.
Pack, s., Maduna.
Pack up, Haboua kahinikahini.
Packing, s., Dogoro.
Paddle, v., Kalo.
Paddle, s., Hode.
Pagan, Dibura tauna.
Page, Buka rauna.
Pain, Hisi.
Paint, s Muramura. v. (the face), Umua.
Pair, Ruaoti.
Palace, Lohiabada na ruma.
Pale, Kurokakuroka.
Paling, Ara.
Palliate, Hamaragia.
Palm (areca), Buatau; (cocoanut), Niu.
Palm (of hand), Ima palapala.
Palpable, Hedinarai.
Palpitate, Rohodae rohodae.
Palsy, Pāda.
Paltry, Maragimaragi.
Pang, Hisihisi.
Pant, Lagadae lagadae.
Papaw, Nita. (Introduced.)
Parable, Parabole. (Introduced.) Hereva hegeregere.
Paralytic, Pāda tauna.
Paramount, Hereaherea.
Parrot (green), Kaikia. (Red), Odubora.
Parcel, Ikumi.
Parch, Marai (by the sun).
Pardon, Dika koauatao.
Pare, Duhia.
Parents, Tamana, sinana.
Parley, Herevahereva.
Paroquet, Kiloki.
Parsimonious, Harihari lasi.
Part, Kahana. Sisina.
Part, v. (from) Tūa. Ahetonia.
Partake, Taina ania.
Participate, Taina abia.
Partner, Bamona.
Party, Veiina.
Pass, v., Hanaia lao.
Passage (boat), Botidalana.
Passenger Gui tauna.
Passing, Hanaia lao.
Passion, Badubada.
Past (time), Idaunegai.
Pastime, Kadara.
Pat, Pataia.
Patch, Bania.
Path, Dara.

Patience, Aheauka.
Pattern, Revareva. Oromana.
Paucity, Hoholasi.
Paunch, Boka.
Pavement, Vevehanaihanai.
Payment, Davana. (*for blood*), Heatotao gauna. Qara henia. (*Of doctor*), Idume.
Paw, Ima.
Pay, Davana.
Peace, Maino.
Peak, Orooro komoge.
Pearl, Kavabukavahu.
Pebble, Nadi kubolukubolu.
Peace, *int*, Maino.
Peck, Koria.
Peculiar, Idau.
Peel, *v.*, Duhia.
Peep, Haigo.
Peerless, Sibona herea.
Pelt, Nadi hodoa.
Pen, Revareva torelaia gauna.
Penalty, Davana.
Pendant, Pepe.
Penetrate, Lalona lao.
Penitence, Helalo karaia.
Pensive, Hade tari.
People, Taunimanima.
Peopled, Mai taunimanima.
Perceive, Itaia.
Perch, *v.*, Rohokau.
Perfect, Namo idoinai.
Perfidious, Koikoi.
Perforate, Budua auru.
Perform, Karaia.
Perfume, Muramura bonana.
Perish, Mate.
Permanent (*durable*), Auka bada.
Permit, Haduaia.
Perpetual, Nega idoinai.
Perpetuate, Hanaihanai.
Persecute, Dagedage henia.
Persevere (*continue*), Malakamalaka.
Persist, Uradika.
Person, Tauna.
Perspicuous, Dina. Ehuni lasi.
Perspire, Varahu.
Persuade, Noinoi.
Pertubation, Kudou vata hetaha.
Peruse, Duahia.
Perverse, Ura dika.
Purvert, Hagagevaia.
Pestilence, Hisi karaia.
Physic, Muramura.
Physician, Muramura tauna.
Piece, Taina. Sisina. (*Of string, wood, &c.*) Tua.

Pierce, Qadaia.
Pig, Boroma.
Pigeon, Pune.
Pile, Senusenu.
Piles (*of house*), Du.
Pilfer, Henao.
Pillage, Dadidadi.
Pillow, Iqina.
Pillow, *v.* Aheqinaia.
Pimple, Usiusi.
Pinch, Hegigi, Hekinitari.
Pineapple, Painapo. (*Introduced.*)
Pipe (*bamboo*), Banbau.
Pish, Hi !
Pit, Guri.
Pitch, *s.*, Muramura koremakorema.
Pitch, *v.*, Tahoa.
Pith, Houkahouka.
Pitiful, Hebokahisi havaraia.
Pitsaw, Ili bada. (*Introduced.*)
Pitted, Budubudu.
Pity, Hebokahisi.
Placable, Manada.
Place, *n.*, Gabuna.
Place, *v.*, Atoa.
Placid (*as a lake*), Vea.
Plague, *s.* (*of sickness*), Hisi.
Plague, *v.*, Hauraia, Hadikaia.
Plain, *n.*, Taora.
Plaint, Tai. Ganagana.
Plait, Bania.
Plane, Naua gauna.
Plank, Leilei.
Plant, Au.
Planting stick, Isiva.
Plaintain (*plant*), Dui ; (*fruit*) Bigu.
Plantation, Uma.
Plaster, Gabaia muramura.
Plat or Plot, Tano kahana.
Play, Kadara.
Plead, Noinoi.
Pleasant (*to taste*), Mamina namo.
Please, *v.*, Hamoalea.
Plenty, Momo. Diagau.
Pliant, Lorekaloreka.
Pluck, Gari lasi.
Pluck, *v.* (*fruit*), Bulukia. (*By pulling down branch*), Dabaia qaidu. (*Birds*) Hui budua.
Plug, Iqadobe.
Plumage, Manu huina.
Plumbago, Ogoa.
Plump, Tau namo.
Plunder, Dadidadi gauna.
Plunge, Paudobi. Edai dobi.
Point, Matana.
Point, *v.*, Duduia.

Poison, Mate muramurana.
Pole, v. Doaia.
Pole, (for poling a canoe), Aivăra.
Polish, Dahua kimorekimore.
Polite, Kara namo.
Polute, Hadikaia.
Polygamy, Hodala.
Pomp, hairaina bada.
Pond, Gohu.
Ponder, Laloa. Hedaraune.
Ponderous, Gaubadabada.
Poor, Ogogami.
Pop, Poudagu.
Populace, Hanua taudia.
Popular, Harina namo.
Populous, Taunimanima momo.
Pork, Boroma anina.
Porpoise, Kidului.
Port, Hedoko gabuna.
Portent, Toana, Qare.
Portion, Ahuna.
Possess, Abia.
Possessed (demoniacally), Boloa.
Possible, Karaia diba. Abia diha.
Post, Autubua. (side), Ihuaihu.
Posteriors, Kunu.
Posterity, Tubudia.
Postpone, Dohore.
Potent, Goada.
Potsherd, Ataga.
Pouch, Vaina ; (marsupial), Mapaü.
Pound, Pauna. (Introduced.)
Pound, v. Qadaia.
Pour, Seia.
Poverty, Ogogami. Asi ganna.
Powder (dust), Gahu. (Gunpowder)
  Pauda. (Introduced.)
Power, Goada; (supernatural) Siahu.
Powerful, Goada tauna. Siahu tauna
Practice, Kara.
Praise, v. Hanamoa. Heatolaia.
Prate, Hereva kava hereva kava.
Pray, Guri. Guriguri kaoulaia.
Prayer, Guriguri.
Preach, Haroro.
Precarious, Moru garina.
Precede, Gunalaia.
Precept, Ahegani herevana.
Precious (of affection), Lalokau. (in
  value) Davana bada.
Precipice, Hagahaga.
Predict, Do vara lasi negana koaulaia.
Pre-eminent, Hereaherea.
Prefer, Abia hidi.
Pregnant, Rogorogo.
Prepare, Hagoevaia.
Prepay, Davana henia guna.

Preposterous, Kavakava.
Presence, Vairana.
Present, v. Henia.
Present (at), Harihari.
Present, s. Herahia gauna. Harihari
  gauna.
Presently, Dohore.
Preserve (to keep), Abia tarikatarika.
Press (in crowd), Hesede matemate.
  (down) Kapuatao.
Pretend, Hedibagani karaia.
Pretty, namo.
Prevail, Qalimu.
Prevaricate, Koikoi.
Prevent, Laoahu.
Previons, Gunana. Gunaguna.
Price, Davana.
Prick, Qadaia.
Prickly, Ginigini.
Pride, Hekokorogu.
Priest, Kohena. (Introduced.)
Prince, Lohia natuna.
Principal (thing), Herea gauna.
  (person) Herea tauna.
Print, v. Revareva karaia.
Print (of foot), Aegabu.
Prior, Gunana.
Prison, Ruma koua (Introduced
  meaning.)
Private, Hamaoroa lasi.
Privately, Ehuniehuni.
Probity, Kara maoromaoro.
Proceed (imp), Aola.
Proclaim, Haroro.
Procrastinate, Dohore koaulaia.
Procure, Abia.
Prodigal, Petapetalaia.
Prodigious, Gaubadabada.
Produce (of garden), Uma anina.
Productive, Anina bada.
Profane, Koau dika.
Proffer, Henia toho.
Proficient, Diba bada.
Profit, Kohu e abilaia.
Progeny, Natudia.
Prognosticate, Dosi vara negana
  koaulaia.
Prohibit, Koauatao. Doha.
Project, v. Herea.
Prolific, Natuna momo.
Prolong, Hahadaia. Halataia.
Promiscuous, Idauidau.
Promise, Koauhamata.
Promontory, Iduka.
Prompt. v. Haragaharaga.
Promptly, Haragaharaga.
Promulgate, Haroro.

Prone, Gorudiho.
Pronounce, Koaulaia.
Proof, Hamomokanilaia.
Prop, Imuta. Itotohï.
Propagate, Havaraia.
Propel (by poling), Doaia.
Proper, Namo. Maoromaoro.
Property, Kohu.
Prophesy, Negana dose vara
   koaulaia.
Propitiate, Hamarumarua.
Propitious (time), Nega namo.
Proposal, Koaulaia.
Propose, Koau.
Proprietor, Biaguna.
Prosperous, Nega namo.
Prostitute, Ariara haine.
Prostrate, Gorudiho.
Protect, Gima.
Protract, Halataia.
Protrude, Herea.
Proud, Hekokorogu.
Prove, Hamomokanilaia.
Proverb, Hereva hegeregere.
Provide, Abia.
Provision (food), Malamala.
Provoke, Habadua.
Proximity, Kahilakahila. Diadau-
   dau.
Proxy, Boloa.
Prudent, Aonega.
Prune, Rigi utua.
Pshaw ! Hi !
Public, Hedinarai.
Publish, Haroro.
Pucker, Magugu.
Pudding (sago), Dia.
Puerile, Meromero bamona.
Pugnacious, Heatu tauna.
Pull, veria. (up grass), Butua.
Pungent, Hegara.
Punish, Davana henia.
Punishment, Davana korikori.
Puny, Maragimaragi.
Pup, Sisia natuna.
Pupil, Hadibaia tauna.
Puppy, Sisia natuna.
Purchase, Hoihoi.
Pure, Goevagoeva.
Purge, Boka hekukuri.
Purloin, Henao.
Purple, Kakakaka.
Purport, Hereva anina.
Purpose (in coming or going), Totona.
Pursue, Gavaia.
Purulent, Hula bamona.
Push, Doria.

Pustule, Sihaurisihauri.
Put, Atoa : (down) Atoa diho ; (on
   clothes), Ahedokia.
Put off (on another), Ahekora.
Putrefy, Epata.

Q

Quake, Gari. Dagu.
Quarrel, Heai.
Queen, Gaubada haine.
Quell, Hatui.
Quench, Hahodoa.
Querulous, Daradara mo.
Query, Henanadai.
Quest, Tahua.
Question, Henanadai.
Quick, Haragaharaga.
Quickly, Lega haraga.
Quicklime, Ahu hegara. Ahu siahu.
Quiet, Asi regeregena.
Quill, Mānu huina.
Quit, Lao. Lakatania.
Quite, Vadaeni. Idoinai.
Quiver, Diba baubauna.
Quotation, Ini koautoma.

R

Rabid, Dagedage hada.
Race (to run) Valān. Heauhelulu.
Radiant, Hururuhururu.
Raft, Pata.
Rafter, Tuidae.
Rag, Dabua sisina.
Rage, Badu.
Ragged, Hedarehedare.
Rail, s. Tabikau āuna.
Rail, v. Hadikaia.
Raillery, Gonagonalaia. Kirikirilaia.
Rain, Medu.
Rainbow, Kevau.
Raise, Abiaisi. Hatoreaisi.
Ramble, Loa.
Rancour, Lalo dika.
Random, Kererekerere.
Rank (growth), Vara rohoroho.
   (Smell) Bodaga.
Rankle, Laloatao.
Ransom, Davana. Qara davana.
Rap, Pidipidi.
Rapid, Haragaharaga.
Rare, Tamotamona.
Rascal, Dika tauna.
Rash, adj. Aonega lasi.
Rash, s. Lari

Rat, Bita.
Ratify, Hamomokanilaia.
Rattan, Oro ; (*larger*) Vakoda.
Rattle, Hataia.
Rave, Koau kava koau kava.
Ravish, Henaohenoa.
Raw, Nadu lasi.
Raze, Rohoa. Buatari.
Razor, Vasika.
Reach, *v*. Eme kau ; (*a place*) Lasi.
Read, Revareva duahia.
Ready, get (*lakatoi*) Laia.
Real, Korikori. Momokani.
Rear, *s*. Murina.
Rear, *v*. Havaraia.
Reason, Badina. Koauna.
Reassemble, Haboua lou.
Rebuke, Sisiba henia. Koauatao.
  Bagu koau.
Recede, Lou. Laka muri.
Receive, Abia.
Recent, Matamata.
Reciprocal, Hekarakaraheheni.
Recite, Koaulaia.
Reckless, Kererekerere.
Reckon (*count*) Duahia.
Recline, Hekure ; (*on the side*)
  Egediho.
Recognise, Toana diba.
Recollect, Hedaraune.
Recompense, Davana.
Reconcile, Herohemaino karaia.
Recover, Abia lou ; (*from sickness*)
  Tauna dainamo. Mauri.
Recount, Koaulaia hegege.
Recriminate, Hepapahuahu.
Rectify, Hamaoromaoroa.
Red, Kakakaka.
Redeem (*a person*), Hamauria.
Reduce, Hamaragia.
Redundant, Gaubadabada.
Reed, Siriho.
Reef, Moemoe.
Reel, *v*. Raraga.
Reflect, Laloa. Helalo karaia.
Reform, Hamaoromaoroa.
Refractory, Koauedeede.
Refrain, Lagaani.
Refuge, Magu.
Refuse, *s*. Momo
Refuse, *v*. Kamonai lasi.
Regard, *v*. Hagerea.
Region, Kahana.
Regret, Helalo karaia.
Rehearse, Koaulaia.
Rein, Hakaua varona.
Reject, Dadaraia. Hihihiraia. Negea.

Rejoice, Moale.
Rejoinder, Haere.
Relapse, Dika lou.
Relate, Koaulaia.
Relative, Varavara.
Relax, Tūa.
Release, Ruhaia nege. Haheaua.
Relent, Lalona lou.
Reliance, Abidadama henia.
Religion, Dirava kara.
Relinquish, Negea.
Rely, Abidadama henia.
Remain, Noho.
Remainder, Orena.
Remedy, Hanamolaia gauna.
Remember, Hedaraune. Helaloune.
Remind, Ahelalca.
Remission, Koauatao.
Remnant, Orena.
Remorse, Helaloa. Karaia.
Remote, Daudau.
Remove, Abiaoho.
Remunerate, Davana henia.
Rend, Hedare.
Rendezvous, Haboua gabuna.
Renounce, Negea.
Renowned, Harina bada.
Repair, *v*. Hamatamataia ; (*a rent*)
  Bania.
Repast, Aniani ania.
Repeal, Koauatao.
Repeatedly, Loulou.
Repeat, Koaulaia lou.
Repel, Lulua.
Repent, Helalo karaia.
Repine, Tāi.
Reply, Haere.
Report, Hari.
Repose, *v*. Hekure.
Represent, Koaulaia.
Repress, Koauatao.
Reprimand, Sisibahenia. Rūa.
Reproach, *v*. Loduheni.
Reproof, Koauhenia. Sisiba henia.
Reptile, Gaigai bamona.
Repudiate, Dadaraia.
Repulse, Lulua.
Reputed, Harina bada.
Request, *s*. Henanadai. Noinoi.
Require, Henanadai. Tahua.
Requite, Davana henia.
Rescue, Hamauria.
Research, Tahua malakamalaka.
Resemble (*a person*), Heidāida ;
  (*things*) Bamona.
Resent, Davana karaia.
Reside, Noho.

Residence, Ruma.
Residue, Orena.
Resin, Domena.
Resist, Koauatubu.
Resolve, Lalo koau.
Respect, *v.* Matauraia.
Respire, Hahoho.
Respond, Haere henia. Ere hadavaia.
Rest, *v.* Lagaani.
Rest, Lagaani gabuna.
Restore, Loulaia.
Restless, Tau mauri.
Restrain, Rūa.
Result, Gau vata vara.
Resurrection, Toreisina.
Retain, Rūa.
Retaliate, Davana karaia.
Retard, Laoahu.
Retch, Mumuta.
Retire, Lao.
Retreat, *v.* Lou.
Return, *v.* Lou.
Reveal, Ahedinarai.
Revenge, Davana karaia.
Revere, Hanamoa. Hemataurai.
Reverse (*end for end*), Sivaia.
Revile, Hadikaia.
Revive, Mauri lou.
Revolve, Hegilohegilo.
Reward, *v.*, Davana henia.
Rheumatism, Lōki.
Rheumatic, Lōki karaia.
Rib, Turiarudu.
Rich, Tāga tanna.
Rid, Abiaoho.
Ride, Gui.
Ridge, Nese.
Ridgepole, Magani bada.
Ridicule, Kirikirilaia.
Rifle, *v.*, Henaoa.
Right, Maoromaoro ; (*hand*), Idiba.
Rigid, Tororotororo.
Rim, Isena.
Rind, Kopina.
Ring, *v.* Gaba doua.
Ring (*finger*), Ima vagivagina.
Ringworm, Huni.
Rinse, Huria. Dairia.
Rip, Bolaia.
Ripe, Mage. Lō.
Ripen (*on the tree*), Hamagea ; (*off the tree, as bananas*) Ikou karaia.
Rise, Toreisi.
Rival, Inai.
River, Sinavai.
Road, Dara.

Roam, Loa.
Roar, Tāi bada. Lolo.
Roast, Gabua.
Rob, Dadidadi.
Robust, Tau namo.
Rock (*flat*), Papapapa ; (*high*), Haga.
Rock *v.* Aheudeheudea.
Roe, Bila.
Roll, Lokua,
Roof, Guhi; (*of verandah*), Bakubaku.
Room, Daehutu.
Roost, Mahuta.
Root, Ramuna.
Root up, Ragaia.
Rope, Qanau.
Rose (Chinese), Vahuvahu.
Rot (*of wood*), Houkahouka ; (*fruit*), Pouka.
Rough, Butubutu ; (*road*), Nadi momo.
Round, Kubolukubolu.
Round (*to go*), Hegegedai.
Rouse, Haoa.
Routed, Aheaua rohoroho.
Rove, Toia vareai.
Row, Ere.
Row, *v. a boat*), Baraia.
Rub, Dahua.
Rubbish, Momo.
Rudder. Tari gauna.
Rude, Guni tauna bamona.
Ruffian, Dagedage tauna.
Rule, *s.* Hahetoho gauna.
Ruler, Lohiabada.
Rumble, Regena.
Rumour, Harina.
Rumple, Magugu.
Run, Heau.
Rush, Heau helulu.
Rust, Hogohogo.

S

Sable, Koremakorema.
Sabre, Ilapa.
Sack, *v.* Dadidadi.
Sack, Nulu. Moda. Puse, (*Introduced.*)
Sacred, Helaga.
Sad, Boka hisihisi.
Saddle, Hosi helai gauna.
Safe, Vata mauri.
Sago, Rabia. (*Small package of*), Kokoara. (*Large package*), Gorugoru,

Sail, *s.*, Lara. Geda.
Sail, Heau.
Sake, Bagu.
Salary, Gau karaia davana.
Sale, Hoihoi.
Saline, Damena bamona.
Saliva, Kanudi.
Sallow, Raborarabora.
Salt, Damena.
Salt, *v.* Damena karaia.
Saltpans, Laguta.
Salt water, Tadi.
Salvation, Ahemauri badina.
Salute, Hanamoa henia.
Same, Bamona. Tamona.
Sanctify, Ahelagaia.
Sand, Raria,
Sandbank, Boe.
Sap, Au ranuna.
Sapient, Aonega.
Sapling, Au maragi.
Satchel, Vaina.
Satisfy, Boka hakunua.
Saturday, Satadei. (*Introduced.*)
Saunter, Laka metailametaila.
Savage, Dagedage.
Save, Hamauria.
Saviour, Ahemauri tauna.
Savour, Mamina.
Saw, Iri.
Sawdust, Au dimura.
Say, Koau.
Scab, Taoha.
Scald, Goua.
Scale, *s.* Una.
Scale, *v.* Unahia.
Scalp, Qara kopina.
Scamper, Heau.
Scar, Kipara.
Scarce, Hoholasi.
Scarcity (*of food*), Dōe.
Scare, Hagaria.
Scarify, Hekisi.
Scarlet, Kakakaka.
Scatter, Gigiarohoroho.
Scent, *s.* Bona.
Scent, *v.* Bonana kamouai.
Scholar, Hadibaia mero.
School, Ahediba karaia.
Schoolmaster, Ahediba tauna.
Scissors, Pakosi. (*Introduced.*)
Scoff, Gonagona.
Scold, Koaukoau.
Scoop, *v.* Kadoa.
Scorch, Halaka
Scorn, Lalo dika henia.
Scour, Hagoevaia.

Scourge, *s.* Dadabaia gauna.
Scout, *s.* Hasinadoa tauna.
Scowl, Vaira hamue.
Scramble, Hetabubunai.
Scrap, Sisina.
Scrape, Naua.
Scratch, Hekagalo.
Scream, Tai lolo.
Screen, *s.* Hamedai gauna.
Screw, *s.* Mogea ikoko.
Scribble, Revareva torea dika.
Scriptures, Revareva helaga.
Scrotum, Apo.
Scrub, Huria.
Scrutinize, Itaia tarikatarika.
Scuffle, Hetabubunai.
Scull, Qara koukouna.
Sea, Davara.
Seacoast, Kone.
Seasick, Gure.
Seaside, Davara badina.
Seawater, Tadi.
Search, Tahua.
Season, Negana.
Seat, Helai gauna.
Seaward, Ataia. Davara kahana.
Secede, Lou.
Second, Rua.
Secret, Hereva ehuni.
Secure, Auka. Kunukakunuka.
Secure, *v.* Koua kunukakunuka.
Sediment, Nuri.
Seduce, Koia.
Sedulous, Goada.
See, Itaia,
See ! Ba itaia !
Seed, Au nadinadina.
Seek, Tahua.
Seemly, Kara namo.
Seine, Reke.
Seize, Dabaiatao.
Seldom, Nega tamo tamona.
Select, *v.* Abia hidi.
Selfish, Anidika.
Self-restraint, Boka auka.
Sell, Hoihoi.
Semblance, Bamona.
Senator, Tau bada.
Send, Siaia.
Senior, Varaguna.
Sentinel, Gima tauna.
Separate, Idau.
Sepulchre, Gara.
Serpent, Gaigai.
Servant, Hesiai tauna.
Serve, Isiaina laoheni.
Set, Atoa.

Set on (*as pot*), Ahelaiakau.
Set on fire, (*as grass*), Doua.
Seven, Hitu.
Seven times, Ahitu.
Seventeen, Qauta hitu.
Seventy, Hitu a hui.
Sever, Utua nege.
Several, Haida.
Severe, Dagedage.
Sew, Turituri.
Shade, Kerukeru.
Shade, *v.* Hakerukerua.
Shadow, Laulau.
Shake, *v.* Aheudeheudea.
Shake, *v.n.* Heudeheude.
Shallow, Qihoho.
Sham, *s.* Dibaka tauna.
Shame, Hemarai.
Shamefaced, Kopi hemarai.
Shameful (*conduct*), Hemarai kara.
Shape, Oromana.
Share, *s.* Ahuna.
Share, *v.* Hagaua.
Shark, Qalaha.
Sharp, Gano.
Sharpen, Segea.
Shatter, Pisi rohoroho.
Shave, Hade huina abia.
She, Ia.
Shed, Ruma kalaka.
Shed, *v.* Hehuhu.
Sheep, Mamoe. (*Introduced.*)
Sheet, Hetaru dabuana. (*Of sail*), Idi.
Shelf, Pata.
Shell, Koukouua.
Shell-fish, different kinds of ; see Appendix.
Shelter, *s.* Medai gabuna.
Shelter, *v.* Hamedaia.
Sherd, Ataka.
Shield, Kesi.
Shield, *v.* Nari. Gima.
Shin, Toratora.
Shine, Hururuhururu.
Ship, Lakatoi.
Shipwreck, Lakatoi tataiakohi.
Shirt, Hedoki gauna.
Shiver, *v.n.* Heudeheude.
Shoal (*of fish, &c.*), Serina. (*Water*), Qihoho.
Shoe, Ae palapala gauna.
Shoot, *v.* Ipidi karaia.
Shoot, Au tuhutuhu.
Shop, Hoihoi rumana.
Shore, Kone.
Short, Qadogioqadogi.
Shortly, Nega daudau lasi.

Shortwinded, Laga tuna.
Shot, Ipidi nadina.
Shoulder, Paga.
Shoulder-blade, Larolaro.
Shout, Lolo ; (*for joy*), Isidae.
Shove, Hesede.
Shovel, Kadoa gauna. Gaga.
Shovel, *v.* Kadoa.
Show, *v.* Hadibaia. Ahedinaraia.
Shower, Batugu.
Shred, *v.* Toia.
Shriek, Tāi lolo.
Shrimp, Pāi.
Shrink (*from cold*), Hegogo. (*Clothes or food*), Hedikoi.
Shrivel, *v.* Magugu.
Shudder, Heguguba.
Shuu, Mata gara.
Shut, Koua.
Shutter, Koua gauna.
Shy, Kopi hemarai.
Sick, Gorere.
Side, Kahana.
Side (*by the*), Badina.
Side to with, Kahaia.
Siege, Koua hegege.
Sigh, Ganagana.
Sight (*eye*), Mata hapapai.
Sight, *v.* Itaia.
Sightly, Namo.
Sign, Toana.
Signal, *s.* Toana.
Signal, *v.* (*with eyes*), Hekunumai.
Signify, Anina.
Silence, Asi regeregena. Hereva lasi.
Silence ! Eremui !
Silly, Kavakava.
Similar, Bamona. (*Preceded by the thing compared with*), Na heto.
Simile, Hereva hegeregere.
Simple, Aonega lasi.
Sin, Kara dika.
Since, Ema bona.
Sincere Momokani.
Sinew, Varovaro.
Sing, Ane abia.
Singe, Duduria.
Singer, Ane abia tauna.
Single, Tamona. Sibona.
Single file, Ilua.
Singly, Ta ta.
Singular, Sibona.
Sink, Mutu.
Sinner, Kara dika tauna.
Sip, Kuri ta ta inua.
Sir ! Lohiabada e !

Sister (*woman's younger*), Tadina. (*Elder*), Kakana. (*Man's*), Taihuna.
Sit, Helai.
Site, Gabuna.
Six, Tauratoi.
Sixteen, Qauta tauratoi.
Sixth, Tauratoi.
Sixty, Tauratoi a hui.
Size, Badana.
Skilful, Aonega.
Skin, Kopi.
Skin, *v.* Kopaia.
Skinny, Varotavarota.
Skip, Roho.
Skipper, Lakatoi tauna.
Skirt (*a woman's*), Rami.
Skull, Qara koukouna.
Sky, Guba.
Slack, Hetu.
Slacken, Tūa.
Slander, *v.* Hadikaia.
Slant, Marere.
Slap, Pataia.
Slaughter, Alala mo.
Slate, Nadi.
Slay, Alaia.
Sleep, Mahuta.
Sleepy, Mata garaia.
Slender, Maragimaragi.
Slide, Dedi.
Slight (*not bulky*), Maragimaragi, Varotavarota.
Slim, Maragimaragi, Varotavarota.
Slime, Qari.
Sling, *s.* Vilipopo.
Sling, *v.* Vilipopo davea.
Slink, Laka magogomagogo. Laka helada.
Slip, Dedi. (*Out of*), Puki.
Slippery, Dedikadedika.
Slit, Hapararaia.
Slope, *s.* Dala hekeihekei.
Sloth, Lahedo. Boka mate.
Slough, Kopukopu.
Slow (*in work*), Lega metau. (*In walking*), Laka metau.
Sluggard, Mahuta tauna.
Slumber, Mahuta maragi.
Slut, Sisia haine.
Small, Maragi. (*Of thread, &c.*), Maimu.
Smart, *v.* Hegara.
Smear, Hedahu.
Smell, Bonana.
Smell, *v.* Bonaia.
Smile, Kiri.

Smite, Huaria.
Smoke, Qalahu.
Smoke, *v.* Kuku ania.
Smooth, Manada.
Smut (*from burnt grass*), Banidu.
Snake, Gaigai.
Snare, Idoa.
Snarl, Gigi.
Snatch, Dadia.
Sneeze, Asimana.
Sniff, Iluhai.
Snip, Sisina utua.
Snore, Udu gogona.
Snout, Kurukuruna.
So, Ini heto. Bamona
Soak, Hadaia.
Soap, Sopu. (*Introduced.*)
Soar, Roho.
Sob, Lagadae.
Sociable, Manada.
Soft, Manokamanoka.
Soil, *v.* Hamiroa.
Soil, *s.* Tano.
Sojourn, Noho.
Solace, Tauhalō.
Sole, Ae lalona.
Solicit, Noinoi.
Solicitude, Kudou hetaha.
Solitary, Sibona noho.
Some (*people*), Haida. (*Things*), Taina.
Somebody, Tau ta.
Something, Gau ta.
Sometimes, Hata.
Son, Mero.
Son-in-law, Ravana.
Song, Ane.
Sonorous, Regena bada.
Soon, Nega daudau lasi.
Sooth, Hamarumaru.
Sooty, Guma karaia.
Sordid, Harihari lasi.
Sore, *adj.* Hisihisi.
Sore, *s.* Toto.
Sorrow, Boka hisihisi.
Soul, Lauma.
Sound, Regena.
Sound, *adj.* Namo. Goevagoeva.
Sour (*acid*), Iseuri. (*Paste, &c.*), Bakobako.
Source, Badina.
South, Diho kahana.
South-east, Laulabada kahana.
South-east wind, Laulabada.
South wind, Diho.
Sovereign, Gaubada.
Sow, *v.* Gigiarohoroho.
Sow, *s.* Boroma haine.

D

Space (*between*), Ihuana. Padana.
Spacious, Lababana bada.
Spade, Gaga.
Spare, *v*. Mia.
Spatter, Petapetalaia.
Spawn, Bila.
Speak, Koau. Hereva
Spear, Io.
Specify, Koaulaia maoromaoro.
Speckle, Toutoudia.
Spectator, Itaia tauna.
Spectre, Vadavada.
Speech, Hereva.
Speed, Heau.
Spell (*a word*), Hagaua.
Spew, Lori.
Spider, Magela.
Spill, *v*. Hebubu.
Spine, Turiamava.
Spirit, Lauma.
Spit, Kanudi.
Spite, Badu.
Spittle, Kanudi.
Splash, Pisipisina.
Splendid, Namo herea.
Splinter, *s*. Au tahana.
Split, Hapararaia.
Spoil, *v*. Hadikaia.
Spoil, *s*. Dadidadi kohu dinana.
Sponge, Puta.
Sport, Kadara. (*In the sea*), Bulu-
bulu.
Spot, Toutou.
Spotless, Toutouna lasi.
Spotted (*as yam, &c.*), Budu-
budu.
Sprain, *s*. Dorua.
Sprain, *v*. Hadorua.
Spray, Pisili.
Spread (*as a cloth*), Lahaia.
Spring, *v*. Roho.
Sprinkle, Nevaria.
Sprout, Tubu.
Spurn, Dadaraia. Hihihiraia.
Spy, Kito tauna.
Spy, *v*. Kito.
Spyglass, Varivari. (*Introduced*.)
Squabble, Heai, Heatu.
Squalid, Dika.
Squall, Guba. Ore.
Squander, Davedavelaia. Piupiu-
laia.
Square, Derekadereka.
Squat (*on heels*), Idori.
Squeak, Tai.
Squeeze (*in the arms*), Gugubaia.
(*Between boards, &c.*), Kapuatao.

Squint, Mata gegeva.
Squirt, Larilari.
Stab, Qadaia.
Stable, Hosi ruma.
Staff, Itotohi.
Stagger, Raraga.
Stagnant, Ranu duhu.
Stair, Vatavata.
Stale, Idaunegai gauna.
Stalk (*of banana, &c.*), Qasi; (*of
mango, &c.*), Adana.
Stallion, Hosi maruane.
Stammer, Lanalana.
Stamp, *v*. Panadagu.
Stanch, Momokani.
Stanched, Vata doko.
Stand, Gini.
Star, Hisiu.
Stare, Raraia.
Start, Hoa. Laumadaure.
Starve, *v.n.* Hitolo mate.
Stay (*to a mast*), Hadeolo. (*At
home when others go*), Anasi.
Steadfast, Badinaia tarikata-
rika.
Steady, Tutukatutuka.
Steal, Henao.
Stealthily, Helada.
Steam, Varabu.
Steep, *v*. (*in water*), Hadaia.
Steep, Hagahaga.
Steer, Tari karaia.
Steersman, Tari tauna.
Stem, Badina.
Stench, Bodaga.
Step, *v*. Laka.
Sterile (*of ground*), Gesegese.
Stern (*of a ship*), Gabena.
Stick, *s*. Au. (*Fencing, small*),
Adira ; (*large*), Pulu.
Stick (*a walking*), Itotohi.
Stick, *v*. Hekahi. Hekamo.
Sticky, Hekamo.
Stiff, Auka. Lokaloka.
Stiff neck, Aio gageva.
Stile, Ikoukou.
Still, *v*. Hatnia.
Stillborn, Mala dika.
Stimulate, Hagoadaia.
Sting *v*. Koria ; (*hornet*), Talaia.
Stingy, Harihari lasi.
Stink, Bodaga.
Stir, Giua.
Stomach, Beka.
Stone, Nadi.
Stone, *v*. Nadi hodoa.
Stony, Nadigabuna.

Stool (*to sit on*), Helai gauna.
Stool (*go to*), Kuku.
Stoop, Haigo.
Stop, *v*. Hadokoa ; *v.n.*, Noho.
Stop ! Vadaeni ! Noho !
Storm, Ore. Guba.
Story (*narrative*), Sivarai.
Stout, Tau gaubadabada.
Straight, Maoro.
Straight, *v*. (*to make*), Ahemaoro.
Strait, Hekahihekahi.
Strand, Ere.
Strange, Idau.
Stranger, Idau tauna.
Strangle, Hemata.
Stratagem (*to deceive*), Koia kara.
Stray, Laka kerere.
Stream, Sinavai. Doga.
Stream forth (*as blood*), Bobobobo.
Strength, Goada.
Stretch, *v.*, Veria.
Strew, Lahaia.
Street, Ariara.
Strife, Heatu.
Strike, *v*. (*with a weapon*), Botaia.
  Lapaia. (*With the flat hand*),
  . Pataia.
String, Varo.
String, *v*. (*a bow*), Rohea.
Stripe, Revareva.
Stripling, Tauhau.
Strive, Goada.
Stroke, *s*. (*with stick*), Qadia.
Strong, Goada. Abidadama.
Strumpet, Ariara haine.
Stubborn, Ura dika.
Stumble, Heqaqanai.
Stump, Au badibadina.
Stunted, Vara lasi.
Stupefy (*as fish with drug*),
  Kekero.
Stupid, Kavakava. Asi aonega.
Sturdy, Goada.
Stutter, Gado lanalana.
Sty (*pig*), Boroma arana.
Stye (*on eye*), Busibusi.
Submerge, Toiadobi. Hadaia.
Submission, Tomadiho henia.
Subsequent, Gabea.
Subside, Dodo.
Substance, Anina. Anitarana.
Substitute, Boloa. Ibodohi.
Subtract, Veria. Abiaoho.
Succeed, Abia. Davaria. Qa-
  limu.
Succour, Kahaia.
Such, Unu heto.

Suck, Toboa.
Suckle, Natuna rata hainua.
Sudden, Hoa. Laumadaure.
Suffer, Hisi ania.
Suffice, Vadaeni. (*Of food*), Boka
  kunu.
Sugarcane, Tohu.
Suicide, Sibona heala.
Sulky, Badu.
Sultry, Siahu.
Sum, Haboua.
Summit, Dorinai.
Summon, Boilia.
Sun, Dina.
Sunday, Sabati. (*Introduced.*)
Sunder, Utua nege.
Sunny, Dina tara.
Sunset, Dina kerekere.
Superior, Namo herea.
Supper, Adorahi aniani.
Supple, Perukaperuka.
Supplicate, Noinoi.
Supply, *v*. Henia.
Support, *v*. (*as a tree or house*),
  Imudaia.
Suppose, Lalo koau.
Suppress, Koauatao.
Suppurate, Hura karaia.
Supreme, Sibona herea.
Sure, Diba momokani.
Surface, Kopina.
Surfeit, Gado lohilohi.
Surmise, Lalo koau.
Surpass, Herea.
Surplus, Orena.
Surprise, *v*. Hahoaia.
Surround, Gegea. Hegege iradai.
Survivor, Hoho tauna.
Swallow, Hadonoa.
Swamp, Kopukopu.
Sway (*by the wind*), Haevaia.
  Helado.
Sweat, Varahu.
Sweep, Daroa.
Sweet, Gaiho.
Swell, Gudu.
Swift, Heau bada.
Swim, Nahu.
Swine, Boroma.
Swing, *s*. Love ; (*Low*) Taupe-
  taupe.
Swing, *v*. Love ; (*Low*) Taupe-
  taupe.
Swoon, Matelea.
Swop, Hoihoi.
Sword, Ilapa.
Symptom, Toana.

TAB (52) TIP

T

Table, Pata.
Tail, Iuna ; (of birds), Tupina.
Take, Abia.   Abikau.   (Away),
   Abiaoho. Laohaia. (Up), Abiaisi.
Tale, Sivarai.
Talk, Hereva.
Talkative, Udu mauri.
Tall, Ganlatalata.   Lata.
Tame, Manada.
Tangle, Heqatu.
Tardy, Halahe.
Taro, Talo.
Tarry, Noho.
Tart, Iseuri.
Taste, Ania toho.
Tattoo, Revareva hatua.
Taunt, Koau henia.
Taut, Rorokaroroka.
Teach, Hadibaia.
Teacher, Ahediba tauna.
Tear, Darea.
Tears, Iruru mata.
Tease, Habadua.
Teat, Rata matana.
Telescope, Varivari.   (Introduced
   meaning.)
Tell, Koau henia.   Hamaoroa.
Tempest, Ore bada.
Temple, Dubu.
Tempt, Dihagani.
Temptation, Idibaganina.
Ten, Qauta.
Tenacious, Āuka.
Tend (as sheep, &c.), Legua.
Tender, Manokamanoka.
Tendon, Varovaro.
Tenth, Qauta.
Termination, Dokona.
Terrify, Hagaria.
Terror, Gari.
Testify, Koaulaia.
Text, Hereva badina.
Thanks (to give), Hanamoa.
That, Enai.   Unai.
Thatch, Ruua guhi.
Their, Idia edia ; (of food), Idia adia.
Them, Idia.
Then, Unai negana.
There, Unuseni.
Therefore, Inai.
These, Inai.
They, Idia.
Thick, Hutuna.
Thief, Henao tauna.

Thigh, Mamu.
Thin, Severasevera.
Thing, Gau.
Think, Laloa.
Thinking faculty, Aonega.
Third, Toi.
Thirst, Ranu mate.
Thirteen, Quata toi.
Thirty, Toi ahui.
This, Inai.
Thorn, Gini.
Those, Unai.
Thou, Oi.
Though, Ena be.
Thought, Lalo koau.
Thoughtful, Aonega.
Thoughtless, Kavakava.
Thousand, Daha.
Thrash, Dadabaia.   Botaia,
Thread, Varo.
Three, Toi.
Threefold, Eretoi.
Threshold, Ikureahu.
Thrive, Vara rohoroho.
Throat, Gado.
Throat sore, Aratnria.
Throb (as the heart), Rohodaerohodae.
   (As a gathering), Hodaehodae.
Throng, Hutuma hada.
Throng, v. Hesedea.
Throttle, Gado gigia.
Through (to go), Hanaia lao.
Throughout, Idoinai.
Throw, Tahoa.
Thrush, Mala rcho.
Thrust, Doria.
Thumb, Sina bada.
Thump, Tutua.
Thunder, Guba rahua.
Thursday, Tarisidei.   (Introduced.)
Thus, Ini heto.
Thwart, Laoahu.
Tickle, Ahemaihemai.
Tide high, Davara bada.
Tide low, Komata gui.   Davara
   maragi.
Tidings, Sivarai.   Harina.
Tie, Mataia.
Tight, Hekahi.
Till, Ela bona.
Time, Negana.
Timid, Gari.
Tin, Tini.   (Introduced.)
Tingle, Ginigini.
Tinkle, Regena.
Tiny, Maragimaragi.
Tip, Matana.

Tipsy, Muramura heala.
Tire, Aheqarahi.
Titter, Kiri maumau.
To (*direction towards*), Dekena
Toe, Ae qaqiqagina.
Together, Ida. Hebou.
Toil, Heqarahi.
Token, Toana.
Tongs, Hakahi gauna.
Tongue, Mala.
Tools, Gau karalaia gaudia.
Tooth, Hise ; (*double*), Gadigadi.
Toothache, Arituma.
Top, Latana. Dorina.
Torch, Kede.
Torment, *v.* Hahisia.
Torrent, Habata.
Tortoise, (*land*), Gelo.
Torture, Hahisia.
Toss, *v.* Piuaisi.
Tossed (*by waves*), Ahekurehe-kure.
Total, Idoinai.
Totter, Raraga.
Touch, Hedaukau.
Touchwood, Alatutu.
Touchy, Badu kava.
Tough, Auka.
Tow, *v.* Veria.
Toward (*to look*), Hagere.
Town, Hanua.
Toy, Kadara gauna.
Tractable, Manada.
Trade, *s.* Hoihoi gaudia.
Trade, *v.* Hoihoi.
Trade-wind (S.E.), Laulabada.
(N.W.) Lahara.
Tradition, Tuputama hereva.
Trail, Lamari.
Train, *v.* Hadibaia.
Traitor, Taotoretauna.
Trample, Aemoiatao.
Tranquil, Vea.
Transact, Karaia.
Transcend, Herea
Transfer, Laohaia.
Transfix, Audelaiabou (*preceded by instrument*).
Transgress, Tataiautu.
Translate (*language*), Hahegere-gerea.
Transparent, Nēga.
Transplant, Ragaia hadoa lou.
Trap, Idoa.
Trash, Gaudika.
Travel, *v.* Laolao karaia.
Traveller, Laolao tauna.

Treacherous, Koikoi.
Tread, Hadaia : (*upon*) Aemoiatao.
Treasure, Kohu.
Treaty, Taravatu.
Tree, Au.
Trees, different kinds of. (See Appendix)
Tremble, Heudeheude.
Tremendous, Gaubadabada.
Tremulous, Heudeheude.
Trench, Dadaila.
Trepidation, Gari.
Trespass, Doha hadikaia, Kamonai lasi.
Trial (*of canoe, &c.*), Dibaia.
Tribulation, Nega dikadika.
Trickle, Veve.
Trifle, Kadara.
Trim, *v.* Hagoevaia.
Trip, *i.* Haheqaqanai.
Triple, Hatoi.
Triumph, *v.* Qalimu.
Troop (*of soldiers*), Tuari.
Trouble, *v.* Haraivaia, Haturiaia.
Troublesome, Haraiva.
Trousers, Piribou. (*Introduced.*)
True, Momokani.
Trumpet, Ivirikou.
Trundle, Hekeialao.
Trunk, Māua (*of tree*), Badina
Trust (*in a person*), Abidadama henia.
Try (*to try a thing*), Dibaia ; (*to do*), Karaia toho.
Tuesday. Tusidei. (*Introduced.*)
Tuft (*of hair*) Hui darolasi.
Tug, Veria. Haroroa.
Tumble, Keto.
Tumult, Herouherou.
Turbid, Duhu.
Turkey (*brush*), Apa.
Turmeric, Raborarabora.
Turmoil, Helogohelogo.
Turn, *v.* (*back*), Lou. (*Round*), Gini-kerehai. (*Over a thing*), Hurea. (*Over one's self*), Hehurehanai. (*End for end*), Sivaia. (*Away*), Idauhai hagerea.
Turtle, Matabudi ; (*green*) Ela.
Tusk, Doa.
Twelve, Qauta rua.
Twenty, Rua ahui.
Twice, Harua.
Twig, Au rakona.
Twilight, Mailumailu.
Twins, Hekapa.
Twine, Varo.

Twirl, Davea.
Twist, Mogea.
Twist (*string*), Aloia.
Two, Rua.
Twofold, Ererua.
Tyranny, Dagedage.

U

Ugly, Dika.
Ulcer, Toto.
Umbrella, Tamalu. (*Introduced.*)
Unable (*to do*), Karaia diba lasi.
Unaltered, Idau lasi.
Unanswered, Haere lasi.
Unarmed, Ima gauna lasi.
Unattended, Bamoa lasi. Sibona.
Unawares, Dagu. Hoalaia.
Unbearable, Ahcauka doko.
Unbecoming, Namo lasi.
Unbend (*as bow*), Kokiaoho.
Unbind, Ruhaia.
Unbounded, Hetoa lasi.
Uncertain, Diba lasi.
Uncivil, Ere dika.
Uncle, Tamana.
Unclean, Miro.
Unclothe, Dabua lasi.
Uncommon, Diahoho.
Uncover, Hulalaia.
Uncourteous, Gaiho dika.
Uncultivated (*land*), Vahu.
Undecided, Daradara.
Under, Henuai.
Underdone, Maeta lasi.
Understand, Diba.
Understanding, Aonega.
Undertake, Karaia koaulaia.
Undo, Ruhaia.
Undress, Dabua dokioho.
Uneasy, Noho namonamo lasi.
Unemployed, Gau karaia lasi.
Unequal, Hegeregere lasi.
Uneven, Hegeregere lasi.
Unexpected, Laroa lasi.
Unfasten, Ruhaia. Kehoa.
Unfold, Kehoa. Hulalaia.
Unfortunate, Dirava dika.
Unfrequented, Dekedekenarahu.
Ungoverned, Lohia lasi.
Unhandsome, Dika.
Unhandy, Lega metau.
Unhappy, Moale lasi.
Unhealthy (*place*), Gorere gabuna.
Unhonoured, Matauraia lasi.

Unhospitable, Heabidae lasi. Se hagerea.
Unhurt, Bero lasi.
Uniform, Hegeregere.
Unintentional, Koaulaia lasi.
Union, Hebou.
Unite (*by tying*), Hiria.
Universal, Idoinai.
Unjust, Kara maoro lasi.
Unkind, Dagedage.
Unknown, Diba lasi.
Unlawful, Taravatu koauabu kara.
Unlike, Bamona lasi.
Unlock, Kehoa.
Unloose, Ruhaia.
Unlucky, Dirava dika.
Unmarried, Headava lasi.
Unmerciful, Boka hisihisi lasi.
Unmovable, Tutukatutuka.
Unneighbourly, Karakara tauna.
Unobserved, Ta itaia lasi.
Unpaid, Davana lasi.
Unpardoned, Koauatao lasi.
Unprepared, Hagoevaia lasi.
Unripe, Mage lasi. Karukaru.
Unroll, Hulalaia.
Unruly, Koauedeede.
Unsatisfied, Boka kunu lasi.
Unsuccessful, Abia lasi. Davaria lasi.
Unthankful, Hananioa lasi.
Untie, Ruhaia.
Until, Ela bona.
Untried, Dibaia lasi.
Untrue, Koikoi.
Unwilling, Koauedeede. Tau se raiva.
Unwonted, Manada lasi.
Up, Dae.
Up ! Toreisi !
Upbraid, Koau henia. Loduhenia.
Uphold, Abiaisi. Durua.
Upon, Latana ai.
Uppish, Dagedage.
Upright, Tupua. Gini maoro.
Uproar, Helogohelogo.
Uproot, Ragaia.
Upsidedown, Kaluhia hebubu.
Upward, Ataiai.
Urge, Ura henia. Noinoi.
Urine, Mei.
Us, Ita (*including those addressed*). Ai (*excluding*).
Use, *s.* Kara.
Use, *v.* Abia.
Usual, Taunabinai.
Uterus, Boka.

V

Vacant (as a house), Ruma gagaena.
Vain, Hekokorogu.
Vainglorious, Heagi.
Vale, Goura.
Valiant, Goada.
Valley, Goura.
Valuable, Hoihoi bada gauna.
Value, v. Davana koanlaia.
Vanish, Lasihia.
Vanquish, Qalimu.
Vapour, Ninoa. Valabu (steam).
Variance, Hebadubaduheheni.
Variety, Idauidau.
Vast, Bada.
Vaunt, Heagi.
Veil, s. Gobaiahu gauna.
Vein, Rara varovaro.
Velocity, Heau.
Vend, Hoihoi.
Venerate, Mataurai henia.
Vengeance, Davana.
Venomous, Mate gauna.
Verandah, Dehe. Ese.
Verify, Hamomokania.
Verse, Siri (Introduced meaning).
Versed, Manada.
Vertigo, Mata madaimadai.
Vex, Habadua. Turiariki
Vexatious, Turiariki.
Vial, Kavapukavapu.
Vice, Kara dika.
Victor, Qualimu tauna.
Victuals, Malamala.
Vigilant, Kito.
Vigorous, Goada.
Vie, Helulu.
Vile, Dika.
Vilify, Hadikaia.
Village, Hanua.   (Small), Hanua motu.
Vindicate, Hamaoromaoroa.
Violate (a tabooed thing), Bokatoto.
Violent, Dagedage.
Viper, Gaigai.
Virgin, Haniulato rami hebou.
Visit, v. (as a sick person), Hegoita.
Visitor, Vadivadi.
Vixen, Koaukoau hainena.
Vocation, Dagi.
Voice, Gâdo.
Volcano, Qarahu orooro.   Lahi orooro.

Voluntarily, Sibona.
Vomit, Mumuta.
Voracious, Aniani bada.
Voyage, Hiri.   (Short), Daiva.

W

Wade, Tulu.
Wag, Hevasea tauna.
Wages, Davana.
Wail, Tai.
Waist, Koekoe.
Wait, Nari.   Helaro.
Wake, Noka.
Walk, Laka.
Walking-staff, Itotohi.
Wall, Magu.
Wallaby, Magani.
Wallow, Hekuhihekuhi.
Wander, Loa kava.
Want, v. Hekisehekise.
Want, s. Ogogami.
War, s. Alala.
War, v. Alala karaia.   Tuari lao (to go to war).
Warm, Siahusiahu.
Warm, v. Hasiahua.
Warn, Rauaia.
Warp, v. Hagagevaia.
Warrior, Alaala tauna.
Wart, Usiusi.
Wash, v. Huria.
Wasp, Naniko.
Waste, v. Petapetalaia.
Watch, v. Gima.   Nari.
Watch, s. Dina gauna.   (Introduced meaning).
Water, Ranu.
Watercourse, Hahata.
Waterfall, Dadahekei.
Watery, Ranukaranuka.
Wave, v. Aheudehendea.
Wave, s. Sinaia.
Wax, Bata.
Way (road), Dara.   (Custom), Kara.
Waylay, Banitao.
Wayside, Dala isena.
We, Ai (excluding the person addressed).   Ita (including).
Weak, Manokamanoka.
Wealth, Kohu.
Wean, Rata kakaianege.
Weapon, Ima gauna.
Weary, Tau e boera.
Weave, Hatua.

Web, Valavala.
Wed, Headava.
Wedge, Hakahi.
Wednesday, Uenisidei. (Introduced.)
Weep, Maragimaragi.
Weed, v. Avarau.
Weed, Ava.
Weep, Tāi.
Weigh, Abiatoho baine metau.
Weighty, Metau.
Welcome, v., Mata papa.
Well, Ranu guri.
Well, adj. Namo.
Well, adv. Namo.
Well nigh, Mokona.
Wellspring, Ranu lohi.
Wench, Kekeni.
West, Tahodiho.
Wet, Paripari.
Whale, Lakara donodono.
What? Dahaka?
Whelp, Sisia natuna.
When? Edauanegai?
Whence? Edeamomai?
Where? Edeseni?
Wherefore? Badina dahaka?
Whet, Segea.
Whether, Iava.
Whetstone, Kaia segea nadina.
Which? Edana?
While, Negana.
Whip, Qadilaia gauna.
Whirlpool, Kavabulobulo.
Whirlwind, Koeahilihili.
Whisker, Vaha huina.
Whisper, Hemaunu.
Whistle, Hioka.
White, Kurokuro.
White hair, Hui buruka.
Whitewash, Ahu ranuna.
Whither? Ede lao?
Who? Daika.
Whole, Idoinai.
Wholly, Idoinai.
Whore, Ariara haine.
Whose? Daika ena.
Why? Dahaka gau?
Wick, Vavae. (Introduced.)
Wicked, Kara dika.
Wide, Lababana bada. Gamoga bado.
Widow, Vado. (In mourning), Vapu.
Wife, Adavana.
Wild, Manada lasi.
Will, Ura.
Willing, Ura henia.
Wind, Lāi.

Wind, v. Lokua.
Windbound, Lai e laoahu.
Window, Varivari. (Introduced meaning.) Ikoukou.
Windpipe, Gado baubau.
Wing (of a bird), Hani.
Wink, Hekunumai.
Winkle, Basisi.
Wipe, Hedahu.
Wise, Aonega. Laloparara.
Wish, Hekisehekise. Ura henia.
With, Ida. Hebou.
Wither, Marai.
Withhold, Rūa.
Within, Lalonai.
Without (outside), Murimuri.
Withstand, Laoahu. Koauatupu.
Witness, Diha tauna.
Woe, Nega dikadika.
Woe, int. Inaio.
Woman, Haine.
Womb, Boka.
Wonder, v. Hoa.
Wont, Kara.
Wood, Au.
Wool, Mamoe huina. (Mamoe introduced).
Word, Hereva.
Work, v., Gau karaia. Heqarahi.
World, Tanobada idoinai.
Worm, Biruka.
Worm-eaten, Manumanu ania.|
Worse, Dika (following the name of the thing or time with which it is compared).
Worship, Tomadiho henia.
Worsted, Darere.
Worth, Davana.
Wound, Bero.
Wrangle, Heai.
Wrap, Kumia.
Wrath, Badu.
Wreath, v., Hiria.
Wrecked, Hurekau.
Wrench, Giua. (Up), Giuaisi. (Off), Giuaoho.
Wretched, Lalo dika.
Wriggle, Heloge.
Wrinkle, Magugu.
Wrist, Ima ganaganana.
Write, Revareva torea.
Writhe, Hegirohegiro.
Writing, Revareva.
Wrong, v.a. Hadikaia. Dagedage henia.
Wrong, v.n. Kererekerere.
Wry, Gageva.

Y

Yam, Maho.
Yard, Dimuna. (*A measure of about a yard.*)
Yawn, Mava.
Ye, Umui.
Year, Lagani.
Yearly, Lagani idoinai.
Yearn, Hekisehekise bada.
Yell, Tāi lolo.
Yellow, Raborarabora.
Yes, Io. Oi be.

Yesterday, Varani.
Yield, Kamonai. Darere.
Yonder, Unuseni.
You, *sing.* Oi ; *pl.* Umui.
Young (*of animals*), Natuna. (*Of trees, &c.*), Karukaru.
Your, *sing.* Oiemu ; *pl.* Umui emui.
Youth, *s.* Tauhau negana.

Z

Zealous, Goada bada.

MOTU AND ENGLISH.

A has the sound of *a* in father. Sometimes it is short, as *a* in mad.

A, *prefix*, Causation.

A, *conj.* but.

Ae, *s.* leg (the entire leg and foot).

Ae badau, elephantiasis in the leg.

Aedudu, relations, adherents.

Ae gabu, a footprint.

Ae gedu, the heel.

Ae komukomu, the ankle.

Ae hemuri, to slip with the foot turning out.

Ae kamodae, paralysed or withered legs.

Ae kepo, to slip with the foot turning in.

Ae moia, Ae moiatao, to tread upon.

Ae meimoi, to rest the feet upon.

Ae palapala, the foot.

Ae qagiqagina, the toe.

Ae sike tauna, a lame man.

Ai, a relative particle of time or place.

Ai, *pron.* we (exclusive of the person addressed).

Ai emai, *pron.* our (exclusive).

Aio, *s.* neck (of person or animal).

Aio gauna, necklace.

Aio gageva, stiff neck.

Aio mareremarere, to nod.

Aiha, *s.* centipede.

Aina, sign of 1st person singular immediate future.

Aita, sign of 1st person plural (inclusive) immediate future.

Aivara, *s.* pole used for poling in shallow water.

Ao, *s.* a sheltered anchorage, a harbour.

Aola, *v. imper.* Go !

Aoma, *v.* come.

Aonega, *s.* the thinking faculty.

Aonega, *a.* wise, clever, acute.

Au, a prefix to numerals in counting dishes, and things of length.

Āu, *s.* a tree ; firewood.

Āu badibadina, a stump.

Āu dimura, sawdust, very small particles of wood.

Āu huahua, blossom, and also fruit.

Āu kopina, bark of a tree.

Āu maragi, sapling. Āu maragimaragi, brushwood.

Āu momoru. See Āu dimura.

Āu nadinadina, seed.

Āu rakena, twig.

Āu ramuna, root.

Āu ranuna, sap.

Āu taha, a splinter, a small piece of wood.

Āu tuhutuhu, a shoot.

Auau, *s.* (1) a stick fork to eat with ; (2) handle, as of an axe.

Auasi, *s.* one who stays when others go on a voyage, or journey. *Auasi tau. Auasi haine.*

Āuka, *a.* firm (not loose) ; (2) Hard (as wood) ; (3) tough (as meat) ; (4) difficult to open (as a door) ; (5) secure.

Āuka bada, durable, immovable.

Auki, *s.* the lower jaw.

Auki bada, swollen lower jaw, mumps.

Auruaoti, *a.* two.

Autuna, Aotuna, *s.* gall.

Autupua, *s.* a mast.

Abae, *s.* the name of a fish.

Abagore, *s.* breastbone of birds.

Abe, *s.* presence ; proximity.

Ahia, *v.* to have, to get, to take hold of.

Abiaisi, to take up.

Abiacho, to remove, take out of the way.

Abia gini, to hold upright.

Abia hidi, to have by choice, to choose.

Abia lasi, fruitlessly.

Abia toho, to weigh on the hands, to try.

Abidadama, *a.* strong.

Abidadama, *s.* a person or thing to rely on.

Abidadama henia, *v.* to trust in or to, to put dependence on, to rely on.

Abihavara, *v.* to take a thing when told not to ; to disregard the taboo of a tree.

Abikau, *v.* to take. A small lean-to on the verandah.

Abilaia, *v.* to obtain with.

Abi mauri tauna, *s.* a captive.

Abitorehai, *v.* to have on trust. Abitorehai tauna, a debtor.

Abona abia, *v.* to castrate.

Adana, *s.* fibre of chewed pandanus fruit.

Adana, *s.* stalk of fruit.

Adavaia, *v.* to be married (mentioning the person to whom married.)

Adavana, *s.* wife or husband.

Ade, *s.* the chin.

Ademela, name of a fish.

Adeolo, or adeholo, *s.* the stay of a mast.

Adia, *pron.* for them, theirs (of food only).

Adia, name of a fish.

Adira, a small stick of fence.

Adorahi, *s.* evening.

Agavaita, one kind of yam.

Agi, *s.* ginger.

Agu, *pron.* mine, for me.

Ahagaia, *v.* to open the mouth ; one's own or another.

Ahakara, name of a fish.

Ahavaia, *v.* to drive, to chase, as a dog or kangaroo.

Abeauka, *v.* (1) to forbear ; (2) to harden.

Aheauka, *s.* patience, forbearance.

Aheudeheude, *v.* to shake. (See Heudeheude).

Aheboera, *v.* to wear out, to fatigue.

Aheboua, *v.* to add to.

Ahebubua, *v.* to turn over, to spill.

Ahediba, *v.* to cause to know, to teach.

Ahediba tauna, one who makes known, instructs, a teacher.

Ahedinaraia, *v.* to manifest, to confess, to expose.

Ahedokia, *v.* to put on (as clothes).

Ahedua, to command, to permit.

Ahegani, to command.

Ahegani herevana, *s.* commandments.

Ahegogo, to collect, assemble.

Ahekora, *v.* to put off on another ; to excuse onself from giving by saying it is another's ; to lay blame on another for one's own fault.

Ahekurehekure, *v.* to be tossed about by the waves.

Ahelaiakau, *v.* to set on.

Ahelaiatore, to cause to sit up.

Ahelagaia, *v.* to make sacred, to consecrate.

Ahelaloa, *v.* to remind, to commemorate.

Ahemaoro, *v.* to make straight ; *s.* judgment.

Ahemauri tauna, *s.* saviour.

Ahemaraia, *v.* to abash, to disgrace.

Aheparia, to wet accidentally (as newly made pottery).

Aheqa, *v.* to tell one to speak.

Aheqinaia, *v.* to pillow.

Aheqaqanaia, *v.* to cause to stumble.

Aberahu, *v.* to smell, from affection, in place of a kiss.

Ahetoni, *v.* to part with friends, to bid farewell.

Ahitu, Hahitu, *s.* seven times.

Ahonua, *v.* to fill.

Ahu, *s.* gourd or bottle in which the lime is carried for chewing with betel nut.

Ahu, *s.* lime (quick or slack). Ahu hegara, quicklime.

Ahu, to close (as a fence which completes enclosure).

Ahu, *adv. in composition,* close.

Ahui, ten (in counting after the first ten, as rua ahui, twenty).

Ahuiahuia, name of a fish.

Ahuota, *s.* a fish so called.

Ahumianimiani, *v.* to stop a crack in *hodu* with melted gum ; to make a vessel water-tight ; to be closed (of a door), having no aperture.

Ahuna, *s.* a share, a division, a portion. Ahugu, my share.

Ahunua, *v.* to make fast a rope.

Ahururua, *v.* to cause to flame.

Akarua, one kind of banana.

Akeva, *s.* beads.

Akudimaia, *v.* to make deaf.

Ala, *v.* from Lao to go, 1st pers. plural present.

Alabore *s.* sinnet (made of cocoanut fibre).

Alaia, *v.* (1) to kill ; (2) to burn (*a house*).

Alaia ore, to exterminate.

Alala, *s.* war.

Alala henia, to give battle.

Alala karaia, making war, fighting.

Alala koaulaia, to speak of fighting; the opposite of peace.

Alatore, *v.* to fish with nets on the shore reef.

Alatutu and Halatutu, *s.* a dry tree or touchwood, burning until consumed. *Rei doua alatutuna.*

Aloia *v.* to twist (as flax into string).

Amai, *pron.* ours, for us. (Exclusive of persons addressed.) Of food only.

Amo, *prep.* from.

Amu, *s.* oven.

Amu, *pron.* yours, for you (sing.)

Amui, *pron.* yours, for you (plural).

Anama, a fish.

Ane abia *v.* to sing.

Ane *s.* a song.

Ane sisibaia tauna, a bard.

Aneru, *s.* angel. (*Introduced from the English*), pl. anerudia.

Ania, *v.* to eat.

Anidika, selfish, eating secretly.

Aniore, to eat up.

Anibou, to eat together.

Aniani, *s.* one kind of mangrove.

Aniani, *n.* food.

Anina, *s.* flesh of the body.

Anina, *s.* primarily, (1) something to eat ; (2) substance, contents of a thing. *Hodu mai anina*, the waterpot has water in it ; (3) kernel. Asi anina, empty, hollow.

Anitorehai, to eat borrowed food.

Anitarana, *s.* body; substance; form.

Anivaga, *s.* a fast.

Āpa, *s.* a brush turkey.

Apo, *s.* scrotum. Apo ivaia, to geld.

Ara and Ala, *s.* a fence of upright sticks.

Arara, one kind of mangrove, the bark of which is used as dye.

Araturia, sore throat.

Are, *s.* nymphæ,

Areto, *s.* bread. (*Introduced from the Greek*).

Aria, *s.* a feast made out-of-doors.

Ariaoda, a fish.

Ariara, *s.* a street, road through a village (distinguished from dala, a road through the bush).

Ariara natuna, a bastard.

Ariara haine, courtesan.

Ariha, *s.* a large lizard, iguana.

Arituna, *s.* toothache.

Aromaia, *v.* to carry a small netted bag round the neck, hanging down the back.

Aru, *s.* (1) current (of river or sea) ; (2) multitude ; (3) *Liq amnii.*

Arua mai, *v.* to flock.

Ase or Ate, *s.* liver.

Asi, *s.* a large canoe. *Asi memero*, crew.

Asi, *adv.* not. Same as *lasi* ; but used before the verb, while lasi follows it. *Asi tauna*, nobody.

Asimana, *v.* to sneeze.

Asi regeregena, *s.* quiet.

Ata, *pron.* ours, for us (inclusive of person addressed).

Atai, *adv. & prep.* (1) above ; (2) the space between earth and sky ; (3) seawards (of the course of a canoe or ship). Ataiai, aloft.

Ataina, *s.* eminence.

Ataga *s.* potsherd ; also Ataka.

Atalata, *a.* ten. (Used in counting long things, as poles, bananas, sugar-canes, &c.

Ate or Ase, *s.* liver.

Atoa, *v.* to place, to set.

Atoahegiro, to turn a thing over.

Atoakau, to place, to lade. As Atoa.

Atogu, *v.* to place me (ato-gu).

Atua, to press pottery into shape.

Atuahu, *s.* a painful swelling without matter, a blind boil.

Ava, *s.* weeds. Avana.

Ava raua, to weed (when a stick is used).

Ava. *Verbal particle, as bava.*

Avararu, *v.* to weed.

Avelo, streamer from lock of hair at back of head. *Gedu avelona.*

E

E is pronounced as in Continental languages.

E, sign of past tense, 3rd pers. sing. and plu. *See* Grammar.

E, sign of present participle, followed by verb and suffix *mu*. *See* Grammar.

E, *adv.* Yes.

E, the sign of the vocative following the noun.

E, *conj.* or.

Eda, *pos. pro, ita eda,* ours.

Edana, *pron. interr.,* which ?

Edana negai, *adv.* when ?

Edaseni, *adv.* where ? in what place ?

Ede, *adv.* (1) where ? oi ede lao ? (2) how ? ede heto ?

Edeamomai, *adv.* whence.

Edeede. *See* Koau edeede.

Edekaratoma ? how was it done ?
  Edekoautoma ? what was said ?
  Ede lao ? whither ?
  Edeseni ? where ? in what place ?
  Ia edeseni ? where is he ?

Edia, *pron.* theirs, for them.

Egediho, *v.* to recline on the side.

Egu, *pron.* mine, for me.

Ehea, *v.* to carry on the shoulder, as a waterpot.

Ehona, to chant or sing.

Ehoro, *v.* to anoint (the head).

Ehuniehuni, } *a.* hidden ; *adv.*
Ehuni, } privately.

Ehuni, *v.* to conceal.

Ekidadiho, to throw down carelessly, to drop or leave on the road.

Ekidaela, *v.* to lie on the back.

Ela, *e.* green turtle.

Ela, *v.* went.

Ela bona, *adv.* till.

Elakaelaka (*geme*), broad chest.

Elaseni, *adv.* where ? *See* Edeseni ?

Eleguna, *adv.* long ago. Syn. Idaunega.

Eleseni, *adv.* where ? *See* Edeseni ?

Ema, *v.* came.

Emai, *pron.* ours, for us (exclusive of person addressed).

Emaimu, coming.

Eme, sign of past tense, 3rd pers. sing. or plu.

Eme kau, *v.* to reach (a place).

Emu, *pron.* for you, yours (*sing.*)

Emui, *pron.* for you, yours (*plural*).

Ena *pron.* his.

Eua. *See* Dekena.

Ena be, *conj.* although, notwithstanding.

Enai, *pron.* that.

Eni, *s.* chunam stick.

Enoeno, *s.* leeside.

Enoeno, *v.* to stay out all night.

Enoatao. *v.* to overlay, as an infant, &c.

Enobou, *s.* cohabitation. (A respectful term.)

Enodele, *v.* to lie on the side.

Enokererekerere, *a.* not sacred, as a man newly married.

Epata, *v.* to putrefy.

Ere, *s.* (1) a row ; a line drawn. Ere rua, two rows. (2) Thicknesses, strands. Ere hani, fourfold.

Ere dagedage, *a.* impudent.

Eredika, *a.* discourteous.

Ere gabe *a.* early manhood, middle-aged.

Eremui ! Silence !

Erena, *s.* speech, voice.

Erere, *v.* to spread, as light at dawn.

Ererua, *v.* to be double, as boards, mat, &c.

Eretoi, *a.* threefold.

Ese, *s.* (1) verandah at side of the house ; (2) gangway outside of the bulwarks of *lakatoi.*

Ese, emphatic particle following a pronoun. *Ta ese karaia.*

Etai, *s.* a fish so called.

Etomamu, *adv.* indeed. (Emphatic word.)

I

I is sounded as in Continental languages.

Ia, *pron.* he, she, it.

Iabina, *s.* one who takes ; a servant.

Iahu, *s.* a woman who is sacred, and who performs certain rights during the absence of voyagers to ensure their safe return.

Ialata, *s.* the name of a fish.

Iana, *pron.* his, hers (*of food only*).

Iareva, *s.* brush.

Iatuatu, the small piece of flat wood used for beating pottery into shape.

Iava, *conj.* or, whether.

Iena, *pron.* his, hers.

Io, *adv.* yes.

Io *s.* a spear.

Iohara, one kind of spear.

Ioheni, *v.* to give a spear to one to kill another with.

Ioheni, *s.* payment given to kill some one.

Iohururu, *s.* a boil.
Iubuna, *adj.* (followed by *tauna*), a cherisher, a feeder.
Iuna, *s.* a tail.
Iutuna tauna, *s.* one who cuts down.
Ibasi, *s.* small bow and arrow, an instrument used for doing the *hebasi.*
Iboudiai, all.
Ibounai, *a.* all, every one.
Ibodohi, ⎱ *s.* a substitute, an ex-
Ibodohina, ⎰ change.
Ibudu gauna, *s.* gimlet.
Ibuni mata, *s.* eyebrows.
Ida, *conj.* together with.
Ida, *prep.* with. (It follows the noun or pronoun of the person accompanied.) *Lau ia ida lao. Oi daika ida?*
Idau, *a.* different, other, foreign, strange.
Idau gau, another thing.
Unai idau, that is different.
Idau tauna, a stranger.
Idauhai lao, *v.* to depart.
Idaunega, usually Idaunegai (past time); (1) just now; (2) a long time ago.
Idaunegai gauna, stale.
Idavarina tauna, finder.
Idi, *s.* the sheet of a sail.
Idia, *pron.* thy, they.
Idia edia, *pron.* theirs.
Idiba, *a.* right (as opposed to left).
Idibaganina, *s.* temptation.
Idibana tauna, one who knows, a witness.
Idita, *a.* (1) bitter (as gall); (2) salt (as sea water).
Idoa, *s.,* a snare.
Idoa, *v.* to ensnare.
Idoa, *v.* (or Itoa) to throw a spear, or stick by putting the finger on the end.
Idoidiai, *a.* every.
Idoinai, *a.* the whole, all.
Idoinai, *adv.,* quite.
Idori or Itori, *v.* to sit on the heels, to squat.
Idori evaeva, to *idori* from place to place in the house. *Oi dahaka idori eraeva helai diho lasi.*
Iduara, *s.* (1) doorway; (2) end of the honse facing the street.
Iduara dehe, verandah at the end of the house facing the street.
Iduaramai, our door.

Iduari, *s.* a comb.
Iduhu, *s.* tribe or family.
Iduka, *s.* headland.
Iduka matana, a point of a head-land.
Idume, *s.* payment to a doctor.
Igāu, *a.* hooked.
Igara, *s.* a barb.
Igedu, *s.* large lashing of the foot of the mast in a native *lakatoi.*
Igigirohorohona tauna, *s.* one who sows seed.
Igimana tauna, a watcher, a pro-tector.
Igiri, *s.* ornamental marking on the edge of pottery bowl. (Trade mark of the maker).
Igo, *v.* to stoop down. See Haigo.
Igoisi, *v.* to look up.
Igodae, *v.* to throw the head back a little so as to look up at some-thing, as on a verandah.
Igodiho, *v.* to bow one's head, to look down abashed. Also of a ship pitching.
Igodiho haniulato, *s.* a bashful young woman, *a.* chaste.
Igui, *s.* bunch.
Igunalaina, *s.* one who leads.
Ihakauna tauna, a leader.
Ihana, *s.* a man's female friend, or, a woman's male friend. *Lau ihagu.*
Ihana, *s.* a brother-in-law.
Iharahai, *s.* With suffix Iharahaigu, &c., a cousin by marriage. A man's wife's cousin is his *iharahai* (of opposite sexes).
Ihareha, *s.* an orphan. Syn. Ogo-gami.
Ihareha, *a.* forlorn.
Ihuhi, a nettle.
Ihihiraia, *v.* to spurn, reject. Syn. Dadaraia.
Ihiria, *v.* to blow with the mouth, as a fire or dust.
Ihoga, *v.* to whistle.
Iholulu, *s.* a boil.
Ihuaihu, *s.* side posts of a house.
Ihuana, *s.* (1) the space between two things, as trees and posts; (2) half-way.
Ihuanai, *prep.* between.
Ihui, a netted bag used as a cradle.
Ikau, *s.* the joining of two nets.
Ikagaibou, *s.* a harlot (an indecent word).

Ikahana tauna, *s.* a helper.

Ikahi, pole which keeps down the thatch of roof.

Ikarana tauna, one who makes.

Ikede tauna, one skilled in canoe making.

Ikeroikero, *s.* the fourth, or top row of caulking on large canoes of *lakatoi*.

Ikou, *s.* an enclosure, as of mats round a newly made grave, in which the widow stays.

Ikcu karaia, *v.* to ripen, as bananas.

Ikoukou, *s.* (1) a stile, the entrance to a garden, where the fence is made low; (2) a window in a house.

Ikoulaina, an enclosure.

Ikoda, *s.* a pole along each side of the canoe in *lakatoi*, caulked between it and the canoe.

Ikoko, *s.* (1) uprights driven into the outrigger of a canoe, to which the cross pieces connecting it with the canoe are tied; hence (2) a nail, a screw.

Ikokou, *s.* a gateway, a stile.

Ikoro tauna, *s.* a skilful canoemaker.

Ikumi, *s.* bale, bundle, parcel.

Ikureahu, sill of door.

Ila, *s.* a hatchet.

Ilau (*generally Ilauta*), small quantity of rice, sago, clay, &c.

Ilaoheni, one who goes to fetch.

Ilaha, *s.* deck.

Ilapa, *s.* sword.

Ilava, *s.* pieces of wood laid across to connect the canoe with the outrigger. In *lakatoi*, cross poles on the top of *ikoda*.

Ileguna, *v.* to watch, to tend.

Iliili, *s.* file.

Ilimo, name of tree and wood of which canoes are generally made.

Ilimoirana, *s.* one kind of hatchet or adze, used after the tree is cut down, and before using the *matapala* or smoothing axe.

Ilua, *adv.* single file, (with verb to go) *Ilualao.*

Iluhai, *v.* to blow down, as the nose, *Udu iluhai.* Iluhai vareai, to sniff up.

Ima, *a.* five. Ima ahui, fifty.

Ima, *s.* the arm (including the hand).
Ima gauna, a weapon.
Ima ganaganana, wrist.
Ima honu, handful.
Ima kavakava, empty handed.

Ima lauri tauna, left-handed.
Ima mauri, mischievous.
Ima mamano, clumsy.
Ima nuana, the lower part of palm of hand.
Ima palapala, the hand.
Ima patapata, to clap the hands.
Ima qagiqagi, finger.
Ima vagivagina, finger ring.

Ima dara, *s.* a return present, as when a friend gives a spear, and the friend to whom he gives it returns him a knife.

Imaguna, *v.* to begin a quarrel or fight.

Imahalataia, *v.* to help with food or goods when visitors come, or when a marriage, &c., is to be paid for.

Imea, a grove of cultivated trees.

Imodai, *s.* a very large native canoe or ship (*Lakatoi*).

Imoga, *s.* pain or sickness supposed to be caused by sleeping in the place where visitors have slept the night or two previous. *Idia imogana ai ese alamai.*

Imuda, *s.* a prop used to support bananas in a strong wind; also a prop to a fence.

Imuda, *v.* to prop. *Dui vata imudaia.* Imuta.

Inā, *interj.* Oh !

Ina, same as *inai*, this.

Inai, *pron.* ; this, as opposed to *unai*, there ; also (2) here ; also (3) an introduction to a speech.

Inai, *adv.* therefore.

Inai, *s.* enemy.

Ināi, *interj.* (with a rough breathing before I). Behold ! What !

Inaio, *interj.* woe be to.

Ini *adv.* here, as opposed to *unu*, there ; as *Ini mai*, Come here. *Ini mai unu loa*, hither and thither.

Inia, as *ini.*

Iniheto, *adv.* like this, so, thus.

Inikaratoma, *v.* to act thus.

Inikoautoma, *v.* to speak thus.

Iniseni, *adv.* here.

Initomai, *adv.* thus. Showing at the same time how.

Initorea, to write thus.

Inua, *v.* to drink.

Inua toho, to taste by drinking.

Ipidi, *s.* a gun, a blunderbuss.
Ipidi anina, a gun charge.
Ipidi nadina, a bullet.

Iqadobe, *s.* a cork, a stopper.

Iqina, *s.* a pillow.

Ira, *s.* hatchet, adze,

Iri, *s.* handsaw.

Irigi, *s.* one kind of coral.

Irohona, one who scatters or destroys.

Iruru mata, *s.* tears.

Ise, *s.* tooth. Ise hahedai, to gnash the teeth.

Iseise, *s.* gunwale.

Iseisena, *s.* edge, brink.

Iseuna, one skilful in house building.

Iseuri, *a.* sour, acid, as unripe fruit.

Isena, *s.* border, brink, edge, hem.

Isi, in composition, up, as *abiaisi*, to take up.

Isi, *s.* wall-plate.

Isia, *v.* (1) to husk a cocoa-nut ; (2) to bite off rind of sugar-cane ; (3) to break a row of bananas from a bunch.

Isiai, *s.* also Hisiai, one who is sent either on a message or to do something.
Isiai manoka, willing, as one sent and not needing to be told twice.
Isiaina tauna, one who is sent.

Isiaina, *v.* (used with *laoheni*) to serve.

Isidae, *v.* to shout (as for joy).

Isiriu, *s.* a scarf or join in wood.

Isiva, *s.* (1) a planting stick ; (2) a crow bar.

Ita, *pron.* we (including person addressed), us.
Ita eda, our (inclusive).

Itaia, *v.* to see, to look. The root ita is rarely used except with suff. *Itagu*, to look at me.

Itaiatao, to look at steadfastly, to watch.

Itahuna tauna, a searcher.

Itadara, *s.* mallet for beating out native cloth.

Itahidi, *v.* to choose by inspection.

Itama, *s.* bows of a canoe.

Itanu, *s.* the small lashing at the foot of the mast in the native *lakatoi.*

Itapo, *s.* fan.

Itoa. See Idoa.

Itohana (with nahuana), *s.* one who looks after, &c.

Itoreahu, *s.* lid, of a pot, &c.

Itorena, *s.* writing.

Itorena tauna, a scribe.

Itori. See Idori.

Itotohi, *s.* (1) walking-stick ; (2) a prop to a house.

Itotohi karaia, *v.* to prop a house.

Ituari, a fish.

Itudobina, *s.* a thing to let down with (followed by varona), a string to draw water with from a well.

Itulu, *s.* small basin with a little knob or leg used to hold the lamp black for tatooing.

Ivaia, *v.* to cut, as one's finger ; to cut up, as a pig ; to mutilate, to flay.

Ivirikou, *s.* a reed musical instrument, a flute, a trumpet.

Ivitoto, a hammock.

O

O has always the round full sound of o in open.

Oi, *pron.* thou.

Oiamu, *pron.* for you, thine (of food and drink).

Oibe, *adv.* yes, just so.

Oiemu, *pron.* for you, thine.

Ouna, *adv.* yonder (near at hand).

Oboro, *s.* capsicum (introduced). See Urehegini.

Oburo, *s.* a small cup-shaped pottery bason.

Odo, small white shell worn by chief.

Odubora, *s.* a red parrot.

Oduga, *s.* the name of a lizard.

Ogoa, *s.* plumbago.

Ogoeogoe, a stranger.

Ogogami, *v.* to be orphaned, to be destitute.

Ogogami, *s.* a poor man, as opposed to *lohiabada.*

Ohe, side.

Ohuduka, *s.* a large scaly lizard.

Ola, *v.* went.

Ole, *s.* large mesh fishing net.

Omada, *s.* chestnut.

Ome, *verb. partic.* for pres. tense, second per. sing. or plur.

Ominuo (from the Greek), *v.* to swear, to take an oath.

Ono, a fish.

Onogo, bastard palm.

Oraia, *v.* to carry on the head, as a waterpot, or a burden.

Ore, *v.* to be finished, done.

Ore, *s.* a short squall (less than *guba*).
Ore, bada, hurricane.

E

Orena, s. a remnant, what is left.

Ori, s. clouds, light rolling clouds; dagadaga, heavy banks of cloud.

Ori, name of a tree.

Oria, v. (1) to grate cocoa-nut; (2) to chew pandanus fruit.

Oro, s. rattan cane.

Oroa, one kind of banana.

Oroaoroa, name of a tree.

Orooro, s. a mountain.

   Orooro beruta, mound. Orooromo, mountainous. Orooro komoge, s. peak.

   Orooro komuta, a hill.

Oromana, s. the fashion, style, order of a thing; as posts of a house; a tree for felling; armlet, &c. Oromana kara, example, pattern.

Oroua, one kind of banana.

Ororobu, name of a fish.

Ōta, fruit of palm called *goru*, chewed as betel nut.

Oti, suffix of dual, and small numbers, as *ruaoti, tatoioti*.

U

U is always sounded as oo in English, as in fool.

Uainananegai, *adv.* three days hence.

Uala, s. crocodile.

Uihala, s. the yard to which one side of the crab-claw sail is fastened, the foot of which is tied to the mast.

Ubama, s. a hornet.

Ubi, s. the name of a bird.

Ubua, v. to feed, as a child, or a pet, to cherish.

Uda, s thick bush, forest.

Udaia, v. to place in a box, canoe, &c.

Udo, s. also Hudo, the navel.

Udu, s. (1) mouth; (2) nose; (3) beak.

   Udu gogona, to snore.

   Udu maduna, nostril.

   Udu mauri, a chatterer.

   Udu bibina, lip.

   Udu honu, mouthful.

Udumotu, name of fish.

Udua, v. to carry a child astraddle on the neck.

Uduguilai, v. to curse.

Udulata, s. the name of a fish.

Udu makohi, s. bleeding from the nose.

Uhau, plural of *tauhau*, young men.

Uhe, s. the end of the yam, which is kept for planting.

Uhea, v. to turn over.

Uhea hebubu, to spill by turning over, to overthrow.

Uhika, s. a wild duck.

Ulaeo, a fish,

Ulato, plural of *haniulato*, young woman.

Ulo, one kind of yam.

Uloulo, s. maggots.

Ulua, v. to climb, as a cocoa-nut tree.

Uma, s. a garden, an enclosed cultivated plot.

Uma hadoa, v. to cultivate.

Umua, v. to paint the face with a device.

Umui, *pron. pl.* you.

Umui emui, *pron. pl.* your. *Umui emui ruma*, your house.

Una, Unauna, s. fish scale.

Una, there.

Unauna, one kind of banana.

Unai, *adv.* there; (opposed to *inai* here); that.

Unai negana, *adv.* then.

Unahia, v. to scale a fish. *Qarume unahi r.*

Unananega, *adv.* four days hence. The unananega of Sunday would be Thursday.

Unia, a fish.

Unu, s. breadfruit.

Unu, *adv.* there.

Unubamona, adv. like that.

Unuheto, adv. thus. (Away from the speaker).

Unukā, *adv.* on the other or off side, further.

Unukaratoma, v. to do thus.

Unukoautoma, said thus.

Ununega, *adv.* an indefinite future time.

Unuseni, *adv.* yonder, in that place.

Upamaino, s. the name of a game of play.

Ura, s. crayfish.

Ura, v. to will, wish, desire.

Ura henia,, to urge.

Urana ura, to desire.

Ura dika, a. self-willed, headstrong.

Urara, name of a tree.

Urea, v. to turn over a thing.

Uregadi, one kind of banana.

Urehegini, s. capsicum.

Uria, s. the month of August.

Urita, *s.* cuttlefish.

Uro, *s.* (1) native earthenware pot; (2) grindstone.

Uro bada, cauldron.

Uru, *s.* (1) deep groaning; (2) stertorous breathing, as when near death. *Varani gangagana karaia hari ia uru mo.* (3) a generation.

Urua, *v.* to climb.

Urua diho, to dip.

Use, *s.* penis.

Usiusi, *s.* pimple, wart.

Uto, *s.* float of fishing-net.

Utu, *s.* flood.

Utu, *s.* louse.

Utua, *a.* (1) to draw water; (2) to cut off.

Utuadae, to rise as a flood.

Utua nege, to sever.

Utugomu regena, rump joint of pork.

Utuha, *s.* a meeting-place, where two villages meet by appointment.

Utuha, *v.* to make an appointment to meet at the *utuha*.

Utubada, *s.* very high tide. *Ututu bada,* deluge.

B

B is pronounced as in English.

Ba, a particle preceding verbs, indicating the future tense, 2 *p.* sing. or pl. as, *Ba oma,* Come thou.

Bae, *v. part.* indicating fut., 3rd pers. pl. *Idia bae karaia.*

Baeha, sign of future, as *ba.*

Baela, *v.* 3rd pers. pl. fut. to go.

Baema, *v.* 3rd pers. pl. fut. to come.

Baia, *v., part.* indicating fut. 1st pers. pl. *Ai baia karaia.*

Baia, *v.* to be near death; hopeless, as from sickness or shipwreck, or surrounded by fire and no way of escape. *Vata baia.*

Baiama, conditional particle 1st pers. pl. (exclusive) if; past time.

Baimumu, *s.* owl.

Baina, *v. partic.* 1st pers. sing. fut. used before verbs. *Lau baina abia.*

Bainala, *v. partic.* 1st person. I will go.

Bainama, I will come, 1st pers. sing. future of verb *m zi,* to come.

Baine, *v. partic.* 3rd pers. sing. fut. before verbs. *Ia baine abia.* If.

Bainela, *v. partic.* 3rd person See Grammar. He will go.

Bainema, *v. partic.* 3rd pers. sing. fut. to come.

Baita, *v. partic.* 1st pers. pl. ft.

Baitala, *v. partic.* 1st pers. pl. ft. of the verb to go.

Baitama *v. partic.* conditional. 1st pers. pl. (inclusive), past time.

Baola, *v.* 2nd pers. pl. fut. to go.

Baoma, *v.* 2nd pers. pl. fut. to come.

Bau *s.* bamboo.

Baubau, *s.* bamboo pipe.

Babaka, one kind of banana.

Bada *a.* large, great. Badana, *s.* size.

Bāda, *s.* (1) wax, used for finger points on the skin of drumheads; (2) honey.

Badau, *s.* (1) penis erectio. *Use badau.* (2) Elephantiasis. *Ae badau.*

Badahobadaho, *v.* to grow. (Of children.)

Badiu regena, tail joint of wallaby.

Badila, *s.* red colour of teeth, from chewing betel nut.

Badina, *adv.* by the side of. Badibadina.

Badina dahaka? *adv.* wherefore?

Badina, *s.* (1) the trunk or stem of a tree near the root; hence, (2) the root or cause of a thing; (3) foundation.

Badinaia, *v.* to cleave to.

Badu, *v.* to be angry.

Badu kava, hasty.

Badubada, passion. *a.* Sulky.

Badukalo, one kind of yam.

Bagara, one kind of yam.

Bagu, *s.* forehead.

Bagu, *conj.* on account of, for the sake of. With suff. baguna, bagugu, &c.

Bagua, *v.* to carry a netted bag hanging in front. See Kiapa.

Bagukoau, *v.* (1) to forbid to come; (2) to send back by scolding.

Baha, sometimes used for *ba* or *bae.*

Bahuna, *s.* food left, and kept to eat cold. Bahudia.

Bakibaki, *s.* a dumpling. (Generally of sago.)

Bakobako, *a.* sour (as paste).

Bakubaku, *s.* roof of verandah.

Bāla, *s.* white wild duck.

Balala, *s.* the name of a fish.

Bala ta, *a.* ten, in counting pigs, dogs, fish, turtle, dugong, &c.

Bama, *conditional partic.* if: 1st pers. sing. and pl. past.

Bamahuta, Good-night! *Ba mahuta o!* May you sleep. Also used in the day-time. Good-bye.

Bame, *ba*, sign of, 2nd pers. sing. fut. with *me* of euphony.

Bamoa, *v.* to accompany another. Bamoa lasi, unattended.

Bamona, *adv.* like, thus.

Bamona, *s.* a companion.

Banaere, one kind of banana.

Bani, *s.* a patch. Banilaia, *s.* to patch with.

Bani, *v.* (1) to plait; (2) to patch; (3) to kindle fire from a spark, as from tinder. Bania, to mend mats.

Bani, *v.* to lay in wait. Banitao, to be laid in wait for.

Banidu, *s.* smut, from burnt grass.

Bara, *v.* to row.

Bara, *s.* oar.

Baragi, *s.* lungs. Also Baraki.

Baribara, *s.* cross. *Au hiri baribara.*

Baribara, to be sprinkled or wetted accidentally, as newly made pottery.

Ba roromamumu. A phrase when quarrelling. "I'll kill you." From roroma to kill.

Baroko, large, as thread or string.

Barua, *s.* muliebria.

Barubaru, the name of a fish.

Basi, *adv.* Not (*Ba* and *asi*).

Basi, *adv.* negative fut. Not.

Basiema, 3rd pers. plural, future of verb *mai*, They will not come.

Basileia, *s.* (from the Greek) a kingdom.

Basina. 1st pers. fut. sing. negative.

Basinama, 1st pers. sing. fut. of verb *mai*. I will not come.

Basine, sign of 3rd per. sing. fut. negative.

Basita, negative with 1st pers. plural (inclusive), let us not.

Bāta. See Bāda.

Batata, name of a shell-fish.

Batu, one kind of yam.

Batugu, *s.* a shower.

Bava, *particle* fut. 2 pers. sing. or pl. Used before verbs beginning with *a*. *Bava abia. Bavi alaia.*

Bava, *s.* a crab.

Be, a connective particle; also used alone with the meaning of Why? What's up?

Bena, to straighten, as a stick by bending.

Bebe, a fish.

Bedaina, where?

Bedebede, name of a shell-fish.

Bedi, *s.* a spoon.

Bedu, one kind of spear, similar to *karagoda.*

Bema, conditional particle, if, 3 pers. sing. and pl. past time.

Bena, as *ena,* there.

Benai, as *enai,* there.

Benaini, *adv.* just so; all right; how now.

Bero, *s.* a wound. *Iena bero hida?* How many wounds has he?

Berusi, *s.* (used with orooro) a small hillock.

Beruta, *s.* See Berusi. Berutaberuta.

Biaguna, *s.* master, owner.

Bio, *s.* cocoanut-shell cup. (Deeper than *kehere*.)

Biobio, *s.* small cocoanut charm.

Bibina, *s.* lips. Udu bibina.

Biku, *s.* the fruit of the banana. Also Bigu.

Bila, *s.* spawn.

Bilailo, *s.* one kind of ant.

Biluka, *s.* earth-worm. Also Biruka.

Binai, as *inai,* here.

Biri, leaf of bastard palm, used for thatch.

Biriakei, *s.* the name of a month (November).

Biriabada, *s.* the month of December.

Biru, *s.* gardening, work in garden or field. Biru eno, to work in the garden, and sleep there.

Bisini, small sunbird.

Bisisi, name of a shell-fish.

Bita, *s.* native rat.

Bitua, *v.* to break, as a stick, spear, &c.; to gather a flower or little branch by breaking the stalk; to gather fruit.

Bivai, *s.* one kind of hawk.

Bo, *euphonic particle,* used much as *bona. Oi ede bo laoumu?* Where are you going?

Boatau, *s.* areca nut and palm.

Boe, *s.* a sandbank.

Boera, *adj.* fatigued, "done up."

Boi, *s.* night. Generally used with *hanua, Hanuaboi.*

Boioboio, *v.* to be lost.

Boiboi, *v.* to call, to summon. Pass. boilia.

Bou, *s.* a small round shell neck ornament.

Bou, *adv.* together, as *anibou*, to eat together.

Boua, *v.* to hammer a rock ; to knock off oysters, &c.

Bobo, *s.* a fool.

Bobo, name of a shell fish.

Bobobobo, *v.* to stream forth, as blood from a wound.

Boboda, name of a fish.

Bobolo, *s.* the hornbill. Also Boboro.

Bodaga, *s.* stench.

Bodaga, *v.* to stink.

Bodaga, *a.* fetid.

Bodo, *v.* to go out, be extinguished, as fire, lamp.

Bogebada, *s.* the name of a hawk.

Boga. *See* Boka.

Bogo, *s.* ear of corn, when first swelling.

Boha, *a.* bald. *Qara boha*, bald head.

Boka or boga, *s.* (1) the stomach, the seat of desire and affection ; (2) the uterus.

Boka kunu, to be satisfied with food, to have a bellyful.

Boka heudeheude (lit., stomach troubled), to desire greatly.

Boka mate, lazy.

Bokabada, name of a shell-fish.

Bokahisi and hisihisi (lit., stomach-ache), to have pity, compassion.

Bokaia, *v.* to disembowel.

Boka auka, *v.* to have self-restraint ; to be strong to work, and not easily exhausted ; to be not nervous and easily frightened.

Bokalau, *s.* entrails, bowels.

Boka hekukuri, diarrhœa.

Boka hisihisi, colic, *v.* to grieve.

Bokani, name of a shell-fish.

Bokani bisisi, name of a shell-fish.

Bokaragi. Bokaragina, *prep.* in the midst.

Bokatoto, *a.* lawless.

Boloa, *s.* possession by an evil spirit.

Boloa, *s.* 1, a substitute ; 2, a successor. Boloa tauna, a deputy.

Boloko, *s.* 1, the name of a gum-tree ; 2, the bush in which the boloko abounds.

Boma, conditional particle, if, 2nd pers. sing. and pl. past time.

Boma, *s.* a hole in the top of the mast through which halyards are rove.

Bomaboma, name of a shell-fish.

Bona, euphonic particle, used in enumerating persons or things.

Bona, *s.* scent.

Bonaia, *v.* to smell.

Bonana, *v.* euphemism for bodaga, to stink.

Bonana namo, fragrant.

Boni, *v.* to return unsuccessful from fishing or trading.

Bonubonu, name of a tree.

Bore, *s.* a narrow road on the reef or the sand, dry at low tide.

Borebore, a fish.

Boroboro, *s.* a painful swelling in the face.

Boroma, *s.* a pig ; also all large animals, as goats, sheep, cows, &c.

Boroma anina, pork.

Boroma arana, pig-stye.

Boroma huina, a bristle.

Boroma maruane, a boar.

Bosea, *s.* a basket.

Bosi, spear of white wood used in hunting.

Botaia, *v.* to beat, to thrash.

Buaki, fruit of *arara*.

Buatari, *v.* to demolish, as a town.

Bubu, *s.* hymen.

Bubudare, hym. rupt.

Bubu e ! term of address to grandmother.

Bubui, one kind of yam.

Bubuni, *v.* to be covered, as trees with water, overshadowed.

Budabuda, name of a tree.

Budia, a loop.

Budia, name of a fish.

Budia, läsi, *v.* to gush out, as blood, when a spear is withdrawn.

Budoa name of a tree.

Budua, *v.* to make a hole through the eye of the cocoanut, to bore a hole.

Buduaulu, *v.* to bore a hole right through. Also Buduauru.

Budubudu, *a.* spotted, rough, pitted, as the face.

Budugara, name of a shell-fish.

Bulelamo, *s.* a caterpillar.

Buloa, *v.* to mix.

Bulubulu, *v.* to duck in the sea in sport.

Bulukia, *v.* to gather, as fruit of mango.

Buna, *s.* the name of a fish.
Bunai. See Unai.
Bunu, *s.* husk of cocoanut.
Bura, *s.* grated cocoanut, after the oil has been expressed.
Burea, *v.* to blossom.
Burena, *s.* pistil of flower.
Buruka, *a.* white. Of hair only. *Hui buruka.*
Burukia, *v.* to gather by breaking off.
Busibusi, *s.* stye on the eye.
Busisi, *s.* a small winkle.
Busibusi, *s.* clitoris.
Butua, *v.* to pull up, as grass ; to pull out, as hair, feathers.
Butuaoho, *v.* to adopt a child.
Butuatao, *v.* to catch hold of one.
Butubutu, *a.* coarse, rough.
Butubutu, clam fish.
Butudiatao. Butu-dia-tao. See Butuatao.

D

D is sounded as in English. In some words it is scarcely distinguishable from t.
Dae, *v.* to ascend.
Dae, *s.* the name of a large fish.
Daea, *v.* to destroy a village, killing its inhabitants.
Daeutu. See Daehudu.
Daeguni, *s.* a corner.
Daehudu, *s.* a chamber.
Daekau, *v.* to ascend.
Daekobi, *s.* a two or three-pronged comb, a solid stem from which two or more prongs are cut.
Daelaia, *v.* to lift up, to exhalt.
Daena, *s.* the top (of a box).
Daena, *v.* to be abreast of, or off a place on the coast.
Daenai, *adv.* on the top.
Dāi hanai, contagious.
Daia, *v.* (1) to rest on, as a foot on the ground, &c. ; (2) to build, of houses or a village. *Hanua daia.*
Daia, *v.* to think.
Daiauru, *v.* to pierce through.
Daiahu, *v.* (1) to close a bag by sewing up the mouth ; (2) used figuratively of the mouth ; (3) to enclose by enemies ; (4) to wound the eye by throwing a stick.
Daiba, *s.* a yam-pit.

Daidai, *v.* to boil.
Daidobi, *v.* to be drifted to sea, as by the current or wind.
Daihanai, *v.* to go out to sea, so as to lose sight of the mountains.
Daika, *pron.* who ?
Dāikau, preceded by *hisi*, to be seized with pain, or an epidemic, as *Hisi eme dāikau, Hisi taina lau taugu ai eme dāikau.*
Dailia, *v.* (1) to water (plants) ; (2) to pour water on a sick person, &c.
Dainamo, *a.* convalescent, as *Taugu eme dainamo,* I am better.
Daipa, a wide space weeded round garden fence.
Dairia. See Dailia.
Dāitao, *s.* a canoe or ship making but little progress from current, head wind, &c.
Daiva, *s.* a short voyage, as to Maiva or Hula.
Dāu, *s.* one kind of banana (very long).
Daua, *v.* to net.
Dāuahuahu, *v.* to bother, as a child or a busy-body, in the way, &c.
Daube, daubedaube, *v.* to swing on a low swing.
Daudau, *a.* distant (place or time).
Daudobi, *v.* to dip into.
Daukau, *v.* to touch.
Dāulao, moon just past full.
Dautu, *s.* the name of a fish. (The porcupine fish.)
Daba, *s.* (lity. morning). Used in counting, &c., for a day.
Daba matana, early.
Daba e kinia, first appearance of dawn.
Daba e rere, morning, after sunrise.
Daba daba idoinai, daily.
Dabarere, morning.
Daba hunua, near morning.
Dabaiatao (Dabaigutao), *v.* to seize.
Dabara, *s.* banana leaf used as a plate to place food on.
Dabaraia, *v.* to serve up food. *Aniani dabaraia.*
Dabari, *s.* male kangaroo.
Dabia, *v.* to put a piece of wood or stone under a canoe, &c., so as to raise it from the ground.
Dabikan, *v.* to lean against.
Dabu, *v.* to be left out in distribution, to have no share.

Dabua, *s.* clothing (general name), cloth.

Dabua hadokilaia, to clothe.

Dabua sisina, *s.* rag.

Dabuia, *v.* to pull, as a rope ; to drag along, as an unwilling child.

Dabutu, *s.* the name of a fish.

Dadaila, trench, gutter.

Dadaba. Dadabaia, *v.* to flog, to beat, chastise.

Dadadaeroha, to rise, as the sun.

Dadadiho, to descend from tree.

Dadadobi, *v.* to go down, as the sun, as food into the stomach.

Dadaraia, *v.* to reject, to decline.

Dadaroa, *v.* to drag, as the anchor.

Dadaroha, *v.* as Dadaroa.

Dadaroha, *v.* to uncover an oven of food.

Dadia, *v.* to snatch.

Dadidadi, *v.* to pillage.

Dadidadi gaudia, *s.* booty.

Daga, material used in preparing *lakatoi* for long voyage.

Dagai, *s.* the name of a fish.

Dagadaga, *s.* (1) heavy clouds, those not carried by the wind ; (2) Groin.

Daga hanai, *v.* to get over, as a fence.

Dagahu, *a.* cloudy, the sun shaded.

Dagahu tauna, *s.* one sent to watch, lest taboo should be broken.

Dagalo, *s.* feathery blossom of cane, reeds, &c.

Dage, excrement.

Dage tauna, a quarrelsome man, challenging others to fight, &c.

Dagedage, *a.* cruel and ferocious,

Dagedage tauna, *s.* a bully.

Dagi, *s.* (1) occupation, trade ; (2) character ; (3) office.

Dagu, *v.* to startle, to quake.

Daha, *a.* thousand.

Dahaka? *pron.* what?

Dahaka gau ? *pron.* why ?

Dahalaia, *v.* to carry a small netted bag (*vaina*) over the shoulder.

Dāhi, *v.* to crouch or go upon the hands and feet.

Dahu, *v.* to rub, to wipe.

Dahua, to rub on, to wipe.

Dahuaoho, to wipe off.

Dahuakamo, to wipe with the hands.

Dahudahu, *s.* the name of a large fish.

Dahudahua, redup of *dahua.*

Dahulu, a fish.

Dakaia, to throw spear.

Dākidāki, *s.* a very large arm-shell.

Dala, *s.* a road.

Dala korikori, highway.

Dala katakata, cross-roads.

Dala, name of a shell-fish.

Daladedi, slippery road.

Dalaia, *s.* the name of a fish.

Dalagi, *s.* the name of a fish.

Daladala, a fish.

Damena, *s.* salt.

Danu, *conj.* also.

Daqai *s.* a bag-net.

Daqaiahu, to enclose, as by a fence.

Daqala, *s.* a sea-eel.

Dara, Daragu, followed by doko. See next word.

Daradoko, *v.* (1) To be sad, on account of absent or dead friends ; (2) to be speechless from fear ; (3) to mourn silently. *Lau daragu eme doko ;* (4) to miss.

Daradae, *v.* to ascend, as mountains.

Daradara, *v.* to doubt, to hesitate.

Daradara mo, *s.* indecision.

Daradara mo, *a.* querulous.

Darahu, *v.* to feel, to grope.

Daralaia, *v.* to hoist ; to take up with one.

Darea, *v.* to be torn.

Darere, *v.* to be vanquished, conquered, weak.

Daria, *v.* to husk a cocoanut with the teeth. *Ise daria.*

Daria, *s.* lanyards.

Darima, *s.* outrigger.

Daroa, *v.* (1) to sweep ; (2) to trim off knots, &c., to adze a plank ; (3) to make passes, and perform sorcery over a sick person. *Gorere daroa.*

Darodaro, *s.* the name of a month (April, May).

Darodaroa, redup of *daroa.*

Darolasi, tuft of hair.

Davadava, *s.* the name of a fish.

Davaha, *s.* coarse cloth worn in mourning.

Davalaia, cost.

Davana, *a.* (1) full, as a house ; (2) sufficient, as sticks for a fence.

Davana, *s.* a payment, a ransom.

Davana henia, to compensate, to punish.

Davana korikori, punishment.

Davara, *s.* the sea.

Davara bada, *s*, high tide.
Davara maragi, low water.
Davaria, *v.* to find, to obtain.
Davea, *v.* to drag, to haul up.
 Davea dae, to launch.
Davedavelaia, to waste.
Davelaia, *v.* to throw a thing or
 person on to the ground, away
 from one ; to swing laden *kiapa*
 round on to the forehead ; to raise
 a heavy box on to the shoulder.
Dea, Deaia, *v.* to bark a tree by in-
 serting a wedge into a slit.
Deadea, name of a tree.
Deure, one kind of banana.
Dedi, *v.* to slip.
 Dedi dobi, to backslide.
Dedeari, sago-palm leaf.
Dedidedi. Dedikadedika, *a.* slippery,
 of the ground, or hands, or object
 held.
Degiro, resort of wild pig or wallaby.
 " *Magani degiro inai.*"
Dehe, *s.* the verandah at the end of
 a house facing the street.
Dehoro, *s.* oil of the cocoanut. fresh,
 mixed with a little water.
Dekea, *v.* to dodge (as a spear, &c.).
Dekedekenarahu, *s.* a quiet, deserted
 place ; *a.* noiseless.
Dekena, *prep.* near to, by the side of.
 Lau ia dekena lao. I went to him.
Dekena tauna, neighbour.
Demaia, *v.* to calk.
Demaiatoho, *v.* to taste.
Demari, *v.* to lick.
Dene, *s.* sandfly.
Depuru, small crayfish.
Dera, *s.* hair on the body, the arms,
 chest, &c.
Dera tauna, a hairy man.
Dere, back and belly fins of fish.
Deredere, *s.* the square edge of a
 board, &c.
Derekadereka, *s.* dimin. of deredere.
Derekaka, *s.* the name of a fish.
Deruha, the well in a canoe.
Dia, *s.* a kind of pudding made of
 sago and bananas.
Dia, negative used in compound
 words.
Dia bada, *s.* anything very small or
 light.
Dia maragi, *s.* anything very big or
 heavy.
Diadaudan, *s.* proximity, nearness.
Diagau, *a.* many.

Diahoho, *a.* not many.
Diaranu, *s.* clear oil.
Diari, *s.* light (as opposed to dark);
 diaridiari, brightness.
Diatau dikana, *s.* a good man.
Diu, *v.* to hit, as with an arrow or
 gun.
Diu, *s.* elbow.
Diua, *v.* to put up the sail of a canoe.
Diuaisi, to lift up, as hands.
Diudiu, successful in fishing, &c.
Diba, *s.* an arrow.
Diba, *v.* to know, to comprehend.
Dibagadi, a long grass.
Dibagani, *v.* to tempt.
Dibaka tauna, *s.* a dissembler.
Dibu, a small light spear used in war.
Dibua, *v.* to carry a bag, &c., sus-
 pended from the forehead (as the
 women do their *kiapas*).
Dibura, *a.* dark.
Dibura tauna, heathen.
Dida, *prep.* with ; syn. Ida.
Didiki, *s.* near the edge of a thing,
 as a table, chair, &c.
Didikididiki, *v.* to be far out to sea.
Digara, *a.* (1) fat ; (2) good (of food
 or drink); (3) lard.
Digu, *v.* to bathe.
Dihina, *s.* a man's sons who will per-
 petuate his name and character ;
 hence sometimes used of inherited
 skill or character.
Diho, *v.* to descend ; to land from a
 boat.
Diho, *a.* south.
Diholoa, *v.* to beat boards and shout,
 as a sign of rejoicing, as when a
 lakatoi comes.
Dihotania, *v.* to be deserted by a
 wife.
Dihu, *s.* a bowl or bath of wood.
Dihudihu, name of a shellfish.
Dika, *a.* bad, foul.
Dika tauna, guilty.
Dika, *s.* (1) a calamity ; (2) guilt.
Dikadika, *adv. intens.* very much.
 Goada dikadika, very strong.
Dilaha, *s.* an old garden (not this
 year's).
Diledile, *s.* a small flying squirrel.
Dima, *s.* (1) one kind of grass ; (2)
 bait for small crabs.
Dimaili, *s.* a small ant.
Dimakau, to catch fire by train of
 dry grass, &c., or by contact as a
 grass petticoat.

Dimona, *s.* a measure of length, less than a fathom, one yard or less.

Dimuradimura, *a.* anything very small, as grains of sand.

Dina, *s.* (1) the sun; (2) a day.

Dina gelona, afternoon.

Dina namo, fine weather.

Dina tara, glare of the sun.

Dina tupua, mid-day.

Dina *v.* to be visible, apparent, as the bone in a wounded leg. *Turi vata dina.*

Dina, prey; also contribution to feast, &c., as *Lau dinagu inai.*

Dina, spear of white wood used principally in hunting.

Dinaha, a fish.

Dina idoinai, *a.* habitual.

Dinika, *s.* a fork.

Diraha, *s.* all children after the first-born.

Dirava, *s.* spirit; god.

Dirava kara, religion.

Divaro, *s.* the name of a month (May.)

Divoi, one kind of yam.

Do, a particle marking future time.

Dõa, *s.* collar-bone.

Doa, *v.* to pole a canoe. (Also Doaia.)

Doa, *s.* (1) a boar's tusk; (2) a horn.

Dõa, to land.

Doadoa, *s.* a scorpion.

Doadoa, *s.* a cage in *lakatoi* for the pottery of the captain.

Doe, *s.* famine, dearth.

Doua, *v.* to set fire to, as dry grass.

Doua, to ring (as a bell).

Dounu, particle future time, not yet.

Dobi, *v.* to be lost in the bush. (Of pigs or dogs.)

Dobi, *adv.* downwards.

Dobi, *v.* to fruit. (When hanging down, as bananas.)

Dobu, *a.* deep.

Dodi, *s.* a debt, *v.* to owe.

Dodo, *s.* very high tide, coming over the street. (Higher than *utubada.*)

Dodo, *v.* to soak up, to absorb, to subside.

Doga, a stream.

Dogo, *s.* anchor.

Dogo atoa, Dogo negea, *v.* to anchor.

Dogoro, *s.* dry banana-leaf packing.

Dogu, *s.* a deep bay.

Dogudogu, *s.* a hollow, depression.

Dogudobi, to set (as sun.)

Doha, *v.* to prohibit.

Doha, *s.* law (introduced meaning.)

Doholodoholo, *a.* dry (of cooked food), dried up (of roast.)

Dohore, *adv.* by-and-bye.

Dohore, *v.* to postpone.

Dokia, dokiaoho, *v.* (1), to pull down a skin without cutting it, as the skin of lizard, or a kangaroo tail; hence (2) to take off one's clothes.

Doko, *s.* anchor.

Doko, *a.* maimed. *Ima doko.*

Doko, to end.

Dokoatao, *v.* to hold, restrain.

Dokoatao, lasi, *a.* free.

Dokokadokoka, *adj.* lonely, distressed.

Dokona, *s.* conclusion, end. Asi dokona, endless.

Doku, *s.* the calf of the leg. *Lau dokugu*

Dola, s. penis erectio.

Dolu, s. back.

Domaga, *a.* one hundred thousand.

Domena, *s.* resin.

Domuadae, to put in mouth.

Dona, name of a fish.

Doria, *v.* to push, to nudge, to jog. Doria dobi, to depose.

Dorina, *s.* the top.

Dorinai, *prep.* on. Also *adv.*

Dorivadoriva, *a.* very high in the air. *Guba dorivadorivana ai.*

Doro, *v.* to stop crying, to be pacified.

Doru, *s.* the back.

Doru laoho, crooked back.

Doru qagugu, *a.* humpback.

Dorua, sprained.

Dosema, for *dosi ema,* not yet come.

Dõsi, *v.* to take care of, to cherish, especially of a wife or child when the husband is away.

Dosi, negative, *do asi.*

Duadua, *s.* the name of a fish.

Duahia, *v.* to count, to read.

Duahihanai or hanaihanai, to count wrong.

Duahia lasi, countless.

Dui, *s.* banana (tree.)

Duba, brown color, dark cloud.

Dubaduba, *a.* dark brown; the color of the skin of Motu natives.

Dubu, *s.* (1) chief's platform. (2) sacred house. (3) church.

Dubina, *s.* the tail of a bird.

Dudi, *v.* to leak (of a canoe).

Dudu, *v.* (1) to gather up, as a squall. (2) to form, as fruit after the blossom falls. (3) to form, as an abscess. (4) to grow, as the teeth of an infant.

Dudu, the name of a shell-fish.

Duduia, *v.* to point.

Duduria, *v.* to singe, to sweal.

Duha, name of a plant, the root and leaves of which are used to stupefy fish.

Duhia, *v.* to prepare yams, &c., for cooking, to pare.

Duhu, *a.* thick, muddy, as water; gross, *boka duhu.*

Dumu, the name of a fish.

Dumu sisia, the name of a fish.

Duna, *s.* the name of a bird.

Dura, *s.* the back end of a house.

Duribaroko, the name of a fish.

Durua, *v.* to help in lifting a weight, &c., to help with anything heavy.

G

G is always hard, as g in good. In some words the g approaches so nearly to k, that words which were heard every day for years, and supposed to be k, are now said by the natives themselves to be g. There is no reason to question the true orthography, although the pronunciation is puzzling. An aspirated k would seem sometimes nearer the truth.

Gaegae, *s.* the name of a green parrot.

Gaiagaia, the name of a shell-fish.

Gaigai, *s.* a snake.

Gaigai bamona, reptile.

Gaiho, *a.* sweet, pleasant to the taste.

Gaiho namo tauna, *s.* a hospitable kind-hearted man.

Gaiho dika, inhospitable.

Gaihona dika tauna, *s.* an abusive churlish man.

Gaili, *s.* a plain or level place on a mountain side.

Gaima, *a.* calm (at night.)

Gaima, *v.* to be becalmed (at night.)

Gaiva, *s.* a projection in the roof over the end of the house.

Gao, *s.* voice. Syn. Gado.

Gau, *s.* a thing.

Gauaia, *v.* to chew, masticate.

Gauaia, *s.* a mouthful (such as infants are fed with.)

Gaubada, *s.* a great chief, a king.

Gaubadabada, *a.* copious, huge, weighty.

Gau karaia, *s.* employment.

Gau lata, *s.* height.

Gaulatalata, *a.* high, tall.

Gau ta, *s.* something.

Gaba, *s.* (1) loins, above the hips ! (2) a belt.

Gaba dona, *v.* to ring a bell.

Gabani, *v.* to be barren (of a woman.)

Gabe, gabea, *a.* last ; *adv.* after, hereafter.

Gabele, *s.* a children's game of spearing cocoanut husks.

Gabena, *a.* last. Gabenai, next.

Gabena, *s.* the stern of a ship, or canoe.

Gabeta, *s.* a death-producing charm.

Gabiruma, *s.* bush near a village, or near a garden.

Gabu, *s.* place.

Gabua, *v.* to roast over the fire.

Gabuna, a site.

Gabugabu, *s.* to talk imperfectly.

Gabugabu ("g" harder than above), to roast, &c.

Gabugabu, *s.* a breaking-out on the lips (as when recovering from illness.)

Gaburu, the name of a fish.

Gāda, s. between the fingers or toes.

Gade, *s.* penis. Syn. Use.

Gadea, *s.* a cable, a chain.

Gadegade, *s.* eye of a rope, link of a chain, &c.

Gādegāde, *v.* to annoy by constantly asking questions, or talking when busy.

Gadigadi, *s.* double teeth.

Gadigadi, *v.* to speak with deep, gruff voice, as in anger.

Gadigadi hahedai, *v.* to grind one's teeth.

Gadili, *a.* thin, poor looking, either from sickness, fatigue, or any other cause.

Gadiva, *s.* knife (superseded by kaia).

Gādo, *v.* to be hungry for meat or fish.

Gādo, *s.* (1) the throat ; (2) voice ; (3) language, speech.

Gādo bauban, windpipe.

Gado lohilohi, *v.* to nauseate, to belch, eructate.

Gadoi, *a.* few.

Gadobada. Gādo, *s.* the ocean, the deep sea.

Gado gigia, *v.* to choke.

Gādo hanai, *v.* to interpret.

Gadokagadoka, *a.* (1) light green, as young leaves, &c. ; (2) blue.

Gado lānalāna, *v.* to stutter.

Gado dika, hoarse.

Gado namo tauna, *s.* a good-tempered man, a courteous man.

Gadn dae, *v.* to comply, to consent.

Gaga, to turn face towards.

Gaga, *s.* a spade.

Gagaena, *a.* unoccupied, waste (of land).

Gagaia, *s.* coition.

Gagaisi, *s.* to look up with the head back, as when looking at the sky.

Gagado, *s.* very young cocoanut, before any kernel has formed.

Gagado, *s.* short tie-beams on the roof.

Gagala, *a.* afraid of falling, &c., dizzy.

Gagalo, *v.* to scratch. Also Hega-galo.

Gagama, *s.* large cocoanut leaf basket.

Gagatao, *v.* to be looked up at, as dogs waiting for a piece of food.

Gageva, *v.* to be crooked (inwards), as a bough of a tree towards the tree.

Gageva (of conduct), crooked, erratic.

Gagevagageva, to curve.

Gahi, *s.* flat stone club.

Gabu, *s.* ; (1) ashes ; (2) dust ; (3) mist, fog at sea, haze.

Gabukagahuka, albino.

Gahuko, *s.* the name of a bird.

Gahulo, to wet with mist, or fog.

Gālo, *s.* the name of a bird.

Galumana, *s.* early morning.

Gamoga, *a.* wide, as a doorway, river's mouth, &c.

Gamoga bada, broad.

Gāna, *s.* plaited armlet.

Ganaia, *v.* to warm oneself at the fire.

Ganagana, *v.* ; (1) to groan, to sigh. (2) to beg, to ask for in prayer.

Ganaganana (*ima*), wrist.

Gani, name of a fish.

Ganiahuota, name of a fish.

Ganikan, to burst out in flame ; also of sudden energy of lazy man.

Ganiva, *s.* cane plaited round the waist when mourning.

Gāno, *a.* sharp, keen edged.

Gāno lasi, dull.

Gānokagānoka, the sharp edge of a board when cut square.

Gara, *s.* sepulchre.

Garaia, burnt, as mouth, from acrid food, or quick-lime, &c. *Udu garaia.*

Garaia, *v.* (proceeded by mata) to be sleepy.

Garahi, *s.* thorn of the sago palm.

Garagara, *v.* to be scorching (of the sun.) *Dina garagara.*

Garia utu, to cut through, as with shell.

Gari, *v.* to be afraid.

Gari, *s.* fear.

Gari tauna, a coward.

Gari, *v.* to fall, as a tree, house, &c.

Gariatao, *v.* to be fallen on, as by a tree.

Garina, *conj.* lest.

Garokoni, one kind of banana.

Gāru, *s.* young fruit of the cocoanut.

Garugaru, *s.* a joint. A hinge.

Garugaru, *a.* immature.

Garugaru bamona, *s.* dotage.

Gata, one kind of yam.

Gatoi, *s.* egg.

Gava, name of a tree.

Gavaia, *v.* to run after one, in order to overtake ; to overtake.

Gave, *s.* feelers of octopus.

Gavena, a lull in wind ; moderate, as of sun not yet high.

Gavera, *s.* edible mangrove.

Gea, *s.* (1) the name of a tree : (2) waste land where such trees stand. *Gea mo.*

Geahu, uncultivated.

Geakone, name of a tree.

Geia, *v.* to dig, as a hole ; to dig up, as yams.

Geia, *v.* to carry a person on the back.

Geohaia, *s.* the name of a small dove. (A Koitapu word.)

Geda, *s.* (1) a mat ; (2) a sail.

Gedu, *s.* back of the head

Gegea, *v.* to surround, enclose, to gird.

Gegeva, *v.* to be crooked (outwards.) See Gageva.

Gēlo, *v.* to swing with a long rope from a cocoanut tree.

Gelo, *s.* fresh water tortoise.

Gelo, turned (as sun).

Gelona, *s.* the time of day, about 3 o'clock. *Dina gelona.*

Geme, *s.* bosom.

Geme elakaelaka, broad chest.

Geme lasikalasika, projecting inflated chest.

Gemegeme, *s.* breast-bone of animals.

Gerebu, *a.* ten thousand.

Geregere. Gerekere, *s.* pandanus tree.

Geregere, *a.* equal, even.

Gero, *s.* fresh-water tortoise.

Gesegese, *a.* sterile (of ground).

Gete, one kind of yam.

Giu, *s.* large long paddles, let down at the side of *lakatoi*, acting as centreboard.

Gina, to stir.

Giua, *v.* to take up young bananas. *Dui giua.*

Giuaisi, *v.* to prize up, as the lid of a box.

Giboa, *v.* to gouge out, as the eye.

Giboa, *s.* muliebria.

Gida, *s.* charcoal, embers.

Gigi, *v.* to snarl.

Gigia, *v.* to squeeze, to shampoo. *Aio gigia*, to throttle.

Gigia, *v.* to scatter, to spread out, as gravel.

Gigiarohoroho, to scatter abroad.

Gigiakan, to throw, as something into the fire.

Gilaki, the name of a tree.

Gili, name of a shell-fish.

Gima, *v.* (1) to look ; (2) to watch ; (3) to protect.

Gima tauna, sentinel ; a protector, applied now to representative of British government, as the Deputy Commissioner.

Gimata, *s.* a single white feather comb ornament.

Gini, *v.* to stand, to be erect.

Ginitore, to stand up (from a sitting posture).

Gini, *s.* (1) a thorn ; (2) tattooing instrument.

Ginibou, to stand together.

Ginidiho, to stand down.

Ginigini, *a.* stinging, prickly.

Ginigini *a.* (the *g* a little harder than the preceding word) prickly, thorny.

Gini hetabila, *v.* to adjoin (of houses.)

Ginikerehai, *v.* to turn round.

Giroa, *v.* to turn round, as the handle of a machine, &c.

Girogiro, *v.* to spin (as a top).

Goada *a.* (1) strong ; (2) clever ; (3) bold, valiant.

Goadagoada, very strong.

Goada bada, zealous.

Goada, *s.* courage.

Goe or Koe, *s.* a small bag-net. (Shorter than *daqai.*)

Goegoe, *v.* to be dinned by the noise of talking, &c.

Goeahu, lowering, as sky.

Goeva, *a.* clean, prepared.

Goevagoeva, *adv.* thoroughly ; *a.* clean.

Goua, *v.* to scald, to blister.

Goua, *s.* a blister.

Goula, *s.* a smooth place for anchoring, as between two reefs, &c.

Goura, *s.* a valley.

Gobaiahu, *v.* to veil, to obscure.

Gobagoba, *s.* a young cocoanut. (Harder than *gogori.*)

Gobea, *v.* to catch.

Gōdi, small stone hatchet.

Gōgō, *s.* a creeping plant. The leaves are used in incantations, and to make yams fruitful.

Gogoa, *v.* to pick up.

Gogoaoho, to gather out of.

Gogoabou, to gather together.

Gogori, *s.* young cocoanut with very soft kernel.

Gogosia, *v.* to keep intact.

Goha, *s.* the name of a month (February).

Gohu, *s.* a lake, a lagoon.

Gohumānu, *s.* water-birds.

Gonagonalaia, *v.* to deride, to mock.

Gore, *v.* to deny.

Goregore, *s.* shelf or rack, formed by the wall-plate at each end of the house.

Gorere, *v.* to be ill.

Gorere, *s.* disease.

Gorere siahu, fever.

Gori, *s.* legend.

Goroto, *s.* gray clay.

Goru, *v.* to lie on the belly, to be prone.

Gorua, *v.* to entice or deceive with food, and then kill while eating.

Gornahu, *v.* to overshadow.

Goruatao, *v.* (1) to be laid on ; to be overlaid, as an infant ; (2) to be sat on, as eggs by a hen ; (3) to fall prone on.

Gorudiho, to fall prone.

Gorugoru, large package of sago, enclosed in two palm fronds, and containing from 6 to 14 *kokoara*.

Gorukau, to lean on a table or box on the elbows, with the face downwards.

Goruparapara *v.* to fall prone.

Guanua or Qanua, *v.* to spear (by throwing).

Guara, the name of a tree.

Gui, *v.* (1) to go on board a canoe or ship ; (2) to ebb ; (3) to ride.

Guia, *v.* (1) to tie, as the hands or feet ; (2) to prepare a torch.

Guia gauna, a band.

Guitau, *s.* the season of S.E. monsoon.

Guba, *s* (1) sky, heavens; (2) heaven ; (3) a squall.

Guba dokona, the horizon.

Guba rahua, *s.* thunder.

Gudu, *v.* to swell, as the hand or leg.

Gudu, one kind of banana.

Gududu, *s.* the name of a fish.

Gugu, *s.* the river bottom, where there are are deep holes.

Gugu, to clasp.

Guguba, *v.* to hold tightly, to grasp with tight fingers.

Gugubaia, *v.* (1) to squeeze by embracing ; (2) to break, as a cocoanut shell between the two hands.

Guhi, *s.* the roof of a house.

Guma, *s.* (1) lamp-black ; (2) bait for fish.

Gumaulu, the name of a shell-fish.

Guma karaia, *v.* to blacken oneself, to be sooty.

Guna, *a.* first ; *adv.* before.

Gunaguna, intens. of guna, first of all (in time).

Gunalaia, *v.* to go before, to lead.

Gunana, *a.* (1) old ; (2) former.

Guni Gunika, *s.* inland.

Gunita, *v.* to eat alone, not sharing to be selfish.

Ani gunita (an abusive term).

Gure *v.* to be sea sick.

Guri, *s.* a pit ; a grave.

Guri, *v.* to bury. Guria

Guri, *s.* a drink, a draught. *Guri tamona*, one draught.

Guria, *v.* to pray. *Dirava guria*.

Guriguri, *s.* a prayer. *Guriguri koaulaia*, to pray.

Gurita, *s.* a draught (of drink).

H

H is not sounded by natives of Pari, and some others ; Hododae, for instance, a part of Hanuabada (Port Moresby).

Ha also He, *interj.* warning, forbidding, look out !

Ha, causative particle.

Haegeadiho, *v.* to cause to recline.

Haeleruaia, *v.* to make of two thicknesses, as boards, mats, &c.

Haeno, moon, two or three nights after full.

Haere, *v.* to answer.

Haevaia, *v.* to sway (by the wind).

Hai, preceded by idau, *adv.* away from.

Haida, *a.* some, any, more (of persons).

Haidaulaia, *v.* to alter.

Haiditaia, *v.* to make bitter.

Haigo, *v.* to peep, to stoop.

Haine, *s.* woman ; female.

Haino, *s.* small white snake

Hainua, *v.* to give drink.

Hairaina, *s.* adornment. *Hairaina karaia*.

Haoa, *v.* to arouse.

Haoda, *v.* to fish. Haoda tauna, fisherman.

Haoda eno, *v.* to go fishing, and stay out all night.

Haodi and Hahodi, *v.* to take breath, as when going up hill.

Haodi *s.* (1) a deep breath ; (2) a sigh.

Haorea, *v.* to demolish, exterminate, to finish.

Hauraia, to teaze, to make cry.

Habadaia, to enlarge.

Habade, *v.* to accuse.

Habadelaia, *v.* to be accused.

Habadua, *v.* to displease, to enrage, to provoke.

Habapatiso, *v.* (*introduced*) to baptize.

Habata, *s.* a rain stream.

Haberoa, *v.* to be wounded.

Habidia, *v.* to rub the eye.

Haboua, v. to collect, to gather together, to assemble.

Habodoa, v. to extinguish, as a fire.

Habubunia, to cover with water.

Hadaea, s. ceremony of a sorceror to find and bring back the spirit of a sick person. *Laulau hadaea.*

Hadaia, v. (1) to place on, as the foot on a mat ; (2) to soak, to steep.

Hadabua, to lack, to be left out.

Hadadaia, v. to make to enter, or go through (as a nose-stick).

Hadagedagea, v. to make savage, to exasperate.

Hadamena, to salt.

Hadaralaia, v. to put *raina* over the arm on the shoulder (as at *Naara* on the appointment of a chief).

Hadavaia, v. to marry. *Inai kekeni lau hadavaia.*

Hadeo, a stone hatchet, used for inside of canoes, &c.

Hadeolo, s. stay (to mast).

Hadedea, v. to frizzle, to burn fat ; to fumigate.

Hadehuina, s. beard.

Hadelea, *adv.* sideways.

Hadetari, v. to brood over, to be pensive.

Hadiaria, v. to make light, to enlighten.

Hadibaia, v. to teach.

Hadibadibaia, as *Hadibaia*

Hadigua, v. to bathe.

Hadihoa, v. to divorce a wife.

Hadikaia, v. to calumniate ; to contemn.

Hado, Hadohado, to plant.

Hadoa (*Hado* with suffix of 3rd person sing.), to plant, as *Maho hadoa.*

Hadokoa, v. to conclude, to stop.

Hadokilaia, v. to put on clothes.

Hadonoa, v. to swallow.

Hadorua, to sprain.

Hadua, v. to tell someone to do a thing ; to give permission. Haduaia, to command.

Hadudua, v. to give food out of respect, as to a chief, or out of compassion to a lazy man.

Haduhua, to make thick, or gross.

Haga, s. crag, high rock.

Hagaia, v. to open the mouth.

Hagana, v. to count (mentally), to distribute to all of a party.

Hagauhagau, a. each one of a company.

Hagabia, to fill partly.

Hagadoia, v. to dwindle.

Hagagevaia, v. to bend, to crook ; (morally) to lead astray.

Hagahaga, s. steep rocks, cliffs, precipice.

Hagania, v. to command.

Hagara, to meet in combat.

Hagaria, v. to daunt.

Hagaru, s. rising tide.

Hagava, v. to bother, to hinder.

Hagavara, one kind of banana.

Hagegeva, a. (with the face *vaira hagegeva*), sorrowful, on the point of crying.

Hagere, v. to look towards, to receive a person. Hagerea.

Haginia, v. to cause to stand, to raise up.

Hagoadaia, v. to stimulate.

Hagoevaia, v. to cleanse.

Hagoria, v. to steer seawards, to put the ship about, to tack.

Haguhi, v. (with lalo) to reflect, to consider.

Hahala, *adv.* lightly, gingerly. (With the verb to hold.)

Hahane, v. to invoke, to call upon absent friends. *O vagi o!*

Haharu, s. a plantation of trees (as cocoanuts unenclosed).

Hahataiaisi, v. to lift and train up, as yam vines.

Haheadavaia, v. to give in marriage, to cause to be married.

Haheaduisi, v. to lift up from the ground, as the tomato vine.

Hahealo, v. to constrain, to encourage, to exhort.

Hahebona, v. to add to, to combine, to congregate.

Hahedai, v. to grind (as the teeth), to gnash.

Hahedinarai, v. to cause to be manifest, to cause to show.

Hahedua v. to extort ; to urge to be quick ; to command.

Hahegani. *See* Ahegani.

Hahegaraheheni, to meet in combat; quarrelsome.

Hahegeregere, v. to compare with, to make equal to. Syn. Hahetoho.

Hahelahua, s. coitio.

Hahenamoheheni, v. *recipr. of* namo.

Haheqaqanai, v. to trip.
Haherahu, v. to smell, to rub noses (instead of kissing).
Hahetoho, v. to compare.
Hahetoho ganna, measure.
Hahisia, v. to cause pain, to afflict, to hurt.
Hahitu, seven times.
Hahoaia, a. to disturb, to surprise.
Hahoho, v. to respire.
Hahohoa, to make plentiful.
Hahururua, v. to make a fire blaze.
Hākau, to reach, to be in contact.
Hakaua, v. to lead.
Hakaua taudia, s. escort.
Hakahi, v. to jam ; to cut wedge-shape. Tarai hakahi.
Hakala, v. to lean forward so as to catch every word, to listen atten-tively.
Hakapua, v. to shut, to close.
Hakara, v. to have killed some one (of returning warriors).
Hakaroho, v. to cause, to scatter.
Hakede, v. to bend forward the ear so as to catch every word.
Hakedea, v. to light with a torch.
Hakerukerua, v. to shade.
Hakerumaia, v. to chill.
Hako regena, leg joint of wallaby.
Haketoa, to cause to fall.
Hakoea, v. to turn round side for end.
Hakunua, v., to cause to be satis-fied.
Hakurokuroa, v. to make white.
Hālā, s. the platform of sticks on which meat is grilled ; a gridiron.
Halaia, v. to broil.
Halaoa, v. to become, to be trans-formed into.
Halababanaia, v. to make broad.
Halahe, v. to delay, to linger, to be tardy.
Halahua. See Hahelahua.
Halaka, v. to burn in cooking.
Halakaia, v. to scald.
Halala, v. to hold lightly or carelessly. Alia halala. Kahua halala.
Halataia, v. to elongate, to lengthen.
Hālatutu, s. fire continuing to burn, after that in the surrounding bush has gone out. Rei doua hālatutuna.
Halasi, s. banana-leaf caulking the third row of caulking in lakatoi.
Halasia, v. to expel, to take outside.
Halō, v. to comfort.

Halōakunu, v. to grate on a rock (as a boat).
Haloua, v. to cause to return ; to bring or send back ; to convert.
Halohiaia, v. to praise, to laud ; to help a chief with presents ; to honour.
Hamaoroa, v. to show, to make kuown.
Hamaoromaoro, v. to make straight, to justify.
Hamau, v. give no answer.
Hamauria, v. to save, to heal.
Hamagea, v. to ripen on the tree.
Hamakaia, to break edge (of knife or axe).
Hamakohia, v. to be dilapidated.
Hamanadaia, v. to habituate.
Hamanaua v. to abase.
Hamane, s. a tree from which oars are made ; (2) the gum of the tree : (3) glue, gum, paste.
Hamanokaia, v. debilitate, to dispirit, to enfeeble.
Hamanu, v. to send for (persons or things).
Hamaragia, to decrease, to abate, to lessen.
Hamarumarua, v. to conciliate, to pacify.
Hamatamataia, v. to mend.
Hamatea, v. to efface, to kill.
Hametaua, v. to encumber.
Hamiroa, v. to defile, to soil.
Hamoalea, v. to cause to rejoice ; to amuse.
Hamomokania, v. to confirm.
Hamomokanilaia, v. to fulfil ; to prove.
Hamu, s. (1) the heated stones for cooking ; (2) a camp oven.
Hamūe, v. (used with the face, raira hamūe), to look away from any one, as a sign of displeasure ; to receive a visitor with disrespect.
Hamūdo, v. to cook with hot stones.
Hamumutaia, s. emetic.
Hanai, v. to cross, to go over, to pass through.
Hanaia lao, v. to pass. See daya hanai. Tulu hanai, &c.
Hanaihanai, a. eternal.
Hanamoa, v. to commend, to give thanks.
Hanamoa koikoi, to cajole.
Hanamoa henia, to salute.
Hanamoa lasi, to disapprove.

Hane, *s.* a woman. Used only (instead of haine) with the place or tribe to which she belongs, as, *hane motu;* or first in a sentence, as *hane namo,* a good-looking woman.

Hani, *s.* the wing of a bird, &c.

Hani, the sign of a question. *Oi gorere hani?*

Hani, *a.* four.

Haniulato, *s.* a maiden, a young woman.

Hanihia, *v.* to appear as a spirit.

Hanogo, to stretch out neck.

Hanua, *v.* village, town.

Hanua motu, a small village.

Hanua taudia, populace.

Hanuaboi, *s.* night.

Hapa, *s.* the side of a house.

Hapapai, *v.* to be bright (of the eyes).

Hapapaia, to give sight to.

Hapararaia, *v.* to split, to separate, to cleave, (of mind) to understand.

Hapariparia, *v.* to moisten.

Hapoua, *v.* to explode.

Haqadogia, *v.* to make short, to clip, to abbreviate.

Hara, *s.* brains. *Qara harana.*

Haraia, *v.* to light a fire or lamp.

Haraiva, *v.* to trouble, to disturb, to bother.

Haraga, *adv.* easily. Haragaharaga, promptly.

Haraga. Haragaharaga, *v.* to be light in weight, to be quick.

Haragaia, to hurry.

Harahua, *v.* to be kissed. (Lit. to be smelt.)

Hare, *v.* to brandish a spear, to defy.

Hari. Harina, *s.* a report, fame.

Harina dika, *a.* infamous.

Hari, *adv.* (1) now, at this moment. (2) Used also as a definite article. *Hari ira,* the hatchet, just used, or spoken of.

Haria, *v.* to divide.

Hari ahui, *a.* forty.

Harioa, to gird.

Hariolaia, to gird with.

Harihari. As hari, but oftener used of to-day ; not so immediate or present as hari.

Harihari ela, henceforth.

Harihari, favour.

Harihari gauna, a present.

Harihara bada, liberal.

Haroro, *v.* to proclaim, to preach, to make a speech.

Haroro tauna, missionary.

Haroroa, *v.* to haul on, to pull taut.

Harua, *v.* to be carried away by a current or flood.

Harua, *a.* twice.

Haruaoho, *v.* to be washed out and carried away.

Hasatauro, *v.* to crucify (from the Greek).

Hasiahua, *v.* to warm, to heat.

Hasinadoa, *v.* to look intently at so as to know again.

Hasinadoa tauna, (1) one who knows a road, place, &c,, from previous observation ; (2) a spy.

Hata, *adv.* sometime, another time, presently.

Hataia, *v.* to clang, to rattle.

Hataisi, *v.* to grow up, as a yam vine by clinging to a stick or tree.

Hataoraia, *v.* to level.

Hatatadaeroha, *v.* to cause to rise, as the sun.

Hatoa, *v.* to pronounce a name.

Hatoboa, to give suck.

Hatolaia, to crown, to put on (as hat).

Hatonia, *v.* to take leave of friends, leaving on a journey.

Hatono, *v.* to gulp, to swallow.

Hatoreaisi, *v.* to raise up.

Hatorotororoa, *v.* to stiffen.

Hatua, *v.* (1) to plait, as mats ; (2) to weave ; (3) to beat a bamboo drum ; (4) to tattoo.

Hatuia, *v.* to quell, to still.

Hatubua gauna, *s.* leaven, *v.* to cause to ferment.

Haturi, *v.* to tire, vex, trouble.

Haturiaia, *v.* to trouble, to tire. See Haturi.

Havaia, *v.* to chase.

Havaraia, *v.* to cause to grow.

Havareaia, *v.* to take inside, to insert.

Havasea, *v.* to banter.

Haveve, *v.* to liquify.

Havevea, to take aim.

Hē. See ha.

Heai, *v.* to quarrel. (Without coming to blows.)

Heai karaia, a disturbance.

Heaiva, *s.* payment to a sorcerer for causing rain, restraining wind, &c.

Heaivaia, *v.* (1) to fee a rainmaker, &c. ; (2) to pay tribute.

Heau, *v.* to run ; to go fast, as a canoe or ship ; to escape.

Heau dara, *v.* to run up, as a mountain.

Heau hekei, to run down.

Heau hekapu, to run two together competitively.

Heau helulu, to run together, to see which can get in first.

Heaulaia, to run off with.

Heautatatata, to run with short steps, like a child just beginning to walk.

Heautania, to be outrun.

Heabidae, *v.* to receive into one's house, to show hospitality (with suffix of person so received). *Lau heabiqu dae.*

Heabidae tauna, one who is hospitable.

Heabiahu, *v.* to go off to meet a ship coming in.

Headava, *s.* the state of marriage. *Oi headava?* Are you married?

Heagi, v. to boast. Heagi herevana, to brag.

Heagilaia, *v.* to ascribe strength, wisdom, &c. ; to praise.

Heagi tauna, *a.* conceited.

Heahu, *v.* to commit suicide by drowning. *Ia sibona heahu.*

Heala, *v.* to be intoxicated.

Healaheheni, *v.* recipr. of alala, to fight.

Healulu, to rush together.

Hearuru. See Healulu.

Heatolaia, *v.* to praise, to extol.

Heatotao gauna, *s.* the payment given to betray or kill another.

Heatotao tauna, the one that pays another to betray or kill a third person.

Heatu, *s.* a combat.

Heidaida, *s.* resemblance, likeness.

Heidaida, *a.* alike.

Heidaida, *v.* to liken.

Heiga, one kind of yam.

Heilu, *v.* to float ; to slip or slide into.

Heinaru, *v.* to cook food for workers.

Heiri, to refuse to allow to accompany, &c. *Idia lau heirigumu.*

Heiriheiri, to dissent, to disagree.

Heita, *v.* (1) two to look at each other. *Oiemu heita tauna.* (2) To see one's self in a mirror. *Ia : sibogu heita*

Heita tao tauna, one who watches or looks after anything ; an overseer.

Heubu, *v.* to make a pet of ; to feed.

Heubu mero, *s.* a boy kept and fed, as servants in a family. *Nao heubu memero.*

Heubu sisia, a pet dog.

Heudeheude, *v.* to tremble, to shake. With boka, to desire.

Aheudeheude, to cause to shake.

Heuduri, *v.* to follow about, as a man after a woman, or to beg something. With suffix, *heudurigu.*

Heukehenke, *s.* a throbbing headache.

Heuraheni, *v.* to desire someone to come to or go with the speaker.

Heuraheheni, to ask anyone to join in an expedition. *Misi Lao heurahcheni koaulaia.*

Hebaduhaduheheni, *v.* recipr. of badu, to be angry one with another, to be at variance.

Hebasi, *v.* to puncture the forehead with a small flint-pointed arrow, so as to draw blood, to relieve headache.

Hebirihebiri, *v.* to sit or stand close together, as trees standing close together.

Hebiri matemate, *v.* to be squeezed, crowded.

Hebou, *v.* to add to, together with.

Hebodohi, *v.* to substitute.

Hebokahisi, *v.* to compassionate.

Hebokahisi tauna, a compassionate merciful man.

Hebokahisi, *a.* humane.

Hebolo, *v.* to take the place of another, to be a substitute.

Hebore, envy.

Hebore karaia, to be envious of success or prosperity of others.

Hebubu, *v.* to spill.

Hebulohebulo, *v.* (1) to be mixed up ; (2) also of the mind, and several stories mixed up in it.

Hedai, *v.* to dive head first.

Hedai dobi, to dive feet first.

Hedaiahu, to enclose (as trees growing all round, troops, &c.).

Hedanatoho, *v.* to touch, to lay hand on.

Hedaukau, *v.* to place the hand on, to touch.

F

Hedahu, *v.* to besmear, to wipe.
Hedahu muramura, liniment.

Hedaqadobi, *v.* to commit suicide by throwing oneself down from a tree or cliff.

Hedalokepokipoa, *v.* (preceded by taia) to disbelieve ; to reject a story as false.

Hedaraune, *v.* to remember, to call to mind (especially when reminded by the sight of something).

Hedare, *v.* to rend.

Hedarehedare, *a.* ragged.

Hedava, to do by turn.

Hedavari, *v.* to meet.

Hedavea *v.* (following hoihoi) to exchange different things in barter.

Hedea, *a.* only, *rara hedea*, only begotten.

Hedibagani, *v.* to dissemble.

Hedibagani, *s.* a temptation, hypocrisy.

Hediho, *s.* a divorcement.
Hediho haine, a divorced woman.

Hedikoi, *v* to shrink (as clothes, or food in cooking).

Hedinarai, *adv.* openly.

Hedinarai, *v.* to make manifest, to show openly.

Hedoa, *v.* to land.

Hedoisi, *v.* to kneel on one knee.

Hedoki gauna, *s.* a shirt.

Hedoko, *v.* to part combatants.

Hedoko gabuna, *s.* anchorage.

Hedoriahu, *v.* to push away or down.

Hedorihedori, *v.* to crowd, to jostle.

Hegabi, partly full.

Hegagaheheni, opposite.

Hegagiudae, *v.* to throw the arms around ; cramp.

Hegagalo, *v.* to scratch.

Hegame *v.* (following noi) to beg.
Hegame tauna, beggar, to look on in hope of getting a share.

Hegani, *v.* to desire (only used with lalona). Used with henia of object.

Heganaia, to warm oneself.

Hegara, *v.* to smart, as the tongue, or a wound.

Hegara, *a.* caustic, pungent.

Hegege, *v.* to encompass.

Hegege, madai, *v.* to enclose.

Hegera, *v.* to coquette.

Hegeregere, *a.* even, equal.
Hegerehegere lasi, *a.* contradictory.

Hegiurai, too long, jammed at ends.

Hegigi, *v.* to nip, to pinch.

Hegigiarohoroho, *v.* to scatter, to throw about.

Hegigibou, *v.* to be full, as a village with people, or a box with goods.

Hegigiraia, to strike with claws (as cat, &c.

Hegida, to hoist sail, of *lakatoi*.

Hegilo, *v.* to turn.

Hegilohegilo, to revolve.

Hegoita. Hegodiaita, &c., *v.* to visit in order to inquire after the welfare, to go to see a sick person.

Hegogo, *s.* a congregation, an assembly,
Hegogo bada, a concourse.

Hegogo, *v.* to shrink (as from cold).

Hegomogomo, *v.* to gargle.

Hegore, *v.* to deny.

Hegore, *s.* denial.

Hegugußa, *v.* to shudder.

Hehea, *v.* to squeeze hard in the hand, to knead in the hand ; to milk.

Hehea, *v.* to carry the waterpot on the shoulder.

Heheni, suffixed to verb to make it reciprocal.

Hehiriraia, *v.* to reject.

Hehona, a recitative song.

Hehuhu, *v.* to shed, to cast leaves.

Hehurehanai, *v.* to turn over oneself.

Hekaßa, *v.* to help with food or goods when visitors come.

Hekabi, *a.* half-full.

Hekagalo, *v.* to scratch.

Hekaha, to help.

Hekahana tauna, *s.* a helper. As Ikahana tauna.

Hekahi, *v.* to stick, to be tight.

Hekahihekahi, *a.* narrow, straight.

Hekakari, as Herarai, onlooker at feast, &c.

Hekakati, *v.* to scratch the face in grief, so as to fetch blood.

Hekalo, *v.*, to beckon.

Hekamo, *v.* to stick ; *a.* sticky.

Hekamokau, *v.* to take hold of a thing, to touch, to cling to.

Hekamonai, *v.* to have labour pains.

Hekamotao, *v.* to clutch.

Hekapa, *v.* twins.

Hekapu, *adv.*, with *heau*, to run competitively.

Hekarakaraheheni, *a* reciprocal of kara, generally of bad conduct.

Hekei, *v.* to descend a mountain.

Hekeialao, *v.* to trundle, to go round and round, as a wheel.

Hekeikan, *v.* to be crushed, fallen upon.

Hekenilaia, *v.* to be filled up by the tide or a flood.

Hekida, *v.* to hoist sail on a native ship (*lakatoi.*)

Hekidaela, or Hekidaera, *v.* to lie on the back.

Hekidadiho, *v.* to throw down carelessly ; to fall down as one dead, or in a fit.

Hekinia (*daba*), peep of day.

Hekinitari, *v.* to pinch.

Hekisehekise, *v.* to desire.

Hekisehekise henia, to covet.

Hekisi, to scarify, to cut.

Hekisia, *v.* to cut oneself with a shell or flint in grief.

Hekoauheheni, *v*, to converse, to talk and answer.

Hekoikoi, *v.* Syn., Herariherari.

Hekoho, *v.* to break off an engagement to marry.

Hekohutania, *v.* to leave, to desert a village.

Hekoka, *v.* to be prevented, to be hindered by what one is doing from going at request. *Lau gau karaia lau hekoka.*

Hekokorogu tauna, *a.* conceited, proud.

Hekopa, *a.* excoriated.

Hekori, savage, untamed.

Hekuhihekuhi, to wallow.

Hekukuri, *s.* diarrhœa.

Hekunumai, *v.* to wink, to make signs with the eyes.

Heknre, *v.* to lie down.

Hekuredobi, to throw oneself down, to lie down carelessly.

Helai, *v.* to sit.

Helai gauna, a seat.

Helai diho, to sit down on the ground or floor.

Helaikau, to sit on, to place, as a pot on the fire.

Helai tore, to sit up, from flying down.

Helai dagadaga, to sit astride.

Helaoahu, *v.* to avert.

Helada, *adv.* stealthily.

Heladadae, *v.* to creep up stealthily, as a thief.

Heladahanai, *v.* to slip out unseen, to escape.

Heladaoho, *v.* to dislocate.

Heladarua, *v.* to start back from fear.

Helado, *v.* to sway, by the wind.

Heladohelado, *a* loose.

Helaga or Helaka, *a.* sacred, taboo.

Helagāu and Lagāu, *v.* to pass before a chief, to be disrespectful. *Misi Lao helagaua garina.*

Helaha, *v.* to kick out behind, as a horse.

Helalo, *v.* to reflect, to consider.

Helalo-dae, *s.* nervous, misgiving, &c.

Helaloune. See Hedaraune.

Helalo karaia, *v.* to repent.

Helaqahanai, *v.* to turn a somersault ; to fall down on the head.

Helaro, *v.* to wait for, to expect some one.

Helarutao, *v.* to sit together with one piece of cloth round both.

Helata, *v.* to moult.

Helavahu, *v.* to be hidden by an intervening object.

Helea, Heleahelea or Herea, *v.* (1) to project. Hence (2) to excel, to exceed. *Namo herea*, very good.

Helide, *v.* to put out of joint.

Heloduhenia, *s.* an accusation.

Heloge, *v.* to enter with difficulty, to wriggle through.

Heloge, *adv.* with difficulty.

Helogea, Herogea, *v.* to store, to garner.

Helogohelogo, *s.* clamour, discord, turmoil.

Hemaia, *a.* tasteless, insipid, of no relish, as food to the sick. *Lau ania hemaia.*

Hemaihemai, *v.* to itch, to tingle.

Hemaunu, *v.* to whisper.

Hemadoi, *v.* to be entangled, or detained in a crowd. *Hemadoia matemate.*

Hemaduala, unwilling, indifferent.

Hemani. See Hetari.

Hemarai, *v.* to be ashamed, to be coy. Hemarai kara, *a.* disgraceful.

Hemata, *v.* to commit suicide by hanging, to strangle.

Hemataurai, *v.* to reverence.

Hemmemeru, *v.* to warm oneself by the fire. Used by those exposed to wind and rain. Let us go asho and *hememeru.*

Hemetaua, *v.* to encumber.

Hemoitao, *v.* to tread upon.

Hemomokāni, *v.* to fulfil, to true.

Henao, *v.* to steal.

Henaohenao, *v.* to have intercourse with the opposite sex, to ravish.

Henaohenao, *s.* illicit intercourse, adultery.

Henamo, a term of address from man to man, or from a woman to a woman. *Henamo e* !

Henanadai, *s.* inquiry.

Hene, spear of white wood used for hunting.

Heni, *v.* to give, to hand to.

Henidoa, to give without payment.

Henia, *v.* to contribute.

Heni hagauhagau, to distribute.

Henigagāe, *v.* to give something when bringing payment for a former gift.

Henihenia, to feed a child or animal.

Henitorehai, to give a thing on credit.

Heno, *adv.* aslant, as *abia heno,* to hold a pen slantingly.

Henu, *prep.* beneath, under. Also Henunai.

Henu, *adv.* seawards (in steering), westwards.

Henuai, *adv.* downwards, under.

Henukahana, in a westerly direction.

Hepalare, *a.* lazy. *Hepalarea tauna* (term of abuse.)

Hepapahuahu, *s.* contention, *v.* to contend, to recriminate.

Hepididae, *v.* to come to mind, to be reminded of.

Hepuhiepuhi, *a.* foolish, erring, crooked (of speech or conduct.)

Hepulai, *v* to run over.

Hepuni, *v,* to sink in, as the feet in mud or sand.

Hepuraidobi, *v.* to boil over, to overflow.

Heqada, to brandish spear, &c., as a demonstration.

Heqaqanai, *v.* to stumble.

Heqarahi, *s.* labour, work.

Heqarahi, *v.* to work, to be busy, to be tired.

Heqatu, *v.* to tangle.

Heqarai, as Heqarahi.

Hera, *a.* personal adornment. *Hera karaia.*

Herai, *v.* to put on the girdle. *Sihi herai.*

Hera gauna, *s.* ornament for personal adornment.

Herage, to take food to women whose husbands are gone on a voyage.

Herahe, *v.* to commit fornication.

Herahia, *s.* a present, an offering.

Herarai. See *Raraia,* to stare.

Heraraho, to take food to women whose husbands are away on voyage, in payment for taking armshells, pottery, &c., for trade.

Herariherari, *v.* to talk about a thing without understanding or knowing the truth. Used with sivarai and koau.

Herariherari, *s.* a "cock and bull" story.

Herea, *v.* to overlap, project, to excel.

Heregeherege, *v.* to be unwilling.

Herekehereke, *v.* as heregeherege.

Hereva, *v.* to talk.

Hereva, euphemism for *gagaia,* sexual intercourse.

Herevaherava, to confer.

Herevaheheni, to talk together.

Hereva, *s.* speech.

Hereva tamona lasi, to disagree.

Hereva hegeregere, fable.

Herogea or Helogea, *v.* to store.

Heroiheroi, *v.* to rub oneself against a post.

Herouherou, *u.* to be excited, to be in tumult (of a village.)

Herohemaino, *v.* to pacify, intercede, to conciliate.

Heroho, *v.* to wash off, to come out (as dirt), to rub off.

Heruruki, *v.* (1) to let slip through the fingers ; (2) to strip by drawing through the fingers, as an ear of corn.

Hesedea, hesedesede, *v.* to be crowded, to push with the shoulder, to jostle, as in a crowd.

Hesedematemate, to stand crowded, jammed.

Hesese, *v.* to be cracked, as the skull, or pottery.

Hesiai, *s.* a message, an errand. As isiai. Hesiai taudia, embassy.

Hetāinturi, *v.* to cry after, as a child after his father.

Hetaoahu, *v.* to put up the hands in forbidding, or in order to save oneself when falling.

Hetaoisi, *v.* to sit up, from lying down.

Hetauadae, *v.* to hang up.

Hetabubunai, *v.* to scramble.

Hetaha. See Kudou.

Hetahahai, *v.* to marry a woman who has left her husband. (She has no wish to return to her husband, though he wishes to get her back. When another marries her, her first husband makes a disturbance, but to no purprse).

Hetahu, *v.* to daub, to anoint the body.

Hetamanu, *v.* to charge, to admonish.

Hetamanu, *s.* a charge, an exhortation.

Hetari, *v.* to coagulate. Syn. Hemani.

Hetaripapara, *v.* to fall backwards.

Hetaru, *v.* to be covered, clothed.

Hetatamatemate, *v.* to push and jostle in a crowd.

Hetavauhe, *v.* to leave, to forget.

Heto, *adv.* like, as (following the *s. Boroma na heto*).

Hetoa, *s.* boundary.

Hetoi hedavari, *v.* to meet on the road.

Hetoi hedavari, *s.* the act of meeting.

Hetoisi, to kneel on one knee.

Hetohotoho, to mock.

Hetorclai, *s.* resurrection.

Hetotao, *v.* to lean one's weight, as on a stick.

Hetova. See Heto.

Hetu, *a.* slack.

Hetū, *v.* to lie off, as a ship from the beach.

Hetubuahu, confined (of bowels), as *Boka hetubuahu.*

Hetutu, *v.* to smite oneself in grief.

Hetuturu, *v.* to drop (of liquids).

Hevago, *v.* to be skinny from illness, and refusing food.

Hevalavala, *v.* to be mildewed.

Hevasea, *s.* fun, jest.

Heveri, *a.* powerless, paralyzed (of an arm or leg).

Hi, *interj.* See Hina.

Hiana, *s.* (1) sister or brother-in-law ; (2) a female friend of a man, or a male friend of a woman.

Hioka, *v.* to whistle.

Hida, *adv.* how many ?

Hidi, *v.* to choose, (Preceded by ita, abia, &c.)

Hidio, *s.* (1) the lean of meat (2) flesh ; (3) the grain of wood. Also Hidiho.

Hidio dika, cross grain (of wood).

Hido, *s.* a wild cane growing by the river side.

Higo, name of a tree.

Hihana. See Hiana.

Hihiria, *v.* to blow with the mouth, as Ihilia.

Hila, *s.* a large species of edible arum.

Hili, *v.* to go a long voyage.

Hili lou, to go a long voyage and return quickly.

Hilia, *v.* (1) to twist round and round ; (2) to tie up a parcel or bundle by twisting string all round it. Also Hiria.

Hilia dabuana, a bandage.

Hiliakau, *v.* (1) to join two pieces of wood lengthwise by tying ; (2) to fasten anything to the end of a stick, to lash at right angles, as the wall-plate to a post.

Hina, *interj.* aha !

Hinere, *v.* to deceive.

Hiri, *s.* a voyage.

Hiria, *v.* See Hilia.

Hisi, *s.* (1) pain ; (2) an epidemic. *Hisi karaia.*

Hisiai. See Isiai.

Hisi ania, *v.* to suffer.

Hisihisi, *v.* to ache, to be in pain.

Hisimo ania, to be in constant pain.

Hisiu, *s.* a star.

Hisiu bada, *s.* (1) a comet ; (2) morning star.

Hitolo, *a.* hungry.

Hitolo, *v.* to hunger.

Hitolo mate, famished.

Hitu, *a.* seven. Qauta hitu, seventeen.

Hituahui, seventy.

Hoa, *v.* to be surprised, amazed.

Hoihoi, *v.* to barter. *Hoihoi davana maragi*, cheap.

Hoihoi tauna, merchant.

Houa, *v.* to paint the face red, when going to fight.

Houkahouka, *a.* rotton, as wood.

Houkahouka, *v.* to be rotten.

Houkahouka, *s.* pith.

Hobe, *s.* houses at each end of *lakatoi* for packing pottery.

Hodaehodae, *v.* to throb, as an abscess.

Hodaia, *v.* (1) to be shaken, as by wind ; (2) to shake out, as cloth.

Hodaia gari. Hodaia keto, *v.* to be blown down by the wind.

Hodaia kohu, *v.* to bo blown down and broken to pieces by the wind.

Hodara, *v.* to have two wives. Also Hodala.

Hodara *s.* bigamy.

Hodava, name of a tree.

Hode *s.* a paddle.

Hodoa, *v.* to throw, as stones.

Hodu, *s.* native waterpot; pl. Hodudia.

Hogohogo, *s.* rust.

Hogo, *a.* complete, sufficient, plenty. Hoho lasi, scarce.

Hohoa, *v.* to be blown by the wind, to be carried away, or to be swaying about in the wind, *Lāi hohoa.*

Hohoa, to inhale, as tobacco smoke.

Hohoga, *s.* a large hole, as in the end of a cauoe, where the heart of the wood is.

Hohotauna, *s.* the survivor, after all the others are killed.

Holoa, *v.* to make a hole in the ground with a pointed stick or crowbar.

Hona, only.

Honebone, a short grass.

Honu, *v.* to be full, as *hodu*, with water, &c. Honuhonudae, quite full.

Honu, *a.* full. Honuhonu.

Hore, *v.* to be above water, as the reef at low tide, or a rock standing up, &c,

Horetao, *s.* a man higher than his fellows. *Sibona horetao.*

Hori, *v.* to grow. Syn. Vara.

Hotamu, name of tree similar to cedar.

Hoto tauna, *s.* survivor.

Hu, *s.* the noise made by the wind. *Lai huna.*

Hu, *a.* to hum.

Hua, to increase, as an ulcer.

Hua, *s.* (1) the moon ; (2) a month ; (3) a cough.

Hua dāulao, moon soon after full.

Hua haeno, moon next to *dāulao.*

Hua karukaru, young moon.

Hua lokaloka, moon about half full.

Hua matoa torea, moon after *haeno.*

Hua. Huaia, *v.* (used with the face, vaira hua) to look angry, not to smile with others. *Ia dahaka vaira hua.*

Hūa, *v.* to cough.

Huaia, *v.* to carry on the shoulder. Huaia boroma, to be carried by four.

Huaia tauna, a bearer.

Huaiakau, to carry on shoulder.

Hūadaehuadae, *v.* to throb, as an abscess.

Huahua, *s.* fruit.

Huarara, *v.* to shine (of the moon and stars).

Huararua, *v.* to carry on a pole between two.

Huaria, *v.* to smash, as pottery ; to strike on the head or limbs in falling ; to clash.

Hui, *s.* hair.

Hui demo, slightly curly hair.

Hui lau, straight hair.

Hui tuma, *s.* hair curly.

Huia, *v.* to put a child or anything large in a netted bag.

Huinaimi, a fish.

Huiraura, *s.* the name of a month (January).

Huitabu, one kind of banana.

Huo, *s.* a kangaroo rat.

Hudo, *s.* navel.

Hudo. *See* Udo.

Huduna, *a.* thick, as a beard or mat.

Hūhū, *s.* single bananas, broken from different bunches, and taken or given to some one.

Huhula, a fish.

Hukea, *v.* (1) to break off, as single bananas ; (2) to gather.

Hula. *See* Hura.

Hulalaia, *v.* to open up, as a parcel, to uncover, to unroll.

Hulekau, *v.* or Hurekau, to be thrown up by the waves on to the beach.

Hulo tauna, *a.* industrious.

Huni, *v.* to cover, to hide. Hunia.

Huuu, *s.* dew.

Hunua, *v.* to make fast, as a rope.

Hura, *s.* matter, of an abscess.

Hura bamona, purulent.

Hura karaia, to suppurate.

Hure, *v.* to drift, to float.

Hureaisi, to be lifted up by tide or flood.

Hureadae, as Hureaisi.

Hurehure, *v.* to be rough, of the sea.

Hurekau, to be wrecked, as *Hulekau* above.

Huria, *v.* to wash, to scrub.

Huro, *s.* grindstone.

Hurokahuroka tauna, an albino.

Hururu, *v.* to lighten with a torch.

Hururu, *s.* a flame.

Hururuhururu, *a.* bright, shining.
Hururuhururua, *v.* to burnish.
Husihusi, *s.* wart or pimple.
Hutuma, *a.* many (of people).
Hutuma, *s.* company.
Hutuma, *a.* thick.

K

K is pronounced as English kettle.
Kaekae, *s.* a green parrot.
Kaemadahu, *s.* sweet potato.
Kaia, *s.* a knife.
Kaiakiri, one kind of banana.
Kaiva, *s.* a cooking pot, with a rim for the lid, a shell-fish.
Kaivakuku. a dancing mask; an idol.
Kau, *v.* (1) to reach a place. *Eme kau.* (2) To be in contact. (3) In composition it is added to verbs of placing, sitting, &c.
Kaua, *v.* to plait a cocoa-nut leaf round a tree in order to taboo it.
Kaubebe, *s.* a butterfly.
Kaukau, *a.* dry.
Kaukau, a prickly creeper.
Kabaia. See *Gabaia.*
Kabana, circumference, waist; hence *orooro kabanaai,* part of way up mountain.
Kabukabu, one kind of yam.
Kadidia, *s.* armpit.
  Kadidia ramuna, hair of the armpit.
Kadara, *s.* fun. Syn. Hevasea.
Kadava, *s.* platform between a double small canoe.
Kadoa, *v.* (1) To dip up water. *Ranu kadoa.* (2) To shovel.
Kagiua, *v.* to put an arm round a post, &c.
Kaha, *v.* to help. Kahai.
Kahau, *s.* (1) claw; (2) nail (finger or toe).
Kahana, *s.* side part of; a district.
Kāhi, *v.* to be jammed, to be too big to enter.
Kahi, *s.* a fence made with sticks, or split bamboos placed lengthwise, hurdle fence.
Kahai, *v.* to spit for roasting, as Hūla fish.
Kahiatao, to press down tight, as thatch with poles lashed.
Kahikahi, *adv.* near, not far.
Kahilakahila, as Kahikahi.

Kahoda, *a.* soft, well done (of cooked yams).
Kahua, *v.* to hold in the clenched hand, to hold tight.
Kahua kubolukubolu, clenched fist.
  Kahuatao, to hold in the clenched hand.
Kahuanege, *v.* to let go, to part.
Kahugo, one kind of yam.
Kakaimege, to wean. *Rata kakaimege.*
Kakabeda, name of a tree.
Kakakaka, *a.* red; any bright colour, purple.
Kakana, *s.* elder cousin, elder brother of brother, or sister of sister.
Kake, *s.* sharp ends of a canoe, &c.
Kakoro, *a.* dry, as withered leaves.
Kalai, *s.* white cockatoo.
Kalaka, *s.* (1) a temporary hut; (2) a tent; (3) a shelter made for sleeping under.
Kaleva, *s.* club (wooden).
Kalo, *v.* to paddle.
  Kaloa helulu, to compete in paddling.
Kaluhia. Kaluhiahu, *v.* to put the lid on, to cover up.
  Kaluhia ganna, lid.
  Kaluhia hebubu, upside down.
Kaluhioho, *v.* to take off the lid or cover.
Kamea, one kind of banana.
Kamea moa, one kind of banana.
Kamela, *s.* (*Introduced*) the camel.
Kamika, *s.* the large sinew of the thigh.
Kamo, *a.* sticky.
Kamoa, *v.* to adhere.
Kamokamo, *s.* that which sticks to the inside of the pot, as when arrowroot has been cooked. *Aniani kamokamo.*
Kamokamo, *s.* a kind of grass resembling wheat.
Kamonai, *interj.* hark !
Kamonai, *v.* (1) to hear; (2) to obey; (3) to believe.
Kamonai lasi, to be disobedient.
Kamonai, *s.* faith.
Kanudi, *v.* to spit; *s.* spittle.
Kanudia, *v.* to be spit on.
Kāpa, *s.* frontlet.
Kapakapa, *s.* a double small canoe.
Kapuatao, *v.* to press down on.
Kara, *v.* (with a suffix, karagu) to catch by contagion.

Kara, s. conduct, custom, habit.

Kara dika, sin.

Kara kerere kerere tauna, one who disregards taboo.

Karai, s. white cockatoo.

Karaia, v. to make, to do.

Karaia diba, can.

Karakara tauna, a worker.

Karaia toho, to endeavour.

Karandi, s. a fish spear with many points ; harpoon.

Karagoda, palm from which spears are made ; also name of spear made from it.

Karakara, a. fierce, as a wild pig ; quarrelsom (of village or individual.)

Karatoma, v. to do thus. (Preceeded by ini or unu).

Karikari, s. barb of arrow.

Karite, s. barley. (Introduced.)

Karoa, v. to divide, when there are many divisions.

Karoa, s. a division. Karoa rua, half.

Karoho, v. to be scattered, as troops defeated and retreating ; to disband. Karohorohoro.

Karohu, ridge cap.

Karu, s. a young cocoa-nut.

Karukaru, s. a babe.

Karukaru, a. immature, young, unripe.

Kasikasi, s. hard cooked sago in cakes ; (brought by Elema people from the gulf).

Kasili, raw, uncooked.

Katakata, s. (Preceded by dala), cross-roads.

Kāva, v. to be out of mind, crazed.

Kāva, a. crazed. Kāva bamona, frantic.

Kavaitoro, a fish.

Kavakava, s. folly.

Kavakava, a. (1) foolish ; (2) empty, without purpose. Hodu karakara; (3) only. Ranu karakava, water only.

Kavahu, s. (1) a bottle ; (2) a smooth white stone used as a charm ; (3) a pearl. Also Kavapu.

Kavabulubulu, s. eddy.

Kavapu, s. a bottle (foreign). See Kavabu.

Kavapukavapu, dim. of kavapu.

Kavera, edible mangrove.

Keadi, name of a shell fish.

Keavaro, name of a tree.

Keia, v. to roll over and over, as a heavy box.

Keiatao, to be struck by a stone rolling down a mountain side.

Keikei, s. a small cooking-pot.

Kebere, s. a cocoa-nut shell drinking-cup.

Keboka, s. megapodius. See Kepoka.

Kede, s. a torch.

Kedea, v. to adze a canoe.

Kehere, s. See Kebere.

Kehoa, v. to open. (The opposite of koua.) To unfasten.

Kekea, v. to coil (as a rope on the deck).

Kekeni, s. girl.

Kekenikekeni, s. dimunitive of kekeni.

Kekerema, name of a shell fish.

Kekero, to be stupified, as fish with duha, to be drunk.

Kema, s. the name of a bird, a coot.

Kemaiore, one kind of yam.

Keme, s. the chest.

Kemerosi, v. to fold the arms on chest.

Kepilakepila, crooked, similar to gagevagageva.

Kepoka. See Keboka.

Kepokipomu, with taia, he dalo, v. to disbelieve.

Keporāi, v. to turn away the head from one speaking. (A sign of disapproval.)

Kepulu, a. blind.

Kerehai, to turn round.

Kerekere, s. sun gone down. Dina kerekere.

Kerepa, s. small native ship, consisting of four or five asi.

Kerere, a. something in the eye, mata kerere.

Kerenai e vara, premature birth.

Kererekerere, v. to do a thing carelessly, heedlessly, without authority ; to blunder ; to err.

Keri, accumulation of drift, brought down by current or flood.

Keroro, name of a tree.

Keru, a. cold.

Kerukeru, adv. to-morrow.

Kerukeru, s. shade.

Kerukeru, a. shady (of place).

Keruma, Kerumakeruma, a. as Keru, cold. (Generally used of food.)

Kesi, s. a shield.

Ketara, s. (1) fresh cocoa-nut oil, without water added ; (2) the same cooked as sauce.

Keto, v. to slip ; to fall.

Keto dele, to slip or fall sideways.

Kevau, s. rainbow.

Kevakeva, name of a shell-fish.

Kevakulu, name of a shell-fish.

Kevaru, s. lightning. See Kibaru.

Kevaruaisi, v. to lighten. From Kevaru.

Kiamakiama, s. aglow (as embers) ; bright.

Kiapa, s. native netted bag.

Kio, s. muliebria.

Kibaru. See Kevaru.

Kibi, s. (1) a quail ; (2) a shéll trumpet.

Kibo, s. (1) a large round basin.

Kibokibo, s. a small basin.

Kibulu, s., a carved cocoa-nut shell pot with cover, for holding oil or fat.

Kidaiadiho, to throw down on ground.

Kidului, s. porpoise.

Kila, a fish.

Kilara. See Kirara.

Kili, or Kiri, v. to laugh.

Kili, s. sinkers to fishing-net.

Kilima, name of a tree.

Kiloki, s. the name of a bird, a parrakeet.

Kimai, s. a hook.

Kimagoi, v. to rob ; to steal continually (a term of abuse). Syn. Vahorita.

Kimore, Kimorekimore, a. bright ; pelished.

Kina, s. key. (Introduced.)

Kinigohina, s. early morning light, before the sun appears. (Preceded by daba.)

Kinoa, arrow flight.

Kinokino, s. a vane ; streamer.

Kipara, s. a scar.

Kirara, v. to open.

Kirara or Kilara, s. an attentive ear.

Kiri, v. to laugh. See Kili.

Kirikirilaia, to laugh at.

Kiriagaibogaibo, name of a shellfish.

Kiririkiriri, s. a chrysalis.

Kiroki, s. the name of a small parrot. Kiloki.

Kiroro, to inflate.

Kisikisi, name of a bird (the spurwinged plover).

Kito, v. to watch, as for an enemy or a thief ; to spy ; to guard.

Kitoa, v. to swoop down and pick up, as a hawk.

Kitokara, s. black cockatoo.

Koau, s. the cause. Oiemu koau, you are the cause. Lau koaugu, &c. Also koauna.

Koau, v. to speak.

Koauahu, to forbid.

Koauatao, to forbid ; to forgive. Pl. koaudiatao.

Koautubu, to counteract ; to frustrate ; to withstand.

Koauedeede, to be disobedient ; to refuse to do as told ; to be unwilling.

Koaubou, to concur ; to agree.

Koauhamata, to promise.

Koaukau, s. a message ; an errand.

Koaukavakoaukava, to guess.

Koaukoau, to growl ; to scold.

Koaulaia, to be spoken of ; to confess ; to bear witness.

Koautao. See Koauatao.

Koautoma, to speak thus. (Preceded by ini or unu.)

Koautora tauna, churlish.

Koautorehai, to borrow ; to have on credit.

Koauna, s. the cause. See Koau.

Koe. See Goe.

Koe, s. a small bag net.

Koea, v. to be turned end for side, to be turned half round.

Koeahilihili, whirlwind.

Koekoe, s. loins, hip, waist.

Koia, v. to betray, to cheat, to mislead.

Koikoi, v. to lie.

Koikoi, s. a lie.

Koikoi, a. untrue.

Koua, v. to enclose ; to block, as a road ; to close, as a door ; to fasten ; to shut.

Kouahu, v. as Koua.

Kouaka, s. the name of a bird.

Koukou, s. outside shell or hard covering. Niu koukouna.

Koukou, name of a tree.

Koupa, s. a chasm ; a ditch.

Koura, s. See Goura.

Kobi, s. (1) a needle ; (2) the name of a fish.

Kobo, Kobokobo, s. the firefly.

Kobo, *v.* to sprout.

Koda, *s.* (1) a man-catcher (a weapon used by Hula natives) ; (2) a pig-net.

Koge, *s.* a projecting point on a roof ; pinnacle.

Kohe, name of a tree.

Kohena, *s.* a priest. (From the Hebrew).

Kohi, one kind of yam.

Kohia, *v.* to break (of hard things).

Kohoro, *s.* tower.

Kohu, *v.* to be wrecked ; broken to pieces (of a house).

Kohu, *s.* property ; wealth ; riches. Kohudia, booty.

Kohua, *s.* a cave.

Kohutania, *v.* to leave, desert, as a village, on account of sickness.

Koke, *v.* to creak.

Kokia, *v.* to draw out, to extract.

Kokiaoho, *v.* to uncork, &c. ; to un-string a bow.

Koko, *s.* (1) a baler ; (2) a gate.

Kokoa, *v.* to nail ; to drive in, as a nail.

Kokoauru, *v.* to break open a cocoa-nut for drinking.

Kokoara, a native package of sago, weighing 30 or 40 lb.

Kokokoko, *s.* the cassowary.

Kokome, one kind of banana.

Kokopa, *s.* a crab.

Kokorogu, one kind of yam.

Kokosi, *v.* to arrange (things).

Kokosia, *v.* to keep intact.   *See* Gogosia.

Kokuroku, *s.* domestic fowl.

Kokuroku, *v.* to be proud, boastful.

Koloa, *s.* notch.

Komata gui, *s.* low water.

Komoge, *s.* the peak of a mountain top ; the top of a tower, spire, &c.

Komu, *v.* to hide.

Komukau, a bird.

Komukomu (preceded by *ae*), an ancle.

Komuta, *s.* a hill.   *Orooro komuta.*

Komutu, *s.* the core of a boil.

Konaka, *s.* the name of a bird.

Kone, *s.* the beach, the sea-coast.

Kopaia, *v.* to skin.

Kopana, *s.* the lap (lit. the front of the body).

Kopi, *s.* (1) the skin ; (2) surface of the earth, sea, &c.

Kopi auka, *s.* (1) a fearless climber, &c. ; (2) indifferent to cold, &c.

Kopi hemarai, *v.* to be ashamed.

Kopukopu, *s.* mud, swamp.

Korema, *a.* any dark colour, brown.

Korema, *s. bêche de mer.*

Koremakorema, *a.* black.

Koria, *v.* to bite, to gnaw, to sting.

Korikori, *a.* true, real, original, native, genuine.

Koroa, *v.* to break off twigs or blaze trees, so as to mark the road.

Koroha, a short spear.

Kororo, *v.* to subside, as water.

Kororokororo, *a.* all (generally used with mate).

Korua, one kind of yam.

Kuadi, name of a shell-fish.

Kuarakuara, *v.* to froth, as a fast boiling pot.

Kuia, to knead.

Kuomenau, the name of a shell-fish.

Kubaba, *s.* a short cocoa-nut tree.

Kubolukuboln, *a.* globular, round.

Kudekude, a long grass.

Kudima, *a.* deaf.

Kudou, *s.* the heart (physical). Kudou hetaha, consternation.

Kuhi, *s.* a skin disease (frambœsia?)

Kuhikuhi, *s.* a painful skin disease, with intense itching.

Kuku, *s.* tobacco.

Kuku ania, to smoke.

Kuku, *v.* to go to stool.

Kuluha, name of a tree.

Kumia, *s.* to wrap ; enfold.

Kunamaka, *s.* the name of a bird.

Kunu, *v.* to be satisfied (always used with *boka*).

Kunu, *s.* (1) anus ; (2) keel of a ship, &c.

Kunu rahubou, to slap buttocks in defiance.

Kunukunu, name of a shell-fish.

Kunuiabiahuna, *s.* the last born.

Kunukakunuka, *adv.* of intensity, added to verbs signifying to tie, to close, &c. ; *a.* secure.

Kurea, *v.* to turn over.   Kureaoho, to roll away.

Kureadobi, to drop down from one's hand.

Kureahu, to turn over.

Kureatao, *v.* (1) to be struck by a large mass, as a landslip ; (2) to be overwhelmed by it.

Knrebou, *s.* a heap of stones, yams, &c.

Kuri, *see* Guri.

Kurita, a little water, oil, &c. *See* Gurita.

Kurokakuroka, *a.* pale.

Kurokuro, *a.* white.

Kuroro, *v.* to inflate, to swell, to distend.

Kuru, *v.* to run at the nose.

Kururu, the name of a shell-fish.

Kurukuru, *s.* long grass used for thatching.

Kurukuruna, *s.* snout.

Kusita, one kind of banana.

L

L is sounded as in English.

La, a prefix to five when counting persons. Laima.

Lāi, *s.* breeze, wind.

Laia, name of a shell-fish.

Laia, *v.* to get ready a large canoe for a voyage.

Lailaia, to prepare, to clear the road.

Laia, postfixed to verbs to mark the instrument.

Lailai, *s.* the name of a month (March).

Laima, *a.* five (men).

Laina, name of a shell-fish.

Lao, *s.* a fly.

Lao, *v.* to go.

Laoahu, to stop, to turn back, to prevent.

Laoevaeva, to go about from place to place.

Laohaia, to take away, to clear away.

Laoheni, to render, to give to.

Laoho, *s.* preceded by dolu, humpback.

Laolao, *s.* a journey.

Lau, *pron.* 1.

Lauagu, *pron.* my (of food).

Lanegu, *pron.* my.

Laukoko, *s.* leaf of banana cut with the fruit,—a superstitious ceremony.

Laulau, *s.* (1) a shadow, a spirit; (2) a photograph; (3) a picture, image.

Laulabada, *s.* South-east monsoon.

Laulabada kahana, *s.* South-east.

Lauma, *s.* a spirit; formerly used only of ghosts of those killed, who appeared in terrible form.

Laumaere, a fish.

Laumadaure, *v.* to be startled, surprised, to be confounded.

Laumea, *v.* to mend nets.

Lauri, *a.* left (hand).

Laba, *s.* an ornament of a house or ship, to fly in the wind. The distinguishing mark of the Mavara family.

Lababana, *a.* wide, as cloth, road, &c.

Lababana, *s.* breadth.

Labana, *v.* to hunt.

Labana eno, to go hunting, and sleep out.

Labolabo, *s.* wild bee.

Lāda, *s.* gills.

Ladana, *s.* name.

Lade, *s.* one kind of coral.

Ladi, a fish.

Lado, to bear down as in labour, to bow the head in dance.

Lado henia, } *v.* to assent by a sign,
Lado, tari, } a nod.

Ladorāi, to nod from sleepiness.

Lāga, *s.* (1) an earthquake; (2) the name of a month (September).

Lāga, *v.* to breathe.

Lagaani, lit, to eat one's breath, to rest. Laga takes suffixes. When an abscess is lanced, and the matter flows out, the patient being relieved says, *Harihari, lagāku name ani varani lau hisi mo ani.*

Lagadae, to pant.

Lagadobu, to be long-winded.

Lagaga, to be frightened, nervous, not speak from fear.

Laganege, to breathe stertorously, as a dying person.

Lagatuna, *a.* breathless.

Lagāi, *s.* the name of a fish.

Lagāua, *s.* disrespect.

Lagadaelagadae, *v.* to pant, to sob.

Lagalaga, name of a shell-fish.

Lagani, *s.* year.

Lagatuna, *s.* dyspnœa, shortwinded.

Lagere, a fish.

Laguahia, *v.* to strike in falling, as the head, arm, &c.

Laguta, *s.* salt-pans.

Laha, *s.* large native ship, consisting of ten or twelve *asi.*

Lahai, *s.* uncle, aunt, cousins.

Lahaia, *v.* to spread a cloth, mat, &c. ; to strew.

Lahalaha, the name of a fish.

Lahara, *s.* north-west wind, and season.

Laharaia, to prepare large sail of *lakatoi*, by renewing strings, patching, &c.

Lahedo, *v.* to be lazy.

Lahedo, *a.* lazy.

Laheta, a fish.

Lahi, *s.* fire. Lahi alaia, a burn. Lahi hururuhururu, a flame. Lahi äuna, fuel.

Lahulahu, *adv.* imperfectly (with verb, to hear).

Laka *v.* to step, to walk, to go. Lakaia hanai, to walk past. Laka diho, to go down to the bottom of the water feet first. (Opp. to *edai*, to dive.) *Davara lalona lakadiho*

Lakaiahu, to cross street.

Lakahaheguna, to walk in single file.

Lakahekako, to walk side by side, with linked fingers or joined hands.

Lakahekapu, to walk side by side.

Laka magogomagogo, to slink.

Lakahelada, to walk stealthily.

Lakakahila, to draw near.

Lakakerere, to lose oneself, to mistake the road.

Laka lasi, to go outside, to walk out.

Laka metailametaila, to saunter.

Laka muri, backwards ; *v.* to recede.

Lakaroho, to take long steps, to stride along.

Laka sili, to step aside.

Lakatania, to be left, left behind.

Lakatoi, *s.* a ship, a native vessel, made by lashing three or more large canoes together. Lakatoi tauna, captain. Lakatoi aniua, freight.

Lakara, *s.* a whale, or some sea monster larger than a dugong.

Lakara donodono, as Lakara.

Laketo, the name of a shellfish.

Lakia, see also Rakia, to draw a pipe.

Lalo, *s.* the inside ; the mind. Lalona, the inside of a thing ; the mind, the seat of the affections. Lalona auka, to be venturesome.

Laloa *v.* to think, to remember.

Lalo auka, to be self restrained.

Lalo haguhi, to cogitate.

Lalo haraga, to desire a thing from seeing, or to do a thing because others are doing it.

Laloa hereqa, to forget.

Laloalu, to cloy.

Laloatao, (1) to bear in mind, to treasure up in the mind and wait for an opportunity of revenge ; (2) to keep a thing to oneself, to keep a secret.

Laloatao, *adj.* secret.

Laloboio, to forget.

Lalo bubu, hymen irrupt. With *kekeni*, a virgin.

Lalo dagu, to exclaim.

Laloharaga, *v.* to do cheerfully, willingly. *See* above.

Lalohegani, to desire from seeing. *Lalogu heyani. Lalogu hahegania.*

Lalokau, (1) to be beloved, endeared ; (2) (of things or food) to be satisfied, or have pleasure in.

Lalokau henia, *v.* to love, to delight in.

Lalokoau, to think, to conjecture.

Lalometau, to do unwillingly.

Lalonamo tanna cheerful.

Laloparara, to be intelligent, to understand.

Lalo tamona, to agree.

Lamaboha, *s.* bald head.

Lamadaia, *v.* to wipe off mud from the feet, &c.

Lamanu, *s.* resin, used when burnt as lamp-black for tattooing.

Lamepa, *s.* a lamp. (*Introduced.*)

Lanalana, *v.* to stammer.

Lapaia, *v.* to strike as with a sword or flat weapon. Lapaiaoho, to smite off.

Laqa, *s.* flax, from which small fishing-nets (*reke*) are made.

Lara, *s.* (1) a large mat sail of *lakatoi*; (2) a ship's sail.

Lara, *v.* to move about while sitting, by propelling with the hands.

Laralara, *s.* the bottom row of chalking in the native ship (*lakatoi*).

Larea, to adjust arrow on string.

Lareba, *v.* to build up stones. *Nadi larebaia.*

Lari, larilari, *v.* to jet out, as blood from a cut artery.

Larilaria, to gush.

Lari, *s.* rash, as in measles.

Laria, Raria, *s.* fine sand.

Laro, *s.* one kind of shellfish ; the shell is used for cutting and paring, &c.

Laroa, *v.* to wait for, to expect.

Larolaro, *s.* shoulder-blade.

Lasi, *v.* to arrive.

Lasi, *adv.* no ; not.

Lasi, *adv.* (the u is slightly shorter than in the negative) outside, as to walk outside, pull outside, &c. Lasilaia.

Lasihia, *v.* to be gone, disappear; Pl. Lasihidia.

Lasi henia, *v.* to receive visitors with respect.

Lasihi, *v.* to be finished and gone, as a year. *Eme lasihi.*

Lasikalasika (*yeme*), inflamed chest.

Lasilāi, *s.* wind from between north and east.

Lāta, *s.* length.

Lāta, *a.* tall.

Lataia, *v.* to condemn to death some one who is absent. Also, Rataia.

Lataba, name of a tree.

Latalata, *a.* long, tall.

Latana, or Ladana, *s.* the top side, on the top of.

Latanai, *prep.* on. Also, *adv.*

Lato. *See* Lado.

Lāva, *s.* a message sent to warn a village of an arranged attack. *Lāva Koiari mailaia.*

Lava, *s.* joists.

Lavara, *s.* a large serpent.

Lave, *s.* halyard (of ship).

Lavu, *s.* a mallet.

Leilei, *s.* a board.

Lebulebu, *s.* boisterous, unseemly mirth.

Lega haraga, *v.* to be quick in doing things.

Lega haraga, *adv.* quickly.

Lega metau, *v.* to be slow in doing things.

Legu Legulegu, *v.* to tend, take care of, as a sick person, animal, goods, &c.

Legua, to nurse a sick person, to tend.

Lele, *v.* to swim, as fish.

Lepeta, *s.* farthing. *(Introd. from the Greek.)*

Leta, *s.* cocoa-nut leaf.

Lioa, *v.* to put on the woman's petti-coat. *Rami lioa.*

Lilia, *v.* to grate, as yams.

Lo, *a* ripe, mature.

Lo, comforted.

Loa, *v.* to walk about.

Loalaia, to walk about with, as with a sick child.

Lou, *adv.* again. Loulou, frequent.

Lou, *c.* to return.

Loulaia, to take back.

Loulou, *adv.* constantly.

Loulou, *s.* spathe enclosing the cocoa-nut blossom.

Loulaia, *v.* to restore.

Lobu, *s.* the name of a fish, grey mullet. *See* Robu.

Loduhenia, *v.* to accuse, to reproach.

Loge. *See* Roge.

Logea tauna, or Rogea tauna, *s.* an industrious man, one who stores.

Logologo, *v.* to talk imperfectly, as a young child.

Logora, *a.* the whole of, many. (Used of numbers.) Great, all.

Lohala, *s.* (1) the edge of a net. *Uto lohala,* the top edge. *Kili lohala,* the bottom edge. (2) The small line which fastens the two edges together.

Lohia, *s.* a chief.

Lohiabada, chief, a gentleman, a courteous term of address.

Lohilohi. *See* Gado lohilohi.

Lohilohia *v.* to bubble up.

Lokaloka, *a.* (1) ripe, mature ; (2) stiff.

Lōki, *s.* pain in the limbs, rheuma-tism.

Lokohu, *s.* the name of a bird, *Paradisea raggiana.*

Lokoru, *s.* the spine at the back of the neck. Lokolu.

Lokua, *v.* to double up, to fold, to roll up.

Lolo, *v.* to shut out, to call out in a loud voice, to brawl.

Lolodagu, to startle by shouting. Tai lololo, to cry out lustily.

Loria, *v.* to vomit.

Lovai, one kind of yam.

Love, *s.* a swing.

Love, *v.* to swing.

Lūa, *v.* to forbid, to restrain.

Lulua, *v.* to drive away, to banish, Luluaoho.

Lulululu, to drive away continuously.

Lulua, *v.* to put on the shell armlet.

Luluki, *v.* to strip off the stem by drawing through the hand or fingers.

Lulululu. *See* Lulua.

M

M pronounced as in English.

Ma, before verbs, marking continued action.

Maela, *s.* the name of a fish.

Maeta, *v.* to be done, of things cooked.

Mai, *conj.* and, with.

Mai, *v.* to come.

Mailaia, to bring.

Maihenia, to fetch.

Maiali or Maiari, *s.* white feather head-dress.

Maikumaiku *a.* very small.

Mailu, *s.* evening twilight.

Mailumailu, *s. See* Mairumairu.

Maimera, a fish.

Maimu, small (of thread, &c.)

Maimumaimu, *a.* very small; wasted by sickness.

Maino, *s.* peace.

Maire, *s.* mother-of-pearl.

Mairiveina, *s.* the East.

Mairumairu, *s.* dusk.

Maita, name of a tree. (Rose apple.)

Mao, *s.* gums.

Maoa tauna, *s.* passenger ; also, Gui maoa tauna.

Maoaia, *v.* to go as passenger.

Maoheni, *v.* to betroth.

Maora, *s.* bowstring.

Maoro, Maoromaoro, *a.* straight, correct.

Maña, *s.* box.

Maula, or Maura, *s.* a small thing, as a spoon, netted bag, &c., given as a pledge to remind the recipient of his promise to return.

Maulu, *v.* (1) to make a hole, as in the skull, *hodu,* &c. ; (2) to be spoilt.

Maumau, *v.* to grumble, to complain.

Maumaulaidia, to grumble at.

Maura. *See* Maula.

Mauri, *s.* life.

Mauri bada, luxuriant.

Mauri maragimaragi, convalescent.

Mabau, *s.* the pouch of a marsupial.

Mabui, a fish.

Madaimadai, *a.* giddy.

Madi be, *conj.* because.

Madinamo, plenty (of food), good harvest.

Madina, one kind of yam.

Mādu, *s.* opening.

Maduna, *s.* a burthen, with the carrying pole.

Māga, *a.* brackish.

Magani, *s.* the wallaby.

Maganibada, *s.* ridge-pole.

Magasi, *s.* very low night tide.

Māge, *a.* ripe, as bananas.

Magela, *s.* a spider.

Magemage, *s.* the name of a bird.

Magi, name of a tree.

Magu, *s.* fortress.

Magugu, *a.* creased, wrinkled.

Magugu, *v.* to crease, to wrinkle.

Maho, *s.* yam.

Maho kavabu, *s.* a smooth stone used as a charm, to make yams grow.

Mahuta, *v.* to sleep. Mabuta tauna, sluggard.

Mahuta gauna, a bed.

Mahuta maragi, to slumber.

Māka, *s.* a crack, notch, as in the edge of a knife, a crevice.

Māka, *v.* to be broken, as a hole in a fence.

Makoa, a fish.

Makohi, *v.* to break, as crockery.

Makohi haraga, *a.* brittle.

Makona and Mokona, *adv.* almost, all but.

Makota, one kind of yam.

Mala, *s.* tongue.

Mala reho, *s.* the thrush.

Mala, *s.* edible stem of banana.

Malaua, *s.* the name of a fish.

Maladoki, to speak a language imperfectly, as a foreigner.

Malakamalaka, *adv.* patiently, persistently, carefully.

Malamala, *s.* food generally.

Malamala, *s.* wide platform at the end of *lakatoi.*

Maloa, *v.* to drown, to founder.

Maloa, one kind of yam.

Malohevani, *s.* about 10 o'clock at night.

Malokihi, *s.* midnight.

Mama e ! child's term of address to his father.

Mamatau, name of a shell-fish.

Mamano, *a.* weak, from sickness.

Mami, *s.* (1) spoil ; (2) prey, as on returning from fishing, &c. *Idia e mami.*

Māmi, *s.* the name of a fish.

Mami. Mamina, *s.* flavour (of food). *Lau mamia toho ia mamina namo.*

Mamoe *s.* sheep. (*Introduced.*)

Mamu, *s.* the thigh.

Manau, *a.* humble. Manau tauna, lowly.

Manada, *v.* to be accustomed to, to be tame.

Manada, *a.* even, smooth, gentle. Manadamanada, to be smooth, tame. Manada tauna, a good-tempered man.

Managa, *s.* land far away from the village.

Managi, *s.* the name of a fish.

Manahala, *s.* the name of a fish.

Manariha, a fish.

Mani, prefix to many verbs in the present tense, *Lau mani ai name itaia.* Sometimes it has the meaning of, to try, *Oi mani a karaia.*

Manoka. Manokamanoka, *a.* (1) weak ; (2) cowardly ; (3) lazy. Of things, weak, soft.

Manokamanoka tauna, coward.

Manonoha, one kind of yam.

Manori, *v.* to faint, to be fatigued.

Mānu, *s.* a bird. Manu rumana, nest.

Manumanu, *s.* (1) beetles, insects ; (2) the name of a stinging fish.

Manumaura, *s.* the name of a month (October).

Mapau. *See* Mabau.

Mara, *v.* to give birth.

Marai, *v.* (1) to wither ; (2) to be exhausted either from work or disease ; (3) to be parched by the sun.

Maraua, *a.* striped.

Maraua, a fish.

Maragi, *a.* small. Maragina, least. Maragimaragi, slender.

Maramara, *s.* umbrella-shaped rock in the sea and on the reef.

Marere, *a.* bent, slanting.

Mari, *s.* ceremony of cracking fingers to know if a vessel (*lakatoi*) is coming.

Mari tauna, one skilled in doing *mari.*

Mariboi, *s.* bat.

Mariva, *s.* after-pains.

Maruane, *s.* the male sex.

Māta, *s.* bandicoot.

Mata, *s.* (1) the eye ; (2) point of anything ; (3) mesh.

Mata dika, lascivious.

Mata gani, to take warning.

Mata ganigani, covetous, greedy.

Mata gara, to shun.

Mata garaia, sleepy.

Mata gegeva, to squint.

Mata kani. *See* Mata gani.

Mata hisihisi, ophthalmia.

Mata kepulu, blind.

Mata madaimadai, giddy.

Mata nadinadi, the pupil of the eye.

Mata paia, to dazzle.

Mata papa, to look pleased.

Mata rauna, eye-lashes.

Mata taia, *v.* to sleep a little when very tired.

Mataatu, name of a shell-fish.

Mataia, *v.* to tie, to fasten.

Matauna, *s.* respect, reverence.

Mataurai, Matanraia, *v.* to respect, reverence.

Matāboi, *s.* a large rope.

Matabudi, *s.* turtle.

Matadidi, *s.* a whitlow, a painful gathering on the hand.

Matakaka, a fish.

Matalahui, to be heedless, to see imperfectly.

Matalahui, *adj.* careless, heedless.

Matama, *s.* beginning. Matamana, Matamaia, *v.* to begin.

Matamata, *a.* new, fresh.

Matana, *s.* tip.

Matana dika, *v.* to be overcast to windward.

Matapala, a stone hatchet, large and broad.

Mate *v.* to die.

Mate diba lasi, immortal.

Mate gauna, venomous.

Mate, *adv.* of intensity, as *tahua mate.*

Matekamateka, languidly.

Matelea, *v.* to faint.

Matemate, used as an intensive with hebiri, hesede, &c.

Matoamatos, *s.* lily. (Introduced name.)

Matoatorea, (of moon) about third quarter.

Mātu *s.* a hole, a channel.

Matuna, *s.* orifice.

Mava, *s.* white matter on the body of a newborn infant.

Mavamava, *v.* to yawn.

Mavaru, *s.* a dance.

Mavaru, *v.* to dance.

Me, particle added to vowel of past time, as, *name*, *eme* &c. It is also used with other particles, but does not seem to add to their meaning.

Meamea, *s.* incantation, prayer. Always in a bad sense, to bring misfortune, trouble, or death on the subject of it.

Mei, *s.* urine.

Menraba, one kind of banana.

Medai, shelter.

Medai, *v.* to shelter.

Medai gabuna, *s.* haven.

Mede, *s.* the temples.

Medu, *s.* rain.

Memeuse, *s.* chip.

Memehute, a fish.

Meqa, *s.* bread-fruit kernel.

Mero, *s.* a boy. Plural, memero. Mero garugaru, a male infant; bigger than *mero karukaru*. Mero karukaru, a male infant. Meromero, dimin. of mero. Mero bamona, boyish.

Metailametaila, *adv.* carefully, deliberately.

Metailametaila, *a.* cautious, deliberate.

Metau, *a.* heavy, arduous.

Mia, *v.* to leave, to allow. Pl., mimia. Mia hanaihanai, to continue, to last.

Miara, *s.* female kangaroo.

Mida, a fish.

Midava, *s.* a grave, after boards, &c., have been removed.

Migu, *s.* the echidna.

Mikamika, an intensive word used with *Herea*.

Mimia, *v.* Plural of Mia.

Minagaminaga, *a.* rotten, of wood. Used after Houkahouka.

Minagoru, one kind of yam.

Minibore, name of a shellfish.

Minimini, name of a shellfish.

Miri, *s.* small gravel.

Mirigini, *s.* (1) north wind; (2) north.

Miro, *s.* dirt.

Miro, *a.* dirty.

Mo, *adv.* only (with *s.*), indeed (*intensive* with *v.*).

Moa, a fish with long projecting lower jaw.

Moale, *v.* to rejoice.

Moale, *s.* delight. Moalena, happiness.

Moemoe, *s.* reef, both barrier and detached.

Moia, to tread on.

Moiatao, *v.* to be trod upon.

Moidedi, steps slipping.

Monkamonka, *v.* to be rotten (of cloth).

Moda, *s.* a bag.

Mogea, *v.* to twist. *See* Mokea.

Mogo, *s.* the name of a tree.

Mokea, *s.* to twist off, as a cocoanut from its stalk.

Moko, *adv.* almost.

Mokona. *See* Makona.

Mokorereva, *s.* the name of a bird.

Momo, *s.* rubbish; *a. fig.*, plenty, many.

Mōmo, *s.* the placenta.

Momokani, *a.* true, faithful. Momokani etomamu, certain.

Momoruna, *s.* crumbs, &c.

Mone, *s.* cakes of sago, taro, &c.; loaf.

Monege, *v.* to race, as canoes.

Moneke, *v.* to be pock-pitted.

Moni, *s.* money. (*Introduced.*)

Mora, *s.* the name of a small land crab.

Moru, *v.* to fall from a height.

Moru, *s.* the name of a fish.

Motu, *b.* to break, as string.

Motu, *s.* the name of a race of natives living at Port Moresby and neighbourhood.

Motumotu, *s.* island; detached portion of the reef.

Mu, *s.* (1) a door; (2) a slab of a tree.

Mu, *v.* (1) to coo as a dove; (2) to be dumb.

Mukia, *v.* to break up and crush leaves in the hand.

Muko, *s.* handkerchief.

Mukoro, *s.* the nose-stick; a beam.

Mukuroa, larvæ of hornet, &c.

Mumu, *s.* turtle egg,

Mumuta, *v.* to vomit.
Muramura, *s.* medicine.
Muramura tauna, doctor.
Murimuri, *s.* outside.
Murina, *s.* the back of anything. *Ruma murina.*
Murina hadikaia, to backbite.
Murina laka, to follow.
Murinai, *a.* next.
Muritai, *a.* younger. With tau or haine.
Musia, *v.* to suck, as a bone, or a cocoanut through the eye, with smacking noise of the lips.
Mutu, *v.* to sink.
Mutu, *v.* to express by squeezing, as cocoanut oil.
Mutuma, *s.* white ant.
Mututania, to sink away from.

N

N is pronounced as in English.
Na, *pron.* 1. Used instead of *lau. Na kamonaimu. Na vasimu.* Particle for 1st pers. sing., and placed between pronoun and verb, as, *lau na diba.*
Na, suffix for 3rd pers. sing., his.
Naidae, *s.* the name of a fish.
Naimenaime, *s.* a flying ornament of house or ship distinguishing the Vahoi family.
Naimuro, one kind of banana.
Nao, *s.* white men.
Nāu, *s.* an eathenware dish or bowl.
Naua, *v.* to scrape, to polish, to plane.
Naua gauna, *s.* plane.
Nadi, *s.* (1) a stone ; (2) iron, metal.
Nadi gabuna, stony.
Nadi larebaia, to build a stone wall.
Nadikuro, a rock in the sea, as coral, &c. (Not so high as *haga.*)
Nadinadi, (1) small stones ; (2) seed ; (3) the kidneys ; (4) shot.
Nadi kubolukubolu, pebble.
Nado, *interj.* of surprise. *Lau dahakai nado.*
Nadua, *v.* to cook by boiling.
Nahu, *v.* to swim.
Nahu hanai, to swim across, as a river.
Nahu, spear of red wood, (used both in hunting and war.)

Nahuana tohoa, to be watchful, to be careful.
Nala, *v.* 1st pers. sing. past, from *lao,* to go.
Nama, *v.* 1st pers. sing. past, from *mai,* to come.
Name, *na* and *me.* 1st person sing. pro with euphonic *me.*
Namo, *a.* good. Namonamo, careful.
Namo herea, becoming, choice.
Namo, *s.* mosquito.
Namumaua, a fish.
Nanaia, *v.* (1) to warm the hands over the fire ; (2) to shampoo a sick person with warmed hands ; (3) to toast.
Nanaia, *v.* (1) to bespeak a thing ; (2) to give payment for praise— *Oi dahaka mamo ? Oi qarume abia lau nanaia.* (3) payment by the one who sees the new moon first.
Nanadai, *v.* to question, to inquire.
Nanadu, *v.* to cook. (A general term.)
Nanadu tauna, a cook.
Naniko, *s.* a wasp.
Napera, cigarette wrapper.
Nara, name of tree, (similar to cedar but harder.)
Nāri, *v.* more commonly naria, (1) to wait for, to expect ; (2) to take care of.
Natuadora, *s.* a child whose parents are living. The opposite of *ihareha,* an orphan.
Natudia, *s.* progeny.
Natuna, *s.* (1) child ; (2) the young of animals.
Natuna karukaru, babe.
Natuna momo, prolific.
Natu rabai, *s.* nephew or niece.
Nega, *s.* time.
Nega daudau, a long time.
Nega dika, a bad time, misfortune.
Nega hoho, often.
Nega idoinai, constantly.
Negana, season.
Nege, *adv.* used in composition signifying, "away from," *Kahuaneye* to let go.
Negea, *v.* to throw away, to relinquish.
Negea dobi, to throw away from one and down.
Nēka, *a.* limpid, clear.
Nemaia, *v.* to name.
Nese, *s.* ridge of mountain or hill.

G

Nese hanai, to cross a river on a fallen tree as a bridge.

Neseriki, crew of boat or ship. *Neseriki memero.*

Nevaria, *v.* to sprinkle.

Niu,*s.* cocoanut tree and mature fruit.

Nihi, *v.* to dream.

Ninoa, *s.* mountain mist, fog, vapour.

Noinoi, *v.* (1) to beg ; (2) to entreat.

Noi hegame, to beg.

Noga. Noka, *v.* to wake.

Nogo, *s.* the name of a crane. Also Noko.

Noho, *v.* to dwell.

Nohobou, to dwell together.

Noho dika, to be in misfortune.

Noho kava negana, leisure.

Nohu, *s.* the name of a stinging fish.

Noka. *See* Noga.

Noko, *s.* a sea-bird, a crane. *See* Nogo.

Nonoa, *v.* to roast on sticks—(of fish only) broil.

Nononono, name of a shell-fish.

Nonu, name of a tree.

Noro, *s.* the name of a fruit. (Similar to *maita.*)

Nua, *s.* inner bark of a tree.

Nuana bada, *a.* corpulent.

Nuia, *v.* to place a water or cooking pot on the ground. *Hodu nuia.*

Nuiakau. As Nnia.

Nuiakubou and Nuiabou, to put food dishes or bowls together in one place in preparation for eating.

Nubagana, *v.* to be unoccupied, waste. (Of land.)

Nudugara, *s.* the name of a shell-fish. (One kind of oyster.)

Nulu, *s.* (1) the fibrous substance which grows round the base of the cocoanut leaf, the *stipule ;* (2) coarse cloth ; (3) a sack.

Nurina, *s.* dregs.

P

P pronounced as in English, sometimes scarcely distinguishable from B.

Pai, *s.* a shrimp.

Paia, *v.* to be bedazzled, as by looking at the sun.

Paila, *s.* pink earth, used for painting the face.

Pailipaili, *v.* to be taut.

Paitapaita, to blaze.

Pāu, *s.* (1) a cardboard-like covering for feather plumes, &c., *Mānu pāu ;* (2) banana-leaf venetian flag.

Paudae, *v.* to jump down into the sea from the beach.

Paudobi, *v.* to jump down into the sea from a canoe, &c.

Pāda, *s.* a disease resembling palsy.

Pāda, *s.* (1) the space between earth and sky, air ; (2) the space between any two places ; distance.

Padaia, *v.* to gather by breaking the stalk.

Pāga, *s.* the shoulder.

Pāko, a small chisel.

Pakosi, *s.* scissors. (*Introduced.*)

Palaheni, *adv.* quietly, carefully.

Palakapalaka, *a.* flat, as a board, &c.

Palapala, *s.* hand, *ima palapala ; ae palapala,* foot.

Panadagu, to stamp with foot.

Pāpa, *v.* to burst, to hatch (eggs) ; to open the eyes.

Pāpa bada, *s.* a flat rock.

Papalau, *s.* (with tauna or haine), sorcerer.

Papapapa, *s.* flat rock.

Pāpu, *v.* to go in mourning. *Ia kakana mate pāpuna.*

Paraoa, *s.* flour. (*Introduced.*)

Parara, *v.* to be split, opened, divided. *Lalo parara,* opened mind, enlightened.

Paravalo, *s.* a shelter, as a roof without walls.

Parikaparika, *a.* clammy, damp.

Paripari, *v.* to be wet.

Paroparo, a frog.

Pasi, a weeded space all round fence of garden.

Pata, *s.* a shelf, a table.

Pata, rotten (as a dead body), corruption ; boiled to pieces.

Pataia, *v.* to pat.

Patakapataka, *v.* to be overdone (of food), to be boiled to rags.

Patapata, *v.* (intens. of pataia), to continue to pat. *Ima patapata,* to clap hands.

Pēka, *s.* spathe of *kamokamo,* from which the ear bursts.

Pepe, *s.* banner.

Pcrepere, *s.* young cocoanut when nearly ripe. *Karu perepere.*

Perukaperuka, *a.* flexible, not stiff. The opposite of *tororo.*

Petaia, _v._ to bale by jerking the water out.

Petapetalaia, _v._ (1) to splash over ; (2) to waste.

Peva, _s._ a bow.

Piu henia, _v._ to spread a report.

Piua, _hari puia_, to spread a report.

Piuaisi. _See_ Piuadae, to lift up on a pole.

Piuadae, _v._ to take a fly, &c., out of of water.

Piupiulaia, _v._ to squander, waste.

Pidia, _v._ to fillip.

Pidipidi, _v._ to knock, to fillip ; hence pidia, to shoot with a gun.

Pilateri, _s._ phylactery. (_Introd. from the Greek._)

Pipitaia, _v._ to clean out a pot or dish by wiping out with the fore-finger.

Pisili, _s._ spray.

Pisipisina, _v._ to splash.

Pisi rohoroho, _n._ to shatter.

Pitopito, _s._ (1) small insects, such as weevils, &c. ; (2) a button. (_Introduced._)

Pou, _v._ (1) to burst, from fermen-tation, &c. : (2) to be crushed, as a reed, &c.

Poudagu, _v._ to explode.

Pouka, _a._ rotten, of fruit.

Podi, _v._ to glance off, as a spear.

Pohuatao, _v._ to beat into, as waves into a ship.

Poporaia, _v._ to be closed up, to have no rain (used only with Guba).

Popoto, _s._ a steep river-bank.

Poruporu, young _nara_ tree before it becomes red.

Pose, cat. (_Introduced._)

Posi, _s._ the bladder.

Pudipudi, preceded by _boka_ ; pain in bowels, followed by diarrhœa.

Puki, to slip off, or out of.

Pūla, _s._ a very high night tide.

Pulu, or Puhulu, large stick for fence-making.

Puue, _s._ the common Torres Straits pigeon.

Pune gobu, large blue pigeon.

Puripuri regena, a rib joint of pork.

Purukia, _v._ } To spit out.
Pururua, _v._ }

Puse, _s._ sack. (_Introduced._)

Puta, _s._ sponge.

Putaro, a lichen which grows on stones under water.

Q

Q. As in English in queen.

Qa, to speak. _See_ Koau.

Qaidu, _v._ to be broken, as stick, bone, &c.

Qauta, _a._ ten. Qauta ima, fifteen. Quata ta, eleven.

Qabira, a stone hatchet, rough and strong, for felling trees.

Qabuqabudia, the remaining few.

Qada, a fish.

Qadaia, _v._ to pierce with a spear ; to wound ; to run a splinter into the foot, to be cut with a stone, to stab.

Qadaqadaia, _v._ to shake, as water in a bottle.

Qadi, _s._ a locust.

Qadia, _v._ (1) to strike as with a rope ; (2) to fan away flies, &c. Qadilaia, that against which a thing is qadia, as to take a dog by its legs and dash its head against a stone.

Qadoa, _v._ to prick out holes, as in a sieve, &c.

Qadobe, _v._ to cork.

Qadogi, _a._ short, concise, low.

Qagiloa, _v._ to go about together, to be inseparable.

Qagiqagi, _s._ toes or fingers, according as it is preceded by _ae_ or _ima_. Qagiqagi dodori, the fore-finger.

Qagu, _v._ (1) to catch a falling thing ; (2) to dodge a spear.

Qagugu, _v._ (preceded by _dolu_) to be bent down with weakness or old age.

Qalaha, _s._ shark.

Qalahu, _s._ smoke.

Qalimu, _v._ to conquer, to overcome, to succeed.

Qama, _s._ phlegm.

Qanau, _s._ a rope.

Qanaki, _s._ tack of a sail.

Qanua or Guanua, _v_ to spear. When a spear is thrown, if it does not miss, it is _qanua_.

Qara, _s._ the head.
    Qara utua, to behead.
    Qara gauna, bonnet, hat.
    Qara gegea gauna, a coronet or crown.
    Qara koukou (shell of the head), skull.

Qara roko, violent headache, sick headache.

Qara tupua, the crown.

Qara harana, brains.

Qara kopina, scalp.

Qara bada, *s.* the sword fish.

Qara haboua, *v.* to collect payment for murder ransom.

Qara qaitu, *s.* American axe.

Qarahu orooro, a volcano.

Qarana, payment for damage, or injury done. *Uma qarana*, &c.

Qare, *s.* sign of death or misfortune, as breaking *hodu*, &c. *Mate qarena*.

Qari, *s.* (1) the bottom of the sea ; (2) a bog ; (3) slime.

Qarotoa, *v.* to take care of, to look well after. Syn. *Dosia.*

Qaru, *v.* to bark.

Qarume, *s.* a fish. (The general name.) Plural, *Qarumedia.*

Qasi, *s.* stalk. *Bigu qasina*, banana stalk.

Qatua, *s.* knot.

Qatuaqatua, knotted.

Qihoho, *a.* shallow.

Qihohoa, *v.* to be aground.

R

R, as in English, but often very light, scarcely distinguishable from L.

Raiva, *v.* to move. With a negative, *se raiva*, to be unwilling, can't be bothered.

Raivaraiva, to move.

Rau, *s.* leaf.

Rāu, *v.* (1) to crawl, as a child, snake, &c. ; (2) to move, as the moon, stars, &c., in the heavens. Rāu tui, to crawl through a small low hole into a house or garden.

Raua, *v.* to scrape, or gather together with two hands.

Rauaia, *v.* (1) to warn of an intended attack ; (2) to shield ; (3) to save.

Raurau, preceded by *gorere*, a slight illness.

Raba, *v.* to go on all fours (as a turtle).

Rabana, *v.* to hunt.

Rabia, *s.* sago ; arrowroot.

Rabora, *s.* turmeric.

Raborarabora, *a.* cadaverous, sallow.

Rabu, particle of enumeration, ten. as *rabu rua*, 20.

Ragaia, *v.* to pull up, to transplant.

Ragaraga, *s.* side, just under the arm-pits.

Ragaraga, *s.* the name of a disease (erysipelas).

Rahala, *s.* north-west monsoon. Also, Lahala.

Rahea, *s.* fornication.

Raho bada, *s.* a term of respect.

Raho namo, *a.* good looking, handsome (of a man).

Rahuautu, to sever.

Rahupou, to slap thigh in bravado. *Kunu rahupou.*

Rahurahu, *s.* (1) ashes ; (2) fireplace.

Raka, *v.* to step, to walk.

Rāki karaia, *v.* to cower.

Rakia, to draw a pipe.

Rako, a twig. *Au rakona.*

Rakua, *v.* to make up the fire.

Rami, *s.* petticoat, waistcloth.

Rami abia, of a girl who has had intercourse with a man (as in Hebrew, uncovered).

Rami hebou, *s.* a virgin.

Ramo, *v.* to chew the betel nut.

Ramu, *s.* root.

Rani, *v.* to be bemorninged, to be overtaken by the morning. Raoirani.

Ranu, *s.* water, juice, liquid.

Ranu buloa, to dilute.

Ranu seia, to bale out water.

Ranukaranuka, *a.* watery.

Rara, *s.* blood. Rara karaia, bloody.

Rara arukubou, a bruise.

Raraia, *v.* (1) to sun, to dry ; (2) to stare, to watch. Raraigu, &c.

Raradikaedae, *s.* dropsy.

Raraga or Raraka, *v.* to stumble on one side, as from a slippery road, or by stepping on a loose stone ; to stagger, to totter.

Raranadi, hunting spear of red wood.

Rari, see Lari.

Raria, *s.* fine sand. Laria.

Raro, clay, (used in making pottery).

Raro duba, dark coloured clay.

Raro kaka, red clay.

Raroa, *s.* a flood which covers the grass.

Rarua, *a.* two (persons).

Raruoti *a.* two persons). Also used as dual with pronouns. *Umui raruoti.*

Rata, *s.* milk. Rata matana, nipple.

Rataia. *See* Lataia, *v.* to condemn an absent one to death.

Ravana, *s.* father-in-law ; son-in-law.

Ravana haine, mother-in-law ; daughter-in-law.

Reaia, *a.* to forget, to lose.

Rei, *s.* grass.

Rege, *s.* a joint of meat.

Regena. Regeregena, *s.* noise, clatter. *Asi regeregena,* Hush !

Reho, *s.* sore mouth.

Reke, *s.* fishing net.

Repati, large white lily.

Revaia, *v.* to condemn to death when the victim is present.

Revareva, *s.* (1) tattooing ; (2) anything striped or variegated ; Hence (3) writing, printed matter. *Revareva hatua.* Pl. revarevadia.

Revo, a fish.

Rioa, *v.* to gird.

Ride, diarrhœa.

Rigi, *s.* branch.

Riki, *v.* to cry passionately, as an infant refusing to take the breast.

Rimuna, *s.* fringe, edge.

Roë, asthma.

Roi, flax. *Vanea roina.*

Roboa, *s.* to adze smooth, as a canoe after *kedea.*

Roboa, *s.* (1) first-born ; (2) first-fruits.

Rodu, a fish.

Roga, *s.* the name of a sweet smelling herb.

Roge, *s.* (1) a store-house ; (2) store-room. Also Loge.

Rogea, *v.* to store in *roge.*

Rogea tauna, one who stores, an industrious man. Also Logea tauna.

Rogoni, *v.* to cook for food for visitors, &c.

Rogorogo, *v.* to be pregnant, to conceive.

Roha, *v.* to look.

Rohadae, to look up.

Roha dobi, to look down.

Roharoha, to look about.

Roha lou, to look back.

Roha, *s.* fathom.

Roha, to measure, to fathom.

Rohea, to string a bow.

Roheahu, *v.* to drum over the dead.

Roherohea, *v.* (1) to dandle a baby ; (2) to shake one in order to awaken.

Roha. *v.* to fly, to leap, to skip.

Rohouda, to leap into, as waves in a boat.

Rohoisi, to jump up.

Rohodobi, to jump down.

Rohohanai, to leap over.

Rohokau, to perch, to light on.

Rohoa, *v.* to cancel ; to rub or wash out, to raze.

Rohodaerohodae, *v.* to palpitate, as the heart.

Rohoroho, intensive ; generally used with *dika.*

Rokohu, *s.* a bird of paradise — *paradisea raggiana.*

Roku, name of a shell-fish.

Romua, to pat pottery into shape.

Ropo, logs on which to launch canoe or boat.

Rorea, *v.* to spread, as branches on the ground, as stones spread out, not heaped up.

Rorokaroroka, stiff, rigid.

Roroma. Roromaia, *v.* to murder a visitor in a village, generally treacherously.

Rosi, *s.* fastenings of sail to yard, robans.

Rosia, *v.* (1) to nurse a child ; (2) to throw the arms around, to hug, as a captive in war, to clasp in the arms, to embrace.

Rovorovo, name of a bird.

Rua, *v.* two.

Rua ahui, twenty.

Ruaoti, a couple.

Rūā, *v.* to detain ; to reprimand, to withhold.

Ruarua, *v.* to dig. Pass. Ruaia.

Rui, *s.* dugong.

Rubea, *v.* to try a stick or spear by holding it in the middle and shaking it.

Rudu, side of chest.

Ruhaia, *v.* to untie, to loosen.

Ruhaia nege, to cast off.

Ruku, *v.* to grunt.

Ruma, *s.* a house.

Ruma gaudia, furniture.

Rumu karaia, to build a house.

Rurua, *s.* small rattan cane.

S

S in purely native words never occurs before *a*, *o*, or *u*.

Sahati, *s.* sabbath. (*Introduced from the Hebrew.*)

Satauro, *s.* a cross. (*Introduced from the Greek.*)

Se, (1) particle added to noun— *Dirava se karaia* ; (2) a negative.

Seasea, *s.* the side of a house on the outside. With *dehe*, side verandah.

Seamata, *s.* ripe cocoanut. *Niu seamata.*

Sei, *s.* flea.

Seia, *r.* to pour.

Senseu, *v.* to look out, as from the masthead ; to look at house or canoe to see if straight, &c.

Sebaka, *s.* back of a house. *Ruma sebakana.*

Sede, bamboo drum or tomtom.

Sedila. Don't know.

Sega, *v.* to clear the bush for a garden. *Sega taraia.*

Segea, *v.* to sharpen a knife or axe.

Sela. *See* Asi ela.

Selaia dobi, to rush down, as a water-fall.

Seliseli, or Seriseri, *s.* a rubbish heap.

Seme, *adv.* not. As asi eme.

Sene, *adv.* long, long ago.

Senu. Senusenu, *s.* a collection of things, a heap.

Senukasenuka, heaped up.

Sepe, *s.* a small white shell, worn by chiefs.

Serina, *s.* a flock of animals or birds.

Seriseri. *See* Seliseli.

Serosero, *s.* the second row of calking in *lakatoi.*

Seseahu, *s.* curtain.

Sesedaeroha, *r.* to rise to the surface, as a diver, dugong, &c.

Seseha, *s.* the sea-coast just inland of the mangroves. *Seseha dala lao.*

Seseha, *a.* brackish, as water in *seseha.*

Sesera, *s.* elegy.

Severa. Severasevera, *a.* thin.

Siaia, *r.* to send. Siaia lao, to dismiss.

Siahu, *a.* hot. *Lalo siahu,* hot-tempered, angry. Siahusiahu, luke-warm.

Siahu. Siahuna, *s.* power, authority (supernatural).

Siaro, *s.* a large red fish.

Sio, a fish.

Sioko, to squat with posterior near ground.

Siokomu, *s.* one kind of banana.

Siusiu, *s.* an indecent dance on *laktaoi* when they are ready for sea.

Sibaka, *s.* a sacrificial offering. (*From the Hebrew*).

Sibaka pata, *s.* an altar.

Sibirere, *s.* light wood, used by children for toy spears.

Sibogu, *pron.* I only.

Sihomu, *pron.* thou only.

Sibona, *pron.* he himself, very self, only, alone.

Sibona namo, to excel.

Sibona heala, to commit suicide.

Sigara tauna, leader of hunt.

Sihaurisihauri, *s.* pustule.

Sihi, *s.* (1) a man's girdle ; (2) the paper mulberry from which the girdle is made ; (3) to abstain from sexual intercourse.

Sihi lasi, naked.

Sihi daudau, *v.* to sleep apart from one's wife a long time.

Sihi kahikahi, *v.* to sleep apart from one's wife for a short time.

Sihi korikori, *v.* to sleep apart from one's wife, not to cohabit.

Sike, *v.* (preceded by ae) to limp, to be lame.

Siko, *s.* prolonged illness.

Siku, *v.* to be perturbed, anxious. (Used with *lalo*).

Sili, *adv.* aside.

Silo, oyster.

Sinaia, *s.* a wave.

Sinaiana, *s.* ocean swell, high waves which do not break.

Sinabada, *s.* (1) thumb; (2) big toe.

Sinahu, *a.* hundred.

Sinana, *s.* mother.

Sinana, *a.* mature (of animals).

Sinavai, *s.* river.

Siniura, a prickly creeper.

Sira, name of a tree.

Siri, *v.* to get out of the way, to move aside.

Siri, *s.* a verse. (*Introduced meaning*).

Siria, *v.* to chip ; to cut up firewood.

Sirigogoha, a shell fish.

Siriho, *s.* a reed.

Sisia, *s.* a dog.

Sisibaia, *v.* to compose a song. *Ane sisibaia.*

Sisiba henia, *v.* to admonish, reprove, advise.

Sisiba tauna, *s.* one who reproves, an adviser.

Sisidara, *s.* feather head-dress.

Sisihu, oyster shells.

Sisimo, light shower.

Sisipo, *s.* the entire outrigger of a large canoe.

Sisisina, *s.* a very small piece.

Sisina, *s.* a small piece.

Sisiria, to sprinkle.

Sisivana, *adv.* equal to, as far as.

Sivaia, *v.* to turn, to reverse (end for end).

Sivarai, *s.* a report, an account, a story.

So, *adv.* not. As Asio.

Sugo, *s.* a yoke. (*From the Greek*).

Suke, *s.* a fig tree. (*From the Greek*).

Sunago, *s.* synagogue. (*From the Greek*).

T

T is pronounced as in English, except before i or e, when it is pronounced as ts. As, *mate* pronounced matse, *raruoti* is raruotsi.

Ta, a contraction of tamona.

Ta, a prefix to toi, for people, as *tatoi.*

Tae, a tree, the bark of which is used for sewing *biri*, and for making thatch.

Tāi, *v.* (1) to cry ; (2) to howl (of dogs). Taitai.

Tai henduri, to cry after a father or mother, as a child does.

Tai lolololo, to cry out lustily.

Tāi momo, *a.* fretful.

Tāia, *v.* to coil in the hand.

Taia, *s.* ear. Pl. Taiadia.

Taia ibuku, *v.* to listen stupidly and not understand what is said.

Taia kudima, deaf.

Taia manoka, *s.* willing obedience.

Taia, *s.* fin at gills.

Taihu, *s.* (1) a man's sister ; (2) a woman's brother.

Taihu rahai, (1) a man's female cousin ; (2) a woman's male cousin. *Rahai* takes the suffix. *Taihu rahaigu.*

Taikotaiko, *v.* to shake the head.

Taina, *a.* some (things).

Taina, *s.* morsel. Taina ania, to partake of.

Taitai, *v.* to weep, to cry. As Tāi.

Taitu, sweet yam.

Taoakunu, *v.* to press down

Taoatao, *v.* to hold down, to press down.

Taoakohi, *v.* to break, as a cocoanut shell by crushing.

Taoha, a scab.

Taola. *See* Taora.

Taona, followed by torea, *v.* to betray As Taotore.

Taora, *s.* level ground, a plain. Taorataora.

Taotao, *s.* necklace (of shells).

Taotore. *See* Taona.

Tau, *s.* the body.

Tau mate, a corpse.

Tau, *s.* a man. *Tau Elema.* Elema man.

Tau ariari, intermittent fever.

Tau mauri, restless, fidgetty.

Tauadae, *v.* to hang up.

Tauihuai, *s.* the sons between first and last born.

Taubadadia, *s.* elders.

Tauguna, *s.* the first-born son.

Tauhau, *s.* a youth.

Tauhalō, *v.* to cheer, to comfort.

Tau manokamanoka, *s.* languor.

Taumuritai, *s.* son subsequent to tauguna.

Tauna, *s.* a man. *See* Tau. Generally used with a noun of quality. *Koikoi tauna,* a liar.

Taunabinai, just so, all right.

Taunabunai, as Taunabinai.

Tauna se raiva, unwilling, can't be bothered.

Taunimanima, *s.* man (generic, including male and female).

Taupetaupe, *s.* a low swing.

Taurahani, *a.* eight.

Taurahani ahui, *a.* eighty.

Taurahani ta, *a.* nine.

Tauratoi, *a.* six.

Tauratoi a hui, sixty.

Tauru, *s.* hades ; unknown ocean space.

Taurubada, *s.* the covering party in an expedition for plunder, &c.

Tau ta, *s.* somebody.

Tau varotavarota, *a.* lean, skinny.

Tāba, to drivel.

Tabaiahu, *v.* to daub with mud, &c.

Tabero, *s.* a shallow bay.

Tabikau, *v.* to lean against.

Taboro, *s.* yam harvest.

TAB (104) TOA

Tabubutabubu, *s.* to shake, as with the wind. *Ima Tabubutabubu*, to shake, of the hand, so as not to take a steady aim.

Tadaia, *v.* to beat out the bark of the paper mulberry, for making native cloth.

Tadi, *s.* sea-water.

Tadikaka, *s.* cousins, family relations.

Tādikāka, *s.* brothers and sisters by the same parents.

Tadi rahai, *s.* younger cousin.

Tadina, *s.* (1) younger brother or sister, (2) younger cousin.

Tadiva, *s.* the name of a fish, red mullet.

Tāga tauna, *s.* a rich man.

Tāge, *s.* excrement.

Tagoa, *v.* to paint one's face all over.

Taguma, a fish.

Taha, used with āu, *s.* a splinter, a small piece of wood. *Au taha. Aegu āu tahana qadaia.*

Taha, used with kudou, *v.* to be distressed, perturbed.

Tahairame, *s.* Syn. Ravana.

Tahia, *v.* to dig out, to take earth out of a hole, to burrow.

Tahoa, *v.* (1) to throw a spear, (2) to throw anything to, but not at any one.
Tahoakau, to throw.
Tahoa dobi, to dash (on the ground).

Tahodiho, *s.* the West.

Tahotaho, *s.* of children playing with light spears, *Tahotaho mo karaia.*

Tahua, *v.* to seek, to examine. Tahu. Tahugumu, with suff. seek me.
Tahu taudia, hunting party.

Tahula, *s.* (1) a slight relapse after a severe illness. *Gorere tahula. Lau gorere ma tahulaia.* (2) A few remaining ill after a general epidemic.

Tahumutāi, *v.* to seek with tears.

Tahuni, *v.* to cover in, as a body in the grave.

Tahure, a fish.

Tāko, one kind of grass.

Takona, *s.* bunch (of fruit), cluster.

Talai, *v.* to chop.

Talaia, *v.* to sting (of the hornet).

Talabili, *s.* bulwarks of *lakatoi.*

Talo, *s.* a vegetable (arum esculentum).

Tamalu, *s.* umbrella. (*Introduced.*)

Tamana, *s.* (1) father ; (2) uncle.

Tama rahai, *s.* uncle.

Tamann, *v.* to charge, to exhort.

Tame, *ta* and *me*, first pers. pl. inclusive, with *me* euphonic particle. *Ita tame moale*, we are pleased.

Tamona, *a.* one.

Tamoru, numb.

Tamotamo, *v.* few, here and there one, rare ; also Tamotamona.

Tanatana, cry of white lizard.

Tanitano, *s.* the name of an evil spirit, supposed to possess a man when in a fit.

Tano, *s.* earth, soil ; country.
Tano ai, ashore.
Tano tauna, a countryman.
Tano bada, *s.* the earth, the land, as distinguished from sky and sea.
Tano gagaena, *s.* a desert.

Tapoa, *v.* to fan.

Tara, *s.* the name of a fish.

Tara, *v.* to shine.

Tarai hepatapata, *v.* to hack.

Tarakia, *v.* to be wounded by an arrow.

Taravatu, *s.* (1) covenant ; (2) hence commandment, law.

Tareko, *s.* hollow seeds used as a rattle on drums, &c. ; also, name of tree to which they belong.

Tari, *s.* rudder, steer-oar.
Tari karaia, *v.* to steer.
Tari tauna, steersman.

Tarikatarika, *adv.* of intensity, thoroughly, continuity.

Taritari, *adv.* continuity, permanence, &c.

Taroma, one kind of banana.

Taru, *v.* to cover, as with a sheet, to wrap oneself in.
Taruahu, to wrap completely.

Taruha, *v.* to camp, to pitch tent.

Taruha hebou, *s.* a camp.

Tataiautu, *v.* to transgress.

Tatakau, Tatakunu, *v.* to strike and be fast on a rock or reef, as a canoe or ship.

Tatakau, *s.* a collision.

Tavanana, *v.* to get food in anticipation of a feast.

Tavea, one kind of yam.

Tōa, to blow, of the wind.

Toa. *See* Dōa.

Toana, *s.* (1) a sign ; (2) a limit ; (3) a mark.

Toea, *s.* white shell armlet.

Toi, *a.* three.

Toi a hui, thirty.

Toia, *v.* to shred, to insert.

Toia hedavari, *v.* to meet on the road.

Toiaroro, *v.* to stretch out, as the arm or leg.

Toia vareai, *v.* to insert, as the nose-stick.

Toutou, *s.* a spot, a mole.

Toutou, *v.* to be spotted.

Toboa, *v.* to suck.

Tobukatobuka, *s.* a shallow vessel, nearly flat, as a dinner plate.

Todena, *s.* gum. *Au todena.*

Togea, *v.* to spear, when the person speared is above. As Christ on the cross.

Togo, *s.* the fruit of one kind of man-grove (aniani), not edible.

Tohē, *s.* a large *uro* for putting raw sago in.

Tohoa, *v.* (1) to try ; (2) to mark for cutting ; (3) to rule lines.

Tohotoho, *v.* to mock. *Umui ia dahaka tohotohoa.*

Tohu, *s.* sugar-cane.

Tohua, a fish with long pointed head, and small mouth.

Tolo, a fish.

Tolumu, *s. See* Tomulu.

Toma, *adv.* like, thus.

Tomadiho, *v.* to prostrate oneself, to worship.

Tomena, *s.* resin. Used as a charm for large dugong and turtle nets.

Tomulu, *s.* the goura pigeon. Also tolumu.

Topoa, *v.* to suck, as an infant, to suck without noise.

Toratora, *s.* shin.

Tore, to rise. *See* Helaitore.

Torea, *v.* to cast the net.

Torea, *v.* (1) to mark the design on tne body with lamp-black and water previous to tattooing ; (2) to write.

Torelaia, written about.

Toreisi, *v.* to raise from a sitting or lying posture.

Toreisina, *s.* a rising up, a resurrec-tion.

Torehai, added to *heni, abia,* &c., to signify repayment.

Toretore, *v.*, to try a *lakatoi* by sail-ing to and fro.

Tororo, *a.* stiff, strong, of a stick or spear.

Tororotororo, stiff, rigid, as the body in a fit.

Tororotororo, *s.* epilepsy.

Toto, name of a tree.

Toto, *s.* sore.

Totōdae, *s.* a very stormy north-east wind, a north-east gale.

Totona, *s.* the object in coming or going to a place. Used with the suffix of the person to whom one goes. *Oi lau totogu dahaka ?* Why have you come to me ?

Tovili, *s.* the kernel, as of the pandanus fruit.

Toviri, *s.* (1) the kernel of the pan-danus ; (2) larvæ of the wild bee.

Tua, a piece (of wood, string, &c.).

Tūa, *v.* (1) to slacken, to let go ; (2) to leave friends.

Tuadobi, *v.* to let down by a rope, &c.

Tuakatuaka, short piece.

Tuara, one kind of banana (eaten by chiefs only).

Tuari, *s.* troops, company of warriors.

Tuari hegegedae, to besiege.

Tuari lao, to go to war.

Tui, *s.* knee.

Tuidaeatari. to kneel on one knee, and bend the other, resting the toes on the ground. Hedoisi.

Tuihadāi, Tuihadaiatari, to kneel on both knees.

Tui hanai, to enter through a low door by stooping.

Tui kebere, *s.* knee-cap.

Tui boio, *v.* to lose the way, to be bushed.

Tuia, *v.* to quiet.

Tuidae, *s.* rafter.

Tubu, *v.* to ferment, to swell.

Tubua, *s.* the crown of the head. With *dina,* noon. Of a post, au tubua, upright.

Tubuahu, *s.* constipation of the bowels.

Tubudia, *s.* (1) posterity ; (2) ancestors.

Tubuka, *s.* feather head-dress for dancing.

Tubukau, to ask permission. *Biaguna tubukau henia.*

Tubukohi, *s.* first appearance of menses. With suffix tubugu.

Tubuna, *s.* (1) grandparent ; (2) ancestor ; (3) descendant.

Tubu rahai, *s.* great uncle or aunt.

Tubu tama, *s.* ancestors.

Tuba tama hereva, *s.* tradition.

Tuha, name of a tree the leaves and root of which are used to stupefy fish.

Tuhutuhu, young shoot.

Tumon, *s.* small pole in *lakatoi*, parallel with *ikoda* but above *ilava*.

Tumuru. *See* Turumu.

Tunua, *v.* to bake pottery. Tunutunu.

Tupina *s.* the tail (of birds).

Tupua, *s.* crown of the head. *See* Tubua.

Tupua, *a.* upright.

Tupuahu, *a.* costive.

Turana, *s.* a friend. (Of the speaker's sex.)

Turi, *s.* a bone. Turia.
Turia mava, backbone.

Turia, *v.* to plait an armlet, to sew.

Turiabada, *s.* the name of a fish.

Turia duhu, *s.* a child who grows slowly.

Turia kirara, *s.* a child who grows fast.

Turiariki, *v.* to discompose, to vex.

Turiarudu, *s.* rib.

Turituri, *s.* native rosewood.

Turoa, *v.* to hollow out (as a canoe or tub).

Turua, *v.* the name of a bird, the laughing jackass.

Turubu, *s.* cassowary feather headdress.

Turu hanai, *v.* to wade across a river.

Turumu, *s.* goura pigeon. *See* Tumuru.

Tutua, *v.* to spear by holding the spear in the hand, to bayonet, to buffet.

Tutuhia, *v.* to strike the foot against a stone.

Tutukatutuka, *v.* to stand firm, as a house or post in a strong wind, to be steady.

Tutututua, *v.* to heat gently with the clenched fist, as a sick person to relieve pain.

V

V is sounded as in English.

Vae, hunting spear of white wood.

Vaia, *v.* (1) to take out of a pot, box, &c. ; (2) to discharge cargo. *Lakatoi anina vaia.*

Vaina, *s.* a small bag, a pocket.

Vainananega, *s.* three days hence. The vainananega of Sunday is Wednesday.

Vaira, *s.* the face, the front.

Vaira hamui, to scowl.

Vaira hūa, *v.* to frown.

Vaira huaia, melancholy.

Vaira lao, *v.* to go to meet some one.

Vairanai, *prep.* before.

Vaisiri, *s.* the name of a fish. Also Vasiri.

Vaitani, *adv.* finished, ended. Used with a verb as, *Daroa vaitani.*

Vaivai, wild mango.

Vaoha, *s.* sea urchin.

Vauto, *s.* wild orange.

Vaura, *s.* cuscus.

Vabala, hunting spear of white wood.

Vabara, vine with fruit like black grapes.

Vaboha, *s.* a lizard.

Vaboha, *v.* to be lowering and gloomy, of the sky. *Tano e vabohaia.*

Vabu, *s.* (1) a widow ; (2) a widower, especially during the time of mourning.

Vabura, *s.* dusk, dark.

Vaburema, name of a shell-fish.

Vadaeni, the end of, the finish ; that's all.

Vadaeni, *interj.* Enough ! *Adv.* Quite.

Vadivadi, *s.* guests, visitors.

Vādo, *v.* (1), to live unmarried, as a widow or widower. *Ia vado noho.* (2) to be barren, of trees, &c.

Vādovādo, *s.* tall cocoanut tree.

Vadumo, stick to which canoe is made fast.

Vāga, *s.* catkin of the betel pepper.

Vāga, (a little shorter than the above) to fast. *See Aniraga.*

Vagaia, *v.* to shell, to take off the shell.

Vagege, *s.* jealonsy, envy.

Vagivagi, *s.* finger ring.

Vagoro, *s.* the bush after the grass has been burnt.

Vadepa, a plant (dracæna).

Vadu, a chisel, a gouge.

Vagoro, *v.* to clear the grass for a garden. *Vagoro karaia.*

Vaha, *s.* the cheek ; the opening at gills of fish.

Vahabada, a swollen cheek.

Vahaleleva, a fish.

Vahorita, *v.* to rob. (A term of reproach.)

Vahu, *s.* uncultivated land, bush.

Vahudagu, *v.* to startle by shouting.

Vahuvahu, *s.* Chinese rose.

Vakera, large native rat.

Vakoda, *s.* a cane.

Valāu, *v.* to run a race.

Valahuvalahu, *adv.* with itaia, to see dimly, not to be able to distinguish persons.

Valakavalaka, *s.* mildew.

Valavala, *s.* cobweb.

Vamu, *s.* animals fit for food,

Vanaga, *s.* the name of a small black fish.

Vanagalau, *s.* the name of a fish.

Vanagi, *s.* a small canoe.

Vanea, *s.* the name of a tree.

Vanea, *s.* flax from the bark of the *vanea*, from which the strongest dugong nets are made.

Vanega, *s.* (usually followed by ai) (1) the day after to-morrow ; (2) the day before yesterday ; (3) hence, past time, not very long ago.

Vapavapa, a fish.

Vapu, *s.* a widow (in mourning).

Vara, *v.* (1) to grow ; (2) to be born.

Vara bada, luxuriant.

Vara, *s.* birth.

Varaia, door fastened by cord.

Varaguna, *s.* (1) the first-born child ; (2) the elder of two persons spoken of.

Varahu, *s.* (1) steam ; (2) perspiration.

Varani, *s.* yesterday.

Varani hanuaboi, last night.

Varavara, *s.* (1) relations ; (2) dependents.

Vareai, to enter. (Applied to going inland to the plantations.) *Ia vareai.*

Vari, name of a tree (the silk cotton).

Varia, dance before going on a voyage to get accustomed to keep awake.

Variri variri, *v.* to blink.

Varivari, *s.* (1) looking-glass ; (2) glass window.

Varo, *s.* (1) fishing-line ; (2) large net (for dugong).

Varo, *v.* to line, as a basket.

Varota, *a.* ten full-grown cocoanuts. *Niu varota.*

Varotavarota. *See* Tau varotavarota.

Varovaro, *s.* (1) veins ; (2) arteries ; (3) tendon.

Varubi, one kind of banana.

Varure, landslip.

Vasea, *v.* to joke.

Vasi, *v.* to go to some one who calls, or to a place near.

Vasiahu, *s.* hot water.

Vasika, *s.* a flint used as a knife ; (2) knife (superseded by *kaia*).

Vasilaia, *v.* to take a thing to one near, or to some definite place spoken of.

Vasiri. *See* Vaisiri.

Vasivasi, *s.* a sign of a coming event, as sneezing, muscular quivering, &c. *Lauegu vasivasi.*

Vāta, *s.* the name of a banana stem from which inferior nets are made.

Vata, sign of present and past time.

Vata, Vatavata, *s.* (1) ghosts ; (2) an unknown spirit supposed to have the power of killing whom he will.

Vataeni. *See* Vadaeni.

Vata dina, *v.* to come in sight.

Vata doko, *a.* stanched.

Vatavata, *s.* (1) a ladder ; (2) a ghost.

Vavae, *s.* wick. (*Introduced.*)

Vea, *a.* calm (in the day.)

Vea, *v.* to be becalmed (in the day.)

Veo, *s.* brass or copper. (*Introduced word.*)

Vedaia, *v.* to pour water in a chatty or any water-vessel.

Vehadi, *s.* the name of a month (June).

Vehadi hirihiri, July.

Vehadi, name of tree.

Verara, one kind of banana.

Veria, *v.* to pull, to draw out, extract, to subtract.

Veriaisi, to pull up.

Veriadae, to draw up.

Veriatao, *v.* to steer towards land, to the left in coming into harbour.

Verina, *s.* a company (of people, as serina of animals), a class.

Vero, *v.* to crawl, as a snake.

Vesi, *s.* semen maris.

Veto, *s.* an abscess.

Vēvē, *v.* to run as water ; to dissolve, to trickle.

Veve hanaihanai, *a.* pavement.

Vilipopo, *s.* a sling.

Vine, *s.* vine. (*Introduced.*)

SENTENCES AND PHRASES.

What is your name? Oi ladamu daika?

Where is your house? Oiemu ruma edeseni ai?

Where is the Chief? Hanua lohia edeseni ai?

What have you come for? Oi dahaka totona mai?

When did you (*plu.*) come? Edananega umui oma?

When will you (*plu.*) go? Aidananega umui baola?

I am hungry. Lau vata hitolo.

I am thirsty. Lau ranu mate.

I want to sleep. Lau mahuta na koaulaia.

Bring some fire. Lahi a mailaia.

Bring some water. Ranu gurita a mailaia.

Bring some young cocoa-nuts. Karu haida mailaia.

Bring some bananas to sell. Bigu haida mailaia baine hoihoi.

What is the price of this? Inai dahaka davana?

What do you want for the fish? Qarume dahaka davana?

I don't want to buy. Lau asina hoihoi.

Go away (*sing.*) and return to-morrow. Oi lao, kerukeru ba lou mai.

I go the day after to-morrow. Lau vanegai bainala.

Put it in the house. Ruma lalonai ava atoa.

Bring in the food. Malamala mailaia.

Be quick. Kara haraga.

Come quickly. Aoma haragaharaga.

Sweep the house. Ruma daroa.

Cook the food. Aniani; or, malamala, nadua.

Is the food ready (cooked)? Aniani vata maeta hani?

Open the door. Iduara kehoa.

Shut the door. Iduara kouahu.

Bring me some water that I may bathe. Ranu mailaia lau baina digu.

Where is the road? Dala edeseni?

Wash all the clothes. Dabua idoinai ba huria.

Wash the clothes to-day; we sail to morrow. Dabua hari-hari huria; ai kerukeru baia heau.

How many canoes have gone? Vanagi auhida vata heau?

All the village has gone fishing. Hanua idoinai haoda lao.

Get the boat ready and we will go. Umui boti hagoevaia ita baita heau.

Lower the sail and put out the oars. Lara ava atoa diho, bara karaia.

The oar is broken. Bara vata qaidu.

Let us keep in-shore because the sea is rough. Ita badibadina lao hurehure garina.

Are you ill? Oi gorere hani?

Where is the pain? Hisi gabuna edeseni ai?

When did your illness begin? Edananegai oi gorere e vara?

Are you costive? Bokamu hetubuahu hani?

My child is very ill. Lau natugu gorere bada.

Where have you come from? Oi ede amo mai?

Where are you going? Oi ede lao; or, Oi ede bo laomu?

Take it carefully or it will break. Abia namonamo makohi garina.

The sea is very rough. Davara vata hurehure bada.

Wait until the wind drops and then go. Umui noho lāi naria, baine mate ba heau.

Come to-morrow and help me. Oi kerukeru baoma lau ba kahagu.

Come (*plu.*) every morning to work. Daba idoinai baoma gau karaia.

I will pay you when you have finished. Oi ba karaia vaitani, lau davana baina henimu.

I did not say so. Lau unukoautoma lasi.

I did not send them. Lau idia asina siaidia.

I gave you plenty of food. Aniani momo lau umui na henimui.

Who will go with you? Daika oi ida lao?

I want to go fishing. Lau hioda lao urana na uramu.

Which hatchet do you desire? Edana ira oi hekisehekise henia?

I will teach you every evening if you will come. Oi baoma lau adorahi idoinai baina hadibamu.

Why does he forbid them? Ia dahaka gau idia e koaudiatao?

We are afraid of the sun. Ai dina garina gari.

The village boys are afraid of the foreigners. Hanua memerodia nao taudia e garidia gari.

What are they doing? Idia dahaka e karamu?

The sun has turned. Dina vata eme gelo.

The sun has gone down. Dina vata dogu dobi vaitani.

The tide is rising. Davara vata hagaru.

It is high tide. Davara vata bada.

The tide is falling. Davara gomata gui.

It is low tide. Gomata vata gui davara maragimaragi.

The sun is hot. Dina vata garagara.

Let us seek a shade until evening. Ita kerukeru gabuna baita tabua, ela bona adorahi.

You go before and we will follow. Oi laka guna, ai oi murimu aia laka.

Call your companions and let us go. Umui bamomui a boilidia ita baitala.

I told you to wait here for me. Lau na koau umui iniseni noho lau narigu.

Tell them to go and sleep in the village. Idia koau henidia idia hanua lao bae mahuta.

Good-night all. Umui iboumui ba mahuta.

APPENDIX.

NAMES OF DIFFERENT KINDS OF BANANAS.

Akarua	Garokoni	Kusita
Oroa	Gudu	Meuraba
Oroua	Hagavara	Naimuru
Uregadi	Hola	Siogomu
Unauna	Huitabu	Taroma
Babaka	Kaiakiri	Varubi
Banaere	Kamea	Verara
Dau	Kameamoa	
Deuro	Kokome	

NAMES OF FISH.

Abae	Bēki	Dumu sisia
Ademela	Borebore	Duribaroko
Adia	Boboda	Gaburu
Ahakara	Budia	Gani
Ahuiahuia	Buna	Ganiahuota
Anama	Dae	Garava
Ariaoda	Dabutu	Huimaimi
Ialata	Dahudahu	Huhula
Ituari	Dahulu	Kavaitoro
Ono	Dalaia	Kila
Ororobu	Daladala	Kururu
Udulata	Daqala	Laumaere
Ulaeo	Daraki	Ladi
Unia	Derekaka	Lagai
Balala	Dinaha	Lagere
Barubaru	Dono	Lahalaha
Bebe	Duadua	Laheta
Bedo	Dumu	Lui

Maimera	Namumana	Taguma
Mabui	Qada	Tabure
Makoa	Qalabada	Tāla
Māmi	Qalaha	Tolo
Manariha	Ramuta	Vahaleleva
Maraua	Revo	Vanaga
Matakaka	Robu	Vanagalau
Matavabu	Rodu	Vapavapa
Memehute	Siaro	Vasiri
Mida	Sio	
Naidae	Tadiva	

Shell Fish.

Batata	Gumaulu	Laketo
Bedebede	Kaiva	Laro
Bisisi	Keadi	Maimai
Bobo	Kekerema	Mamalāu
Bokabada	Kevakeva	Mataatu
Bokani	Kevakulo	Minibore
Bokani bisisi	Kiribogairigaio	Mininuni
Bomaboma	Kirigaibogaibo	Nononono
Budugara	Kuadi	Nudugara
Butubutu	Kunnkunu	Qamenau
Dala	Kururu	Roku
Dihudihu	Laia	Sirigogoha
Dudu	Laina	Siro
Gaiagaia	Lagalaga	Vaburema
Gili		

Names of Trees.

Auiani	Budoa	Kavera
Araara	Gava	Keakone
Ori	Gea	Keavaro
Oroaoroa	Gilaki	Kerolo
Urara	Higo	Kilima
Besere	Hodava	Kohe
Boroko	Hotamu	Koukou
Budabuda	Kakabeda	Kuluha

H

Lataba	Nala	Turituri
Maita	Niu	Totō
Magi	Nonu	Vaivai
Mogo	Sira	Vari
Mudoru		

NAMES OF YAMS.

Agavaita	Gete	Madina
Alo	Heiga	Makota
Ulo	Kabukabu	Maloa
Badukalo	Kahugo	Manonoha
Bagara	Kemaiore	Minagoru
Batu	Kohi	Papakadebu
Bubui	Kokorogu	Taitu
Divoi	Korua	Tavea
Gata	Lovai	

NAMES OF BIRDS.

Odubora	Haba	Koisere
Ogororo	Kaekae	Kouaga
Uage	Kalai	Kunumaga
Baimumu	Kauage	Lokohu
Bisini	Keboga	Manubarara
Bogibada	Kema	Nogo
Digudigu	Kibi	Pune
Duna	Kiloki	Pune gobu
Gahuga namo	Kisikisi	Turua
Galo	Kitogala	Turumu
Gobu	Kivivi	

COMPARATIVE VOCABULARY OF SEVEN NEW GUINEA DIALECTS.

THE first column in the following vocabulary represents the language spoken by the Motu tribe (see page 1 in Grammar). The second column is the dialect of Kerepunu or Hood Bay. The people of Hula, or Hood Point, speak the same language with slight variations. The inland villages, and also the large village of Kalo, speak almost the same dialect.

The third column is the language spoken in the large distric of Aroma, a few miles east of Hood Bay.

The fourth column is that of South Cape. This dialect is spoken with some variations by the tribes scattered from Orangerie Bay to Milne Bay. The languages spoken at Heath Island and at East Cape are as different as those of Hood Bay and Aroma. Want of space has prevented these being included in the vocabulary.

The next column is from the west of Port Moresby, and represents the districts inland of Redscar Bay. Between Kabadi and Hall Sound are the villages of Naara; and these speak a language with more of the Maiva or Lolo element in it.

The sixth column represents the language spoken by the people of Maiva, Kivori, &c., west of Hall Sound. Closely allied to this is the Lolo dialect, spoken by the tribes in that large and populous district.

The last column is a specimen of the languages spoken by the tribes in the Gulf of Papua. It is in many particulars essentially different, both in grammar and vocabulary, to the others, and is spoken by people darker in colour, and different in habits to those in the Eastern peninsula.

The words have been collected as follows :—In our college at Port Moresby we have youths from almost all the places above-mentioned. These have been there long enough to have a thorough knowledge of the Motuan. I printed the list of words and gave them out, a slip at a time, to be filled in by the most intelligent of the students. In this way several of them were completed by natives only, while in other cases the original lists were filled in by Rarotongan or Samoan teachers employed in our Mission. With the exception of Kabadi and Motumotu the whole of the words have been carefully read over with the natives of the several districts, and are as accurate as they can be made without a personal knowledge of the languages. In the case of Motumotu, the murder of Tauraki, the mission teacher, has deprived me of the opportunity of correcting the slips from there. The teacher was one of our most intelligent men, and by far the best linguist we had. Philology has sustained a loss in his untimely death. Some of the words collected by him were revised by Mr. E. G. Edelfelt, a gentleman who resided for some time at Motumotu. He objected to many of the words spelt with *d* and thought *r* should be substituted, such as *siare* for *siade*, *da* for *ra*, &c., but as I have had no opportunity up to the time of going to press of deciding, I have left the words as the deceased teacher wrote them, merely pointing out the probability that in some cases *r* might be substituted for *d* and *vice versa*.

W. G. LAWES.

COMPARATIVE VIEW OF NEW GUINEA DIALECTS.

English.	Motu.	Kerepunu.	Aroma.	South Cape.	Kabadi.	Maiva.	Motumotu.
above	atai	ahai	rai	eva	aruna	uvi	orari
afterwards	gabe	gabi	gabi	muriai	avea	muri	aite
all	ibounai	naparana	maparaia	gamagari	bounana	ikoinai	forouai
anchor	doko	rogo	roba	ro	itoo	too	fave
and	mai	na	ma	ma	mai	nanu	eata
angry	badu	baru	paruparu	siaiau	idnava	vakia	kitouroi
arm	ima	gima	ima	nima	ima	ima	mai
arrow	diba	riba	ripa	....	dibana	paki	farisa
ascend	daelkau	rakeau	larage	uavasee	kaekae	karaau	patai
ashamed	hemarai	nuagoberagi	mara	taumamaea	emaridiva	haumaea	memariti
ask	nanadai	verenagi	lenaki	hesio	ranaina	vakaivakai	....
awaken	haoa	vahoa	baoa	auhanoi	vanoa	vaona	sukaputapai
back	doru	kinipara	ou	dakira	pulipuli	kape	avasa
bad	dika	raava	rabaraba	balaa	kaka	kia	maroro
bag (*small*)	vaina	goroa	bola	tana, tojo	kana	mahoa	oroa
bamboo pipe	baubau	baubau	baubau	bauban	kemona	ireire	kika
banana fruit	bigu	hani	gabua kalova	asai	lamana	uarupi	meae
banana-tree	dui	pukave	pakave hui	asailiena	koroi	akaea	arikaka
basket	bosea	baiaa	poea	bosa	kakana	polea	posea
bat	mariboi	mahoba	maopa	mariboi	....	apoapo	taino
bathe	digu	rigu	riku	eledui	kuru	uele	masukai
beach	kone	one	one	kerekere	kepaana	poe	miri
bech-de-mer	korema	papua	ava	ieduba	kupa	uapula	korema
beg	noinoi	noginogi	noginogi	avanori	nonina	noinoi	meamearokiriki
bird	manu	manu	manu	manu	manu	rovorovo	ori
bite	koria	olia	olia	ieretai	arasiava	urina	pitovai
black	koremakorema	ruparupa	ruparupa	dubaduba	kupakupa	napulaupula	menru
blind	matakepulu	ma ele	mai abuabu	nata kibukibu	makaerere	iau	oiaesosoro
blood	rara	rala	rara	osisina	rara	aruaru	ovo
board	leilei	vua	bua	niorumoru	papaona	lailai	susu
body	tau	hau	hau	tau	kau	hau	....

English.	Motu.	Kerepunu.	Aroma.	South Cape.	Kabadi.	Maiva.	Motumotu.
boil, v.	nadua	nanua	nalua	lauriga	nakuna	tatuna	epai
bone	turi	iliga	iliga	siata	kuriana	uria	uti
bottle	kavabu	ma	ima	ile	kavapu	kavapu	kavapu
bow, s.	peva	riba	peva	siri	dipa	humu	apo
boy	mero	melo	mero	nerumeru	urane	miori	siare
branch	rigi	raha	laka	lagana	reena	kaka	rakai
breadfruit	uuu	uuu	gunu	unuri	aarupu	oki	seo
break (*string*)	motu	ruhi	pelui	iemotu	okova	mohu	rarae
break (*stick*)	qaidu	oru	oru	takoeu	para	healaurina	topukavai
break (*skull*)	kokoauru	panuru	panuru	oirapai	karanru	ahruruna	sukai
bring	mailaia	veaamaia	veamaiagia	nreama	maiaina	omaiaina	ankoatiria
bring forth	mara	rugu	kapi	hisu	paiau	mauri	uri
broken	makohi	maa	avalua	taesi	pajava	paa	toharai
brother (*younger*) or sister	tadina	arina	arina	anataumurita	kadina	hatina	marehari
brother (*elder*)	kakana	arina	kuine	tuahana	kadina	aana	paua
butterfly	kanbebe	bebe	pepe	bebe	poioo	petopero	kaokao
buy (*or sell*)	hoihoi	voivoi	hoiboi	uneune	inaina	kavakava	itaialoi
cane	ema	veamai	veamai	ilaoma	kemaiva	emai	lakoati
cassowary	kokokoko	kirapu	gilabu	guabon	viona	vio	niiva
centipede	aiha	aiva	gaiva	alihei	eeraka	raaraa	eope
chest	geme	oba	komakoma	kapakapa	pasipasina	haharana	haifae
chief	lohia	vere	helegana	knuau	ovia	ovia	pukari
chief (*high*)	lohiabada	vereot	beletaku	vasavasa	oviapaka	oviapaka	pukarirovaea
chin	ale	liare	gari	gaeagaea	vakeana	ate	uale
clothes	dabua	rapuga	labua	ruru	kupuna	havuni	puta
cloud (*light*)	ori	iloha	lauba	lada	ori	ori	mea
club (*stone*)	gahi	gabi	paila	putuputu	sapia	amaria	maholo
club (*wood*)	kaleva	lepe	leke	erepa	okuna	puraa	poti
cocoanut (*tree*)	niu	auma	palovu	niu	niu	tona	da
cocoanut (*young fruit*)	karu	lao	rao	aru	mauka	vei tona	rataure
cocoanut(*mature fruit*)	niu	niu	niu	niu	niu	kilokilo	da
cold	keru	nakula	nagula	vaoo	viona	ama	mekoko

English.	Motu.	Kerepuna.	Aroma.	South Cape.	Kabadi.	Maiva.	Motumotu.
come?	soma	onoveamai	onobeamai	uraoma	omamai	omai	koatiria
come	mai	veamai	beamai	raoma	mai	omai	koatiria
conduct	kara	'ala	ala	lanlauna	vavai	vavai	mai
conquer	qalimu	walimu	belavi	adidiri	oaka	aivala	ivara
cook, v.	nanadu	nanunanu	nalunalu	selauriga	nakunaku	tatutatu	epai
cooked (*done*)	maeta	behara	gala	imaisa	eara	anate	sanai
cooking pot	uro	gulo	ulo	gureva	nrona	uro	eraera
crayfish	ura	gula	tlalava	vagina	o'una	aihi	hahearoi
crocodile	nala	bngaha	buala	varagohe	nã	puaea	sapea
crowbar (planting stick)	isiva	gari	qalaki	gori	si'o	ihiva	sima
cry	tai	agi	agiagi	tani	diareva	hai	fi
cup	kehere	beri	peri	bia	ini'au	otou	kakumoisa
cut	ivaia	voroa	boroa	inigoi	ivaia	ivana	eraraia
dance	mavaru	bara	palapala	saga	varia	euã	eoi
dark	dibura	mhnna	inuna	masikiri	vapune kaiva	vabnra	murumuru
day (*to*)	harihari	ivagomona	evanamo	nauta	iavaruna	bariu	melu
day (after to-morrow)	vanegai	vaomanai	walelepokoni	huana	maranina	elani	a
deceive	koia	wapa	wapa	bora	erepaniava	ooina	rohorai
descend	diho	rigo	ripo	besa	naedo	riri	fankai
desire	ura	ula	ririwamagi	heinna	uranadaeurava	arina	kaisi
dew	hnnu	amo	qaraqara	benbeu	ameru	peu	seo
die	mate	wareha	walega	mate	ekeo	ari	opai
dirty	miro	milo	miro	bita, bil	mirona	opu	sirisiri
dish (*earthenware*)	nau	nagu	libu	gaeba	kavia	ororo	saisa
displeased	lalodika	aona rahava	ao raba	nuana baea	aokaka	aona ckia	hai maroro
distant	dandan	laulau	raurau	roharoha	paana	homa aehai	safari. ala
do	karaia	'ala	ara	selanlauci	vavaia	vavai	pisosi, &c.
dog	sisia	waeha	waga	vanuhe	oveka	uneha	ave
don't know	sedila	bana	pilamu	hai	inanõ	iamotaina	anaro
doorway	idnara	vanagivanagi	apagana	dobila	akena	pihia	utapi
dream	nihi	nivi	nipi	enosuvai	inivi	nivi	hivahitatai
drink	inua	niua	niua	unomu	intra	moinu	laria

English	Moru	Kerepunu	Aroma	South Cape	Kabadi	Maiva	Motumotu
drive (*away*)	lulua	iua	gina	uaiduei	o'ona	uuna	rarivatai
drum	gaba	gaba	gaba	boiatu	apa	iraravu	opa
dry	kaukau	anau	kui	bitapitari	akarona	ororo	haha
dwell	noho	alu	alu	mia	miava	miaho	avai
ear	taia	eha	ega	bea	kaina	haia	kirori
earth	tano	wano	arima	tano	kanona	hano	oti
east	mairevéina	abuano	walau	vaeau	kaeaona	tototaina	kauritnpe
eat	ania	ania	kanikani	nai	eaniva	moana	laria
eight	tauralaui	anravaivai	anravaivai	harigigi haiona	kararani	avavani	....
elbow	diu	ima uaouaona	ina galugaluma	nimasu	otuou	ova	maikiri
enclose	koua	kanahabu	kanakabu	ugudu	avina	kaiavuna	sasankeia
evening	adorahi	lavilavi	labilabi	mailahi	raviravi	lavilavi	mefautn
excrement	tage	age	age	koe	kae	hae	e
eye	mata	na	nana	mata	maka	maha	ofao
face	vaira	waira	pirana	anaao	ioinana	uaira	soso
fall	keto	leo	peo	guvi	kedi	eho	pitoi
fall (*from height*)	moru	heorigo	peovali	beu	vairaasi	eho	oai
fat	digara	mona	uana	momona	mera	olo	saqare
father	tamana	amana	amana	tamana	atanana	hamana	oa
fear	gari	gari	gali	matautsi	mekauva	mariki	tore
feast	aria	verewa	lewa	soi	naktu	uadena	sosoka
fierce	dagedage	aoraava	aoraba	mananaubara	vaioo	lipulipu	otite
find	davaria	lavalia	rawalia	rolai	kavaria	tavuahaina	eovai
finished	ore	beaigi	begabuwagi	ihoiho	eveova	eore	mareke
fire	lahi	arova	alova	vaki	auaraara	iruva	ahari
first	guna	gune	reparepa	ibaguna	avai	uai	onopa
fish	garume	mahani	nagani	cana	veana	naia	ekaka
fish, v.	haoda	veabu	peabu	taueaina	burua	vacha	tapora
fish-hook	kimai	gahu	kau	auri	kapona	naktu	farama
five	ima	inaima	inaima	bariggi	ima	ima	oroka oroka me farakeka
fly, s.	lao	nagama	nagama	nrouro	aokama	aomaha	oropea
fly, v.	roho	rovo	lobo	ieroi	rova	rovo	itoi

English.	Motu.	Kerepunu.	Aroma.	South Cape.	Kabadi.	Maiva.	Motomotu.
food	malamala	aniani	wala	aiai	kepana	pohama	rariaetau
foolish	kavakava	avaava	avaava	eaueanre	poopoo	poopoo	meakakari
foot	ae palapala	ake	kapuna	ae tapatapa	aenana panarana	aepanava	molakou
forbid	koaualu	ila havu	ilagavu	ribagudu	seiakao	hinavuna	soa sasaukai
forehead	bagu	bagu	paguna	deba	paunana	pau	halihali
forget	reaia	ugamagi	lewalewala	ilauponori	reanava	reana	haisafavai
four	hani	vaivai	baibai	hasi	vani	vani	oroka oroka
fowl	kokorogu	horo	bolo	kanukamu	kokoroo	kokoro'u	kokolo
fowl (jungle)	keboka	wario	wario	korauto	kepoo	kepoko	hahanka
friend	turana	hana	gana	enaheriamu	enakanina	enahan	morattai
fruit	huahua	vuavua	buana	uauana	vekopi	vuana	fare
full	hom	vonu	bonu	mnonan	eakava	vonu	soauai
garden	una	araha	laraga	oaia	ropa	uma	oru
gird	rioa	rigoa	ligoa	nrio	evara	verama	aravai
girdle (men)	sihi	ivi	ibi	sihi	sivi	ihavuri	si
girl	kekeni	iao	iao	sin	vaisi	uahoucho	liori
go!	aola	ouoao	onoluo	anlau	onakana	mouo	tereia
go	lao	ao	lao	ierau	kana	ao	tereia
t;ool	dirava	barahu	balau	eanbaala	dirava	tirama	karisu
good	namo	nama	nama	iroro	noinoa	namona	ladeva
good-night	bamahuta	bamalu	alovaialu	aioni	kamaeno	haparua	iavaino
grand parents	ttubuna	upuna	nbuna	tubuna	kupuna	kupuna	papa
grass	rei	legi	regi	rei	reina	tuvu	kavuru
grow	vara	wara	wara	ietubu	kupu	lama	maiauai
hair	hui	bui	bui	uru	iduna	vui	tui
hatchet	ira	giro	gilo	ilama	ira	uapila	nao ita
have, take, get	abia	abia	gabia	uabi	kavarava	iina	ovaia
he	ia	ia	ia	ia	iaua	ia	areo
head	qara	repa	lepa	nagara	roona	ara	arofave
head (*back of*)	gedu	keru	keru	keduna	ekuna	eku	ameasuta
heart	kudou	lau	malaha	tutneveu	muana	aoakoi	hai
heavy	metau	meau	meau	poroe	sinaa	puma	pason
heel	ae gedu	ake waguna	qalili	ae keduri	ekueku	aeaena	molakiri

English.	Motu.	Keropunu.	Aroma.	South Cape.	Kaoadi.	Maiva.	Motumotu.
here (opposed to there)	inai	enai	enai	inai	iinana	eincaia	mehe
here (in this place)	iniseni	enai	enai	teina	iinanai	eineia	rehe
his, hers	ena	gena	gena	cnana	ena	ena	areve
his (food)	iana	iahana	iagana	iana	nomaena	iana	areve
his	iena	iagena	iagena	iaena	ena	iena	areve
house	ruma	numa	numa	numa	ruma	itu	uvi
house (sacred or plat- form).	dubu	lubu	rubu	dubu	ro'e	marea	elamo
how	ede heto	rahaemiaraiwa	raeniaraiwa	edoha	adiveka	aehamiho	lafeare
hundred.	sinahu	inavu	inabuna	tataoharigigi simate.	poupon	hinavu	....
hungry	hitolo	vio	laka	guriamu	orana	mare'a	eroasauai
hunt	labana	apana	labana	bcbetura	apana	apana	tapora
I	lau	au	lau	eau	nana	au	ara
ill	gorere	vivi	kaka	asiebo	epaova	inaoa	ekaloi
inside	lalo	ao	laona	arona	aona	aona	hai iri
jaw	auki	are	garc	gadigadi	nainainana	ate	uale
jealous	vagege	vagege	wagege	siaiau	vaiora	vaki'a	hai alala
kill	alaia	wagia	bagia	unui	akunia	ahuna	paeaia
kiss	aberahu	veveravu	pebarabu	alagoi	kevaipauva	pauna	ineresisi
knee	tui	wa'uwa'u	kalnkalu	turi	acna	ovaova	arikoka
knot	qadna	wahua	pawau	hesio	podina	pova	fasai
know	diba	riba	ripana	ata	isanava	iovina	ore
lamp-black	guma	milo	guluma	dumu	nma	nnu	alo
large	bada	gamu	para	lailai	babaka	apauana	rovaea
lash (a large canoe)	laia	rigoa	ligoa	seolin	vaia	virina	fasai
laugh	kiri	mamai	mamai	maruhi	vainai	ilili	area
lead	bakaua	laagia	baia	voeai	omakanaina	vakana	rariovi
leaf	ran	lau	ran	lau	meka	ran	toro
leave alone	mia	mia	mia	iota	miava	menoho	areaea
left hand	lauri	auri	auli	seuseuri	earina	aoari	maiava
leg	ae	ake	gage	ae	ae	ae	mola
lie, s. and v.	koikoi	vapaau	owaba	borabora	reparepa	macao	apevā

English.	Motu.	Kerepunu.	Aroma.	South Cape.	Kabadi.	Maiva.	Motumotu.
lie down	hekure	maho	mao	eno	enodo	enoti	auiavai
life	mauri	maguri	mauri	mauri	mauri	mauri	makuri
light	diari	maea	malagani	marana	rani	eä	ovava
lightning	kevaru	rama	rama	namanamari	iamana	eimare	....
lips	bibina	bibina	pipigana	soba	bibinana	pinana	taipi
listen	kamonai	amonagi	amonaki	nataiei	onova	avahaona	mapai
liver	ate	ae	gae	ate	nuana	ahe	hai
loins	koekoe	veo'e	warimo	duaduarina	oeoena	hoana	koapisi
look	itaia	gia	ia	ita	isanava	ihana	ofaeavai
louse	utu	gu	u	tuma	amuni	uhu	ape
lungs	baraki	launa	nuanua	ateburoburo	apaapa	aoakoi	....
male	maruane	maruwane	maruane	tamoana	kauna	koa	kaisava
man	tannimarima	aunirimarima	aunilimalima	tatao	kanda	maearima	karu
man (as opposed to woman).	tau	hau	au	tau	kau	hau	vita
many	hutuma	guma	uma	kamagari	ko'unana	mako	ranapo
marry	headava	vearava	begarawa	hetavasora	vevavine	haoainive	laeai
mat	geda	kera	gepa	leiaha	eka	irc	kiti
milk (and breast)	rata	la	la	susu	rakana	ae	ko
mine	egu	gegu	geku	enagu	euna	e'u	arave
mine (food)	lauegu	angegu	geku	eauenagu	euna	auen	arave
mine (drink)	lauagu	auagu	auagu	eauagu	anna	aua'u	arave
moon	hua	vue	bue	navalai	uena	naoa	papare
morning (to)	daba	lapa	lapa	maraietomu	kabaerere	lani	miori
morrow (to)	kerukeru	laparua	pogipogi	maraitomu	marana	nara	bevere
mother	sinana	inana	inana	sinana	aidana	hinana	lou
mother (or father) in-law.	ravana	ahama	agama	bosiana	ravana	ravana	ova
mountain	ororo	olo	golo	uduuri	aapu	oeo	laepa
mouth	udu	muru	nuru	ava	ake	pina	ape
name	ladana	arana	arana	esana	akanana	atana	rare
navel	udo	vuro	bulo	usoma	puko	botoa	rarave
neck	aio	aigo	gaigo	gado	kemona	aio	kavarehau

English.	Motu.	Kerepunu.	Aroma.	South Cape.	Kabadi.	Maiva.	Motumotu.
net (*fishing*)	reke	rehe	lē	hiana	reena	lee	rehe
new	matamata	valiguna	walibuna	harihariuna	makamaka	mahamaha	are
night	hanuaboi	vanngabogi	bannabogi	eanuaboni	vapukana	lavi	faita
no	lasi	aikina	noaia	nige	ve'o	ahai	kao
nose	udu	ilu	iru	isu	itu	itu	everape
offspring	natuna	nahuna	nauna	natuna	nakima	nahuna	atuti
olden time	sene	lahuveha	laubagi	mumuga	avainana	naivaha	evera
one	taunona	obuna	abuna	esega	kapea	hamomona	farakeka
only	sibona	gerehana	kerekana	iabomu	sipona	kipona	haria
ours (*exclusive*)	ai emai	aigema	aigemai	aienamai	naida emai	aiemai	erove
paddle v.	kalo	leva	lepa	nimaoi	aona	vote	saita
paddle s.	hole	leva	lepa	vose	ode	vote	taisa
pain	hisihisi	vivi	bibi	amumuna	nuunuuva	haiara	hehea
palm (*of hand*)	ima lalona	ima aona	labalaba	nima alona	panava	panavana	morakou
paradisea raggiana	lokohu	diake	tiake	siai	oon	inehi	ho
peace	maino	maino	maino	roni	maino	vaivua	tairu
pearlshell	maire	alo	alo	gininba	mairi	maire	....
penis	use	wúi	wái	duga	usina	ani	mate
petticoat	rami	lami	awai	nogi	divana	kiva	taheka
piece	taina	iaha	iara	begana	ka	hana	taheka
piece (*small*)	sisina	kirikirina	lipilipi	begana	vaku'a	papana	ita
pig	boroma	bac	pae	salai	boroma	aiporo	sua
pigeon	pune	pnne	pune	gabubu	ratríea	rauria	oti
place v.	gabuna	kapuna	aba	alinai	apuna	ekana	aviavai
place v.	atoa	haoa	olea	utore	koreado	horotina	havaroi
play	kadara	nla	pelelc	aihea	enopoo	papura	hai iri rareva
pleased	lalo namo	aona nama	ao nama	ntana iroro	aononoa	aona enamo	maurisa
porpoise	kidului	irdlui	iln	ururiabolo	uriana	kaipu	hiveia
pour	seia	limaha	rimarima	uini	poura	laina	aihehea
power (*generally supernatural.*)	siahu	iavu	iabu	gigibori	siau	hiavu	
pregnant	rogorogo	uviuvia	imuimu	ieboga	memeroa	puma	ereovai
pull	veria	olia	golia	uiuri	verina	verina	aruavaia

English.	Motu.	Kerepunu.	Aroma.	South Cape.	Kabadi.	Maiva.	Motumotu.
rain	medu	gupa	kupa	nabu	upa	avara	rai
rainbow	kevau	baeva	lalanpu	vari	evau	opa	lavai
rat	bita	uruve	urupe	ibou	kana	kana	aili
red	kakakaka	viraravirara	ralarala	butabuiana	pairapaira	viro	mohari
refuse, (reject)	koanedeede	ilapereovo	ilaraperape	tauotaota	paoava	uva	kaevauvi
rejoice	moale	verere	berele	kode	raauva	aonamo	bairareva
relations	varavara	warawara	warawara	ehana	koaena	hatiaana	paumarehari
return	lou	vaiure	labuure	nio	erö	mue	eata
riches	kohu	dinaha	lanla	gogo	dinada	kepu	etau
right (*hand*)	idiba	riba	riba	tutuna	idibana	itipa	toare
ripe	mage	mera	mela	buina	mairoo	aiva	mea
river	sinavai	wai	wai	saga	akena	ate	mai
road	dara	raopara	lara	dopila	kere'a	taeara	otiharo
rope	qanau	wanau	aiai	tari	onau	anau	horou
run	heau	laka	rabu	aitautau	veau	veau	soea
sacred	helaga	veaha	begaha	hasisi	rove	rove	....
sago	rabia	lapia	rapia	rapia	rapia	pareo	poi
sail, *s.*	lara	la	lara	vorivori	idiuna	raea	auvia
salt	damena	rama	rama	arita	diaa	tamena	soare
sandbank	boe	epouuna	rina	daudau	rore	pau	mili
satisfied	boka kuau	inage vonu	belaguna	boka sese	amoukuva	amiari	elefefese
scatter	karoho	arovo	arobo	setaagorigori	kapanana	otaraina	hariaharia
scold	koankoau	ilaila	ilaila	diraha ariri	ekäuva	aviavi	oauai
sea	davara	rama	rama	gabogabo	kavara	aku	saea
sea (*deep*)	galobada	rawapara	rawapara	gabotuuu	kavarapakana	akupaka	kaikara
sea (*rough*)	hurehure	ahu	raboa	vovori	röia	roio	aroro
seek	tahua	avua	abuabu	iovi	kaura	tavuna	erie
send	siaia	ugua	unagi	hetamari	uraina	uhuna	omoia
seven	hitu	mahere aura-vaivai	auraoi wabuna	harigigi rabui	karakoi kapea	avahau hamo-mona	
shark	qalaha	baewa	paowa	laeva	oava	etoeto	itari
shelf (*table*)	pata	ropi	palapala	hata	varana	itara	posa
shield, *s.*	kesi	gehi	mali	opea	oroau	kehi	reua

English.	Motu.	Kerepunu.	Aroma.	South Cape.	Kabadi.	Maiva.	Motumotu.
ship	lakatoi	lakaoi	rakaoi	vaka	annakoi	annohi	vavaea
short	gadogi	upa	upa	kunkun	'ope'ope	kookoona	harua
shoulder	paga	alo	aro	dabaearona	aropakuna	aro	solohou
shout	lolo	oho	gogogogo	vovo	oova	eio	uhotoai
side (by the)	dekena	lahanai	elena	arinai	apauana	herena	man
sign	toana	iriana	bairia	heiheinoi	koana	hoana	pupusukai
sink	mutu	maguhu	pulupulu	sariri	inukeo	euhu	......
sister	taihuna	arina	arina	rouna	a'opana	haivuna	uaroa
sit	helai	aluari	aluari	nbava	mialo	miati	auavai
six	tauratoi	auraooi	aulaoi	harigigi esega	karakoi	avaihau	......
skin	kopi	opi	opi	opi	vaerana	paraua	ruru
sky	guba	guba	buenuluku	gareva	kaakaana	kupa	kauri
sleep	mahuta	mahu	man	eno	enova	parua	vutniavai
small	maragi	kiri	kiri	gakiri	mara'i	papana	seieka
smell, v.	bona	bona	bonana	panena	makaana	timi	suru
smoke	qalahu	kovu	mugo	asu	siauna	atu	aikoela
snake	gaigai	gerema	ma	mota	paipai	elau	ikaroa
song (hymn)	ane	mari	mari	vana	rari	hui	fara
south	diho	aburigo	gaburigo	......	asiaona	ahidaina	seipi
speak	koau	ila	ila	riba	esiava	ieavi	onuoi
spear	io	olova	olova	alahia	uka	auarai	hola
speech	ere	garo	garo	arina	maora	aiana	o
speech (language)	gado	garo	karo	arina	lauma	avi	uli
spirit	lanma	avnavu	laupa	earuiarua	ainuku	autva	ove
spit, v.	kanudi	aninu	aniulu	gariso	koore	atoti	pea
stand up	toreisi	gulurahai	gulurai	utoro	visiu	mikiri	itoia
star	hisiu	givu	bin	ibora	vainao	vihiu	koru
steal	henao	lema	rema	aivahari	sinae	vainao	torea
stomach	boka	inage	uliina	boka	vakuna	ma	erchorou
stone	nadi	vau	bau	veu	vrunava	pihara	fave
tone, v.	hodoa	abaa	rari	ntarai	roke	ahuna	toaia
store house	roge	loke	wala numa	sanala		itukoikoina	uvi seieka
straight	maoro	rori	lagoa	dudurai	meoro	vero	haura

English.	Motu.	Kerepunu.	Aroma.	South Cape.	Kabadi.	Maira.	Motumotu.
strike (*downwards*)	botaia	waria	varia	ntarrai	upinava	ovina	toaia
string	varo	waro	waro	maina	poana	uaro	ela
strong	goada	iriga	iliga	adidiri	iraa	tavura	rofo
substance (*flesh*)	anina	anina	ganina	aina	anina	anina	maea
sugar-cane	tohu	omu	obu	garu	ake	ovaova	ase
sun	dina	haro	garo	mahana	akona	veraura	sare
sweet potato	kaemadahu	nokela	nokela	kanua	iniveu	taakaema	kauari
swim	nahu	nabu	nabu	tuba	na'uva	na'u	riveai
tail (*quadruped's*)	iuna	iguna	giuna	delena	iuna	aarena	aru
take	laohaia	aoagia	laoagia	uraei	ekaniina	aoaina	ovitereia
taro (*plant*)	talo	ale	keu	udo	rire	hovoo	soera
teach	hadibaia	vaariba	vebariba	heaheata	vaisavaisa	ovaiovina	satiriraraia
ten	qauta	harana	kapanana	saudoidoi	onka	harauhaea	....
theirs	edia	geria	geria	enadi	eda	ekia	eleve
theirs (*food*)	adia	haria	garia	adi	ada	akia	eleve
there	unai	vanai	wanai	ururi	aarupu	uaa	seo
they	unuseni	vanai	wanai	neiai	aananai	uaa	rau
them	idia	ila	ira	isi	iada	ia	ereo
thigh	mamu	maava	paga	gasa	di'udi'una	ape	ukae
thin	severa	magivi	magipi	earoearo	kevekeve	nivinivi	sesera
thine (*food*)	emu	gemu	gemu	enamu	emuna	emu	ave
thine	amu	amu	ganu	amu	amu	amu	ave
this	oiemu	oigemu	goigemu	oaenamu	emu	oiemu	ave
thing	gau	hau	gau	giuauri	kanuna	nanu	etau
think	laloa	ugamagi	uamagi	nautui	rasava	laonana	haikaeai
thou	oi	oi	goi	oa	orina	oi	ao
three	toi	oi	oi	haiona	koi	ailau	oroisoria
throat	gado	orolo	ronorono	gado	akonana	ako	havarehau
throw	tahoa	biaha	laqa	utu	viuna	kapona	toapaia
throw away	negea	pihaoa	laqaoa	ugabaei	viuna	neena	butapai
thus	bamona	vciana	beaina	anasagu	boinana	avana	mafeare
tide (*falling*)	komatagui	bearu mamara	lina	magu iesiva	eomaku	pura eahi	maraovai
time	nega	homana	arioma	huiana	enona	homaa	mea

English.	Motu.	Kerepunu.	Arona.	South Cape.	Kabadi.	Maiva.	Motumotu.
tobacco	kuku	kuku	kuku	kuku	kuku	kuku	kuku
toe	ae gagigagi	ake ririna	ake lirina	ae gigi	ola'olana	ae uauau	mora keka
tongue	mala	nae	malana	memena	mala	maea	tepa
tooth	ise	rua	rua	mo'a	nise	nihe	tao
tree	au	au	garbu	oeagi	au	matin	tora
true	momokani	aunauna	aunauna	mamohoi	momooi	tohamu	kofa
turtle	matabudi	haoao	gaokao	vonu	a'ea'ena	vonu	akeake
two	rua	lualua	lua	rabui	rua	rua	oraokaria
two days hence	uainananegai	vavaanuo manai	warerepogoni	imaisina	maraniaoma	uelani	iso
two days hence (more than)	unananegai	......	wauliraga	galilima	tapaverere	naelani	poaru
two (men)	rarua	lualha	ralua	rabii	kaudaruda	terarua	erenka
untie	ruhaia	rugaha	ruvaea	uiaili	riiasa	ruvuna	ferankeia
village	hanna	vaniga	banna	eanua	vanua	aiara	karikara
visitor	vadiradi	wariwari	varivari	taumana	kodina	vaki	sarina
vomit	mumuta	mumna	mumua	marive	urave	aiora	munsiavai
voyage (to go)	hiri	viri	rapu	ivotu	lio	viri	salima
walk	laka	laha	loa	nrau	kana	kaa	tereia
walk (about)	loa	lahalaha	loa	seharebarensi	epoepo	kaoao	moraveita
wallaby	magani	vagi	wagi	vavauri	vaaru	itavala	pisoru
war	alala	veali	bedi	iala	akuaku	on	sasari
warriors	tuari	veaui	bedi	iala	akuaku kauda	hnari	maora
wash r.	huria	vuligia	purigia	denri	ru'ana	uttunaina	ukeia
water	ranu	nanu	nalu	goila	vena	vei	ma
we (exclusive)	ai	ai	ai	ai	naida	ai	ero
we (inclusive)	ita	ia	ia	ita	isada	aika	leao
weak	manokamanoka	moiramoira	lepeilepei	bemberu	manomanova	aveave	meamafu
went	ela	hao	lao	ulau	kekana	eao	sisisi
west	tahorliho	avurigo	bagiriwa	eavana	variana kaivanai	tivotaina	diho
wet	paripari	bevenanu	korekore	iebuta	eveiva	veivei	maroi
what?	dahaka?	raha	ragan	saha	kava	tava	rarevekoru
where	edeseni?	arikinai	arai	aidinoeai	aenaiva	aeae	lenoa

English.	Motu.	Kerepunu.	Aroma.	South Cape.	Kabadi.	Maiva.	Motumotu.
which?	edana ?	arikina	arigau	haedi	aenava	aeana	deva
white	kurokuro	hurohuro	urouro	posiposi	raraa	rauarana	ncsea
who?	daika ?	rāi	liai	eai	kāi	tai	reisa
widow	vabu	wapu	vabu	vabu	opu	uapu	toai
wind	lai	agi	agi	mana	avivina	vanra	mirurn
wind (north)	mirigini	valaka	gabuano	bembeu	narairana	maraira	marurn
wind (south-east)	lanlabada	vahau	wāiau	aruabu	vareana	vanla	inauta
wind (north-west)	rahara	avala	eapala	lalasi	revona	varuru	avara
woman	haine	vavine	babine	sine	vavine	vavine	ua
wound (*by spear*)	qadaia	kinia	kinia	uaidibai	ooua	komona	sukeia
yam	maho	marawapa	gani	apoi	pure	taa	maho
yes	oi be	ina	namu	e. aboiesalia	ea.	aia	a
yesterday	varani	varahani	waragani	lahi	ravina	uarani	area
you	umui	omi	mui	omin	uida	uai	co
young man	tauhau	haugoroa	koloa	hevari	oreore	hivitoi	milofu
your's (food)	amui	ami	gami	ami	amui	ami	cve

I

Sydney : Charles Potter, Government Printer.—1888.